A Guide to National Security

Threats, Responses, and Strategies

Julian Richards

With contributions from Lord Carlile of Berriew,
Andy Dancer, and Sir Ian Andrews

OXFORD
UNIVERSITY PRESS

OXFORD

UNIVERSITY PRESS

Great Clarendon Street, Oxford OX2 6DP
United Kingdom

Oxford University Press is a department of the University of Oxford.
It furthers the University's objective of excellence in research, scholarship,
and education by publishing worldwide. Oxford is a registered trade mark of
Oxford University Press in the UK and in certain other countries

British Library Cataloguing in Publication Data
Data available

Library of Congress Cataloging in Publication Data
Library of Congress Control Number: 2012932076

ISBN 978-0-19-965506-9

Printed in Great Britain on acid-free paper by
CPI Group (UK) Ltd, Croydon, CR0 4YY

Preface

My early years of awareness of foreign affairs and national security were formed largely in the 1970s and 1980s. If you had asked me then which issues constituted national security concerns for the UK, I would have pointed first towards the threat of nuclear oblivion initiated by the Soviet Union. I would also have identified the threat of terrorism from the IRA, both within Northern Ireland and in public spaces within the UK. In 1982, there was the brief anomaly of the seizure of the Falkland Islands by Argentina, and the bold military venture to take them back. At that time, I remember having breakfast before going to school, listening to reports on the radio of events in the far South Atlantic. These included Brian Hanrahan's famous report from an aircraft carrier, in which he circumvented restrictions on reporting of operational details by saying of a group of Harrier fighter jets returning from a sortie over the Falklands that he 'counted them all out, and counted them all back'.[1]

Nearly a decade later, I was listening to the radio again, this time to reports of NATO fighter jets flying into Iraq to repulse Saddam Hussein's invasion of Kuwait. The Soviet Union had not yet completely collapsed, but was in the process of doing so, with the Berlin Wall having been breached to unleash a wave of democratic transformation across Eastern Europe. The Cold War was more or less over, but the security picture to follow was not yet clear.

State-on-state conflict, plus some domestic terrorism, therefore, would have headed my list of national security concerns during my youth. If asked the same question now as to what constituted national security concerns in the UK, I would probably recount a much longer list of issues and threats, encompassing several different strands of terrorism; threats of involvement in military conflicts overseas; threats from domestic unrest and extremism; cyber-security threats; and possibly the risk of natural disasters or accidents, to name but a few.

The issues we have gathered together under the umbrella of national security concerns have broadened considerably in the few years since the end of the Cold War. The picture is fairly unrecognizable from what we would have imagined in the 1980s. A government's National Security Strategy written at that time would have looked very different from one written in 2012.

This book explores the processes and developments which have shaped this transformation over the last three decades, and critically examines

---

[1] See B. Hanrahan and R. Fox, *I Counted Them All Out, and I Counted Them All Back: The Battle for the Falklands* (London: BBC Books, 1982).

processes of politicization and securitization that have delivered the new strategic vision.

The book takes as its point of reference the National Security Strategy and Strategic Defence and Security Review delivered by the newly elected government in the UK in late 2010. I argue that this process of strategic review is more than just a milestone in the gradual development of securitization during the post-Cold War period. It is also a review that claims many firsts. It claims to be one written in a truly strategic way, where the exigencies of budgetary considerations are placed to one side in favour of an in-depth and objective risk assessment. This is a bold claim given the almost unprecedented downward pressure on defence budgets in the light of the global financial crisis that has unfolded since 2008. Of the many casualties of the latest review are the Harrier jets that were so iconic in the Falklands campaign, and which have now been consigned to the history books.

The 2010 strategic review also tackles a particular political issue within the UK government of the right way to deal with major national security issues in a modern democracy. The trauma of the second campaign in Iraq, in 2003, was made worse—claim the current government—by the manner in which the Blair government of the time had instituted a new culture of 'sofa government', in which chats with the Prime Minister and the role of unelected special advisers set the course. This was hardly the way, claimed the Conservatives, that major issues of foreign policy in which British troops would be committed to war should be decided at the top of government. The 2010 strategic review therefore comes with the establishment, for the first time under this name, of a new National Security Council. This is set to end the sofa government model and reinstitute a proper process of collective Cabinet decision-making on major national security issues.

In these ways, the 2010 strategic review in the UK marks a particularly significant juncture in the process of national security strategizing in the post-Cold War era. As such, this process not only provides a number of fascinating and critical points for those interested in the UK's own national security posture, but also provides much of value to anyone involved in such issues across the Western world in the contemporary era of globalization. There is much with which the UK is grappling that will ring bells in Washington, Paris, and many other places.

The production of this analysis requires a number of people to be thanked. First, the experts who provided specific advice and comment for the text of this book deserve special thanks, and specifically Sir Ian Andrews, Lord Alex Carlile, and Andy Dancer. Numerous other officials in the National Security Secretariat in London, and in Local Resilience Forums in various parts of the country have also provided invaluable expertise and advice. In terms of the book itself, Lucy Alexander, Emma Hawes, and colleagues at Oxford University Press must be thanked for providing patience, good humour, and professionalism. Finally, my family, as ever, have provided the most important support in terms of encouragement and understanding, and my father has added to this some forensic proofreading. Without all of this, the book would never have seen the light of day.

Julian Richards
October 2011

Contents

Abbreviations   xii

Part One Threats

1 Introduction   3
The 2010 National Security Strategy—breaking new ground   3
Priority risks and threats   5
National security in the UK—a modern history   7
Defining 'national security'   14
Key points   17

2 Setting the Scene: The Threat Picture in a Globalized World   19
'Wider' security risks   19
The political backdrop   20
The strategic context—globalization and transnational threats   25
Key points   30

3 Tier One Threats   32
Risk and resilience   32
Terrorism   35
Cyber threats   41
Natural hazards and disasters   44
International military crisis   48
Key points   50

4 Tier Two Threats   52
Overlapping risks and capabilities   52
An attack using 'unconventional' weapons   53
Unstable and failed states   56
Organized crime   60
Disruption to satellite communications   64
Key points   66

5 Tier Three Risks   67
Backdrop—security in Europe   67
Wider regional conflict   70

Contents

Energy security   72
The risk of a nuclear emergency   76
Border security   78
Key points   80

Part Two Responses

6 Responses   83

The response framework   83
Administrative organization   86
Response capability—an 'adaptable posture'   90
National security 'tasks'   91
Key points   96

Part Three Strategies

7 Administering National Security: Governmental Strategies and Structures   101

The political origins of the National Security Council   101
Why an NSC?   103
Presidentialization and prime ministerialism   106
NSC process and machinery   109
Departmental organization outside the Cabinet Office   111
Key points   115

8 Boots on the Ground: Restructuring Military Capability   116

Introduction: the case for restructuring   116
Britain's place in the world   117
The changing character of conflict   119
Inter-service issues   121
Proposed restructuring   123
The nuclear question   126
Key points   128

9 Fighting Asymmetric Conflicts   129

The challenge of Afghanistan   129
Selling the strategy—the battle of the narratives   130
Peacekeeping, peace-enforcement, and counter-insurgency   133
Future force requirements   137
Key points   139

10 Domestic Policies: Counter-Radicalization and Counter-Terrorism **140**

Old and new threats 140

The evolving nature of the terrorist threat 141

Counter-terrorism strategy in the UK 143

Prevent 147

Key points 151

11 Partnerships: EU, UN, NATO, and the 'Special Relationship' **153**

Chance encounters and shifting alliances 153

The 'special relationship' 154

Existing alliances 156

Europe, and France 161

Counter-terrorism 163

Key points 166

12 Conclusions **167**

Key points 176

Index 177

Abbreviations

ACPO	Association of Chief Police Officers
AQAP	Al Qaeda in the Arabian Peninsula
AQIM	Al Qaeda in the Islamic Maghreb
ANA	Afghan National Army
ANP	Afghan National Police
BBC	British Broadcasting Corporation
BERR	Department for Business, Enterprise and Regulatory Reform
BIS	Department for Business, Innovation and Skills
BNP	British National Party
BSOS	Building Stability Overseas Strategy
BTC	Baku-Tblisi-Ceyhan pipeline
BTWC	Biological and Toxin Weapons Convention
CADO	Community and Diversity Officer
CBRN	chemical, biological, radiological, and nuclear weapons
CCS	Crisis Contingencies Secretariat
CDSN	Conseil de défense et de sécurité nationale
CESG	Communications-Electronic Security Group
CIA	Central Intelligence Agency
CIRA	Continuity Irish Republican Army
CJEF	Combined Joint Expeditionary Force
CNI	Critical National Infrastructure
CNN	Cable News Network
COBR	Cabinet Office Briefing Room
COIN	Counter-Insurgency
CONTEST	Counter Terrorism Strategy
CPNI	Centre for the Protection of National Infrastructure
CSDP	Common Security and Defence Policy
CSOC	Cyber Security Operations Centre
CWC	Chemical Weapons Convention
CYBERCOM	Cyber Command (United States)
DCDC	Development Concepts Doctrine Centre (Ministry of Defence)
DCLG	Department for Communities and Local Government
DCOG	Defence Cyber Operations Group
DDR	disarmament, demobilization, and reintegration
DECC	Department of Energy and Climate Change
DEFRA	Department for Environment, Food and Rural Affairs
DfID	Department for International Development
DOPC	Cabinet Defence and Overseas Policy Committee

EC	European Community
ECHR	European Convention on Human Rights
ECSC	European Coal and Steel Community
EDL	English Defence League
EEC	European Economic Community
EMU	Economic and Monetary Union
ENISA	European Network and Information Security Agency
ERRF	European Rapid Reaction Force
ESDP	European Security and Defence Policy
EU	European Union
FATA	Federally Administered Tribal Areas (Pakistan)
FCO	Foreign and Commonwealth Office
FIEP	France, Italia, España, Portugal (Police union)
FOB	Forward Operating Base
FSB	Foreign Security Service (Russia)
G8	Group of Eight leading industrialized nations
G20	Group of Twenty leading finance ministers and central bank governors
GCHQ	Government Communications Headquarters
GDP	Gross Domestic Product
GPS	Global Positioning Satellite
HMS	Her Majesty's Ship
HVT	High Value Target
IAEA	International Atomic Energy Agency
ICTY	International Criminal Tribunal for the former Yugoslavia
IED	improvised explosive device
IISS	International Institute of Strategic Studies
IMINT	Imagery Intelligence
INSTINCT	Innovative Science and Technology in Counter Terrorism
IRA	Irish Republican Army
ISAF	International Security Assistance Force
ISC	Intelligence and Security Committee
JIC	Joint Intelligence Committee
JIO	Joint Intelligence Organisation
JRRF	Joint Rapid Reaction Force
JTAC	Joint Terrorism Analysis Centre
LAA	Local Authority Agreement
LeT	*Lashkar-e Toiba* (Pakistan)
LIC	Low Intensity Conflict
LIFG	Libyan Islamic Fighters Group
LRF	Local Resilience Forum
MI5	Security Service
MI6	Secret Intelligence Service
MOD	Ministry of Defence

MP	Member of Parliament
MRBM	Medium-Range Ballistic Missile
MSU	Multinational Specialised Unit
NATO	North Atlantic Treaty Organization
NCA	National Crime Agency
NDS	National Directorate of Security (Afghanistan)
NGO	non-governmental organization
NHTCU	National High-Tech Crime Unit
NI35	National Indicator 35
NPT	Nuclear Non-Proliferation Treaty
NRA	National Risk Assessment
NSC	National Security Council
NSID	National Security, International Relations and Development Committee
NSRA	National Security Risk Assessment
NSS	National Security Strategy
NSSB	National Security Strategy Board
NSSM	National Security Study Memorandum
NWS	Nuclear Weapons States
OAE	Operation Active Endeavour
OCSIA	Office of Cyber Security and Information Assurance
ODA	Overseas Development Assistance
OPCW	Organisation for the Prohibition of Chemical Weapons
P5	Permanent Five members of the UN Security Council
PASC	Public Administration Select Committee
PCeU	Police Central e-Crime Unit
PEO	Prevent Engagement Officer
PIRA	Provisional Irish Republican Army
PRM	Presidential Review Memorandum
PSNI	Police Service of Northern Ireland
PVE	Preventing Violent Extremism
RAF	Royal Air Force
RIRA	Real Irish Republican Army
RMA	Revolution in Military Affairs
RUC	Royal Ulster Constabulary
RUF	Revolutionary United Front (Sierra Leone)
RUSI	Royal United Services Institute
SDSR	Strategic Defence and Security Review
SEAD	Suppression of Electronic Air Defence
SFOR	Stabilisation Force in Bosnia and Herzogovina
SOCA	Serious Organised Crime Agency
SRU	Security Resilience Unit
SSR	Security Sector Reform
TPIM	Terrorism Prevention and Investigation Measure

TTP	*Tehrik-e Taliban Pakistan*
UAV	Unmanned Aerial Vehicle
UKBA	United Kingdom Border Agency
UKTA	United Kingdom Threat Assessment
UKTI	United Kingdom Trade and Industry
UKUSA	United Kingdom–United States of America intelligence agreement
UN	United Nations
UNAMSIL	United Nations Mission in Sierra Leone
WMD	weapons of mass destruction

PART ONE

Threats

Introduction

The 2010 National Security Strategy—breaking new ground

At the end of 2010, the newly installed UK government (a coalition of Conservatives and Liberal Democrats which had taken power from the Labour Party in May) published a new National Security Strategy (NSS), entitled 'A Strong Britain in an Age of Uncertainty'. A day later it published a comprehensive Strategic Defence and Security Review (SDSR), and the day after that, its first spending review. The NSS and SDSR, which link closely together, constituted the first major review of the UK's defence strategy since 1998, which was itself the first major foreign policy-led review in the post-Cold War period in Britain, delivered by the new Labour government at a time when military operations were under way in the Balkans. The NSS and SDSR were the product of a new National Security Council (NSC), the first time Britain had established such an institution under that name, although it was built on an existing National Security Secretariat within the Cabinet Office. The new Conservative Prime Minister, David Cameron, had established the NSC on the first full day in government, in line with a pre-election pledge, reflecting the importance he attached to this area of government.

Although the UK has experienced a number of major defence reviews in the past, including the 1994 Defence Costs Review in the immediate aftermath of the collapse of the Soviet Union and end of the Cold War, the 2010 NSS and SDSR were heralded as being a first in many respects. Officials in government claim that the 2010 reviews were the first to be properly based on a considered strategic risk assessment, drawing on the expertise of a wide range of analysts, and were thus the first such reviews that were truly 'strategic' in the proper sense of the term.[1] They were also more than just a defence review, but were the

---

[1] Interview with National Security Secretariat official, August 2011.

first time a complete review of the UK's capability and posture against the widest range of security threats had been fully considered. Finally, the reviews were intended not to be simply musings on the nature of contemporary security threat, as many previous reviews could aptly be described, but as rigorous and structured documents that drove security policy and allowed government to make sensible decisions about resources and actions.[2] The timing was also significant and novel, in that the spending review came after the strategy review (albeit very closely after), which meant that the one could not be unduly influenced by the other. Theoretically, the strategy could not have been constrained and shaped by the available resources but considered objectively, and the subsequent decisions on spending allocations across defence and other sectors could not drive strategy, but rather work in the other direction.

These were bold claims, and, as I will discuss, they have proved to be fiercely contested ones. In many ways the whole process was conducted under a certain air of crisis, as the financial implications of the global economic slowdown after 2008, and the subsequent discovery of a massive budget deficit at the heart of the government's finances, coloured all discussions about policy and expenditure. Security and defence were not to be exempt from such considerations, as every area of government foresaw a bleak period of cutbacks and belt-tightening. Some critics have suggested that this means the NSS and SDSR could not be entirely objective.

This book provides a comprehensive analysis of the NSS and SDSR of 2010, exploring what they say about threat, strategy, and policy in twenty-first century Britain. It also explores the processes and debates that underpin the launch of the new strategies, including the NSC and its formulation at the centre of government decision-making. The detail clearly says much that is specific to the UK, not least contemporary conceptions of where Britain sees itself as rightfully being in the twenty-first century, globalized, and multilateral world. It also touches on issues of security threat and perception within the UK itself, not least in relation to domestic terrorist threats and issues. Beyond the shores of the UK, however, the 2010 NSS and SDSR processes are also fascinating case studies in contemporary threat perception and strategizing, which have parallels with, and implications for, any industrialized nation getting to grips with how to structure and refocus its security and defence capabilities in the contemporary world, not least during the midst of a global financial earthquake that threatens to reverberate for some years to come. In some ways, as Clarke argues, we are no longer in the post-Cold War world, but in the 'post-post-Cold War era'.[3] Such a condition of postmodernity is uncharted territory indeed. In this way, this study should provide much of interest to practitioners, analysts, and

---

[2] Ibid.

[3] M. Clarke, 'The United Kingdom's Strategic Moment' in M. Codner and M. Clarke (eds), *A Question of Security: The British Defence Review in an Age of Austerity* (London: I.B. Tauris, 2011), 9.

academics of security well beyond the UK in mapping a course through this new era.

The book is structured around three Parts. Part One ('Threats') take a detailed look at the risks that were identified as security threats to the UK in 2010, and the way in which they have been prioritized within the NSS. Part Two ('Responses') maps the detailed policy responses the government has proposed to this canvas of threats. Part Three ('Strategies') ties the analysis together within the context of a number of strategic themes and issues, including how Britain sees its 'place in the world', and what this means for threat assessment and policy responses.

Priority risks and threats

The core of the NSS and the risk assessment on which it is based, is a three-tiered prioritization of a batch of risks assessed to be the most significant for the UK's national security at the present time. The analysis that went into the production of the NSS was based on the foundation of a National Security Risk Assessment (NSRA), conducted in autumn 2010 by a collection of 'subject matter experts, analysts and intelligence specialists.'[4] Again, the government claimed that this was the first ever NSRA of its type, and certainly the first which assessed and prioritized 'all major areas of national security risk—domestic and overseas'.[5] The exercise built on the findings of the classified National Risk Assessment (NRA), and extended the time frame of analysis to 20 years.[6] The results of the NSRA were put to the NSC, which subsequently summarized them as 15 'generic priority risk types', allocated across three tiers of priority (see Fig 1.1 below). These risks form the core of this book's analysis in terms of which risks were securitized by the government at the end of 2010, and the strategy it proposes adopting to tackle these risks. I will say a little more about the NSRA process in Chapter 3.

Chapter 2 will examine the backdrop to this picture of risk assessment, by considering the manner in which security threat has evolved since the end of the Cold War. Chapters 3, 4, and 5 will then examine each of the three tiers of priority risk identified in Figure 1.1 in detail. Before commencing such analysis of the contemporary threat picture, however, it is instructive to consider the historical pathway that led to the NSS and SDSR in 2010.

---

[4] HM Government, 'A Strong Britain in an Age of Uncertainty: The National Security Strategy' (London: TSO, October 2010), 25.

[5] Ibid.

[6] Cabinet Office, 'Fact Sheet 2: National Security Risk Assessment', available at <https://update.cabinetoffice.gov.uk/sites/default/files/resources/Factsheet2-National-Security-Risk-Assessment.pdf> (accessed 7 November 2011).

Figure 1.1 UK National Security Strategy (2010)—priority risks

Tier One: The National Security Council considered the following groups of risks to be those of highest priority for UK national security looking ahead, taking account of both likelihood and impact.

- International terrorism affecting the UK or its interests, including a chemical, biological, radiological, or nuclear attack by terrorists; and/or a significant increase in the levels of terrorism relating to Northern Ireland.
- Hostile attacks upon UK cyberspace by other states and large-scale cyber crime.
- A major accident or natural hazard which requires a national response, such as severe coastal flooding affecting three or more regions of the UK, or an influenza pandemic.
- An international military crisis between states, drawing in the UK, and its allies as well as other states and non-state actors.

Tier Two: The National Security Council considered the following groups of risks to be the next highest priority looking ahead, taking account of both likelihood and impact. (For example, a CBRN attack on the UK by a state was judged to be low likelihood, but high impact.)

- An attack on the UK or its overseas territories by another state or proxy using chemical, biological, radiological, or nuclear (CBRN) weapons.
- Risk of major instability, insurgency, or civil war overseas which creates an environment that terrorists can exploit to threaten the UK.
- A significant increase in the level of organized crime affecting the UK.
- Severe disruption to information received, transmitted, or collected by satellites, possibly as the result of a deliberate attack by another state.

Tier Three: The National Security Council considered the following groups of risks to be the next highest priority after taking account of both likelihood and impact.

- A large-scale conventional military attack on the UK by another state (not involving the use of CBRN weapons) resulting in fatalities and damage to infrastructure within the UK.
- A significant increase in the level of terrorists, organized criminals, illegal immigrants, and illicit goods trying to enter the UK.
- Disruption to oil or gas supplies to the UK, or price instability, as a result of war, accident, major political upheaval, or deliberate manipulation of supply by producers.
- A major release of radioactive material from a civil nuclear site within the UK which affects one or more regions.
- A conventional attack by a state on another NATO or EU member to which the UK would have to respond.
- An attack on a UK overseas territory as the result of a sovereignty dispute or a wider regional conflict.
- Short- to medium-term disruption to international supplies of resources (eg food, minerals) essential to the UK.

National security in the UK—a modern history

In March 1948, the British Foreign Secretary, Ernest Bevin, wrote in a top secret memo entitled 'The Threat to Western Civilization' about the issue that had become central to conceptions of national security in Western nations. Bevin noted that Soviet expansion was not only a security concern, but an existential threat to civilization in Western democracies.[7] 'It is their intention', he noted of the Soviets, 'to endeavour to expand their activities to cover the whole of Europe at the earliest possible date'.[8] Indeed, 'physical control of the Eurasian land mass and eventual control of the whole world island is what the Politburo is aiming at—no less a thing than that.'[9]

These were not idle words. Bevin noted that 'the immensity of the aim should not betray us into believing in its impracticability'.[10] The clear threat he perceived from expansionary Soviet communism was one that required 'the active organisation of all those countries who believe in parliamentary government and free institutions'. Bevin proposed a strategy of a 'multilateral economic, cultural and defensive' union between Britain and its immediate West European neighbours, which would be 'left open for accession by other European democracies'. In March 1948 this progressed with the signing of the Treaty of Brussels between Britain, France, and the Benelux countries, which, in turn, paved the way for the establishment a year later of the North Atlantic Treaty Organization (NATO). The intention was unambiguous: here was a clear and comprehensive threat to security that required robust action based on a broad range of national interests, and that the action had to be multilateral and forged around shared values of democracy and liberty.

The immediate postwar period, therefore, was one in which a single, existential security threat loomed large over national governments in the Western world and particularly in Europe, as the Soviets made firm their gains in the Second World War to establish an arena of communism across Europe. It was perceived as an ideological, political, and raw military threat, as it became established in Western political thinking that the Soviet Union was hell-bent on expanding communism as far as possible, by force if necessary, the main evidence for which was the rapidly expanding size of Soviet military forces which appeared to far exceed any requirements for mere defence from attack.

If we wind the clock forward to the mid-1970s, we see Western governments deep in the planning and implementation of what had become the Cold War with the Soviet Union. National security and defence strategizing and planning was still wholly oriented towards the perceived Soviet threat. In a statement on the UK defence estimates of 1974, put forward by the recently installed Defence

---

[7] 'The Threat to Western Civilization', Memorandum by the Secretary of State for Foreign Affairs, 3 March 1948 (CP (48) 72), p 1.

[8] Ibid.

[9] Ibid, p 2.

[10] Ibid, p 2.

Secretary, Ian Gilmour, the opening words noted that 'Britain's security rests upon the strength of the North Atlantic Alliance'.[11] It was further observed that 'Under the protection of the Alliance, the West has remained secure; and Western Europe has been able to develop its institutions undisturbed.'[12] The continued and rapid development of the Soviet military capability and its deployment across the Warsaw Pact arena was assessed to have delivered 'strategic nuclear parity' with the United States. 'This makes it more than ever necessary', the 1974 statement noted, 'that the West should possess strong and credible conventional deterrent forces, as well as adequate tactical nuclear forces, so as to make clear to a potential aggressor that he cannot launch an attack with any certainty of being able to gain his objectives.'[13]

Here, therefore, was a strongly military conception of security, whereby a balance of hard power was the underpinning principle of national security. Western security, defined as an ability to 'develop institutions undisturbed' required a protective military ring around it to deter any notion of successful military attack from an aggressor. The logic was a simple one of numbers: it was noted in 1974 that 'The forces now deployed by the Warsaw Pact are greater than could possibly be needed for garrison duties, or for defence against an attack from the West, supposing such a thing to be conceivable.'[14] The deterrent force needed to include the most capable and destructive elements, from a large standing army right up to nuclear weapons, and the delivery systems for them, including a fleet of nuclear-powered submarines (of which the UK had eight by the end of 1974).

By the late 1980s, the Soviet system was clearly starting to fray at the seams, a perception underlined by the withdrawal of the mighty Soviet army from Afghanistan in 1989. The revolutions in Europe that accompanied the dismantling of the Berlin Wall in the same year, marked the endgame of communist dominance across postwar Europe. In 1991, the Soviet Union itself collapsed as a political unit, to be replaced by a number of sovereign, nominally democratic states (with the exception of Belarus). As Ronald Reagan had noted, 'Freedom is never more than one generation away from extinction. We didn't pass it to our children in the bloodstream. It must be fought for, protected, and handed on for them to do the same.' The notion was of an ideological battle—between communism and 'freedom'—and that it had to be contested with military might. The Cold War had never descended into all-out military conflict, but the threat of it doing so was always there in the shape of massive and very real military arsenals on both sides.

With the euphoria in the West of the breaching of the Berlin Wall and the end of the issue that had defined national security since the end of the Second

---

[11] 'Statement on the Defence Estimates 1974', Memorandum by the Secretary of State for Defence, 21 January 1974 (CP (74) 5), p I-1.
[12] Ibid.
[13] Ibid, p I-2.
[14] Ibid, pp I-3–4.

World War, much speculation arose as to the nature and shape of the post-Cold War world. Immediate security preoccupations at the macro level seemed to revolve primarily around regional conflicts that had arisen with the removal of the totalitarian communist state, and particularly those in the Balkans. The gradual and painful collapse of the state of Yugoslavia that began in 1991 unleashed a series of conflicts between pre-communist communities and states whose complexity caused many analysts to struggle to articulate what was happening, and how the international community should respond. The Dayton Accords signed in Paris in 1995 brought an end to the first phase of immediate conflict, but only after NATO had undertaken a bombing campaign against Serbia to bring it to the negotiating table.

As Fearon and Laitin note in their analysis of civil war, the post-Soviet conflicts were increasingly described in 'culturalist' terms rather than in terms of conflicts over economic disparity or grand political ideology.[15] Certainly, the conflicts erupting between Croats, Serbs, and 'Bosniaks' in the former Yugoslavia seemed to be most aptly described as 'ethnic' and nationalist conflicts. The 1995 US National Security Strategy presented in the Clinton administration noted that 'ethnic conflict is spreading', while also recognizing that this was just one of a much more 'diverse' set of security challenges than had been faced during the Cold War.[16] The thinking accorded with the data at the time. As Fearon and Laitin's analysis of the prevalence of civil war through the twentieth century shows, the end of the Soviet Union saw a spike in civil, intrastate conflicts. In 1990, approximately 30 countries around the world were afflicted by such conflicts, but by 1994 this figure had risen to above 40.[17]

The conflict in Yugoslavia had also posed some very difficult questions for the NATO alliance, which had been established 40 years earlier to confront the massed Soviet threat in Europe. Here was a new form of conflict, very much on Europe's doorstep, which threatened to conflate into wider regional conflict and burden Western Europe with serious human and resource burdens. The conflict was also punctuated with grave human rights abuses, the likes of which had not been seen in Europe since the Second World War. The establishment of the International Criminal Tribunal for the Former Yugoslavia (ICTY) in May 1993—the first such tribunal to be established by the UN and the first international court since the Nuremberg and Tokyo tribunals—also marked a shift in macro political philosophy. 'Realist' thinking of the twentieth century had suggested that hard military power backing up individual states' interests would always trump attempts to forge meaningful international alliances committed to mutual peace. The failure of the League of Nations in the 1930s to prevent territorial aggression and expansion, the subsequent horrors of the

---

[15] J.D. Fearon and D.D. Laitin, 'Ethnicity, Insurgency and Civil War', *American Political Science Review*, 97/1 (2003), 78.

[16] The White House, 'A National Security Strategy of Engagement and Enlargement', February 1995, p i.

[17] Fearon and Laitin, n 15, at 77.

Second World War, and the frozen chapter of the Cold War, had reinforced such notions. Institutions such as the ICTY, however, started to suggest that a more Kantian 'idealist' policy could have traction in a way that it had not been able to do for many decades. At the same time, there were questions for NATO and the West about 'intervention' in conflict scenarios such as the Balkans. As I will discuss in Chapter 8, the later period of conflict in Serbia involving the Kosovo enclave at the end of the 1990s, saw the British Prime Minister Tony Blair articulate a doctrine of military intervention for reasons of 'self-interest and moral purpose', in what became known as his Chicago speech.[18] In 2012, some analysts and commentators are pondering whether Prime Minister David Cameron is portraying a renewed 'Blair doctrine' in his foreign policy pronouncements about Britain's intentions in the area of military intervention overseas.[19]

While the Yugoslav wars were getting underway, another situation was developing in the Middle East which also set the tone for some of the post-Cold War scenarios that would be faced by the international community. Iraq's invasion of Kuwait in 1991 and Saddam Hussein's subsequent refusal to withdraw in the face of strong pressure from the UN ultimately led to an international military intervention, led primarily by NATO countries, in January 1992. The operation was interesting on a number of levels. First, the role of the UN was significant, in that a number of resolutions were passed ultimately authorizing military force against Iraq, culminating in Resolution 678 which stated that 'all necessary means' would be used if Iraq failed to comply with earlier demands to withdraw from Kuwait. Here, then, was a post-realist conflict in which, on the face of it, the international community had collaboratively set the policy instead of individual states taking matters into their own hands (notwithstanding a number of disagreements along the way within the UN Security Council).

From a military perspective, the intensely asymmetric nature of respective military capabilities in the conflict, which led to a rapid victory by the invading Coalition forces, led to much talk of a Revolution in Military Affairs (RMA). Here, ultra high-tech military equipment could both deliver to the living room exciting pictures of ordinance hitting targets through 24-hour news channels, but also restrict casualties (at least on the coalition side) to miniscule proportions. In the 1992 Gulf campaign it is estimated that the Coalition forces suffered 240 battle deaths, of which 148 were US service men and women.[20] This compares to more than 47,000 US battle deaths during the nine years of

---

[18] 'The Blair Doctrine', PBS News, 22 April 1999, available at <http://www.pbs.org/newshour/bb/international/jan-june99/blair_doctrine4-23.html> (accessed 16 September 2011).

[19] M. Savage, 'Words not enough against tyrants, Cameron tells UN', *The Times*, 23 September 2011, 7.

[20] Imperial War Museum, see <http://www.iwm.org.uk/server/show/ConWebDoc.2480> (accessed 27 June 2011).

the Vietnam conflict,[21] and represents an extraordinary change in the dangers of waging war over just 20 years of military development. (As with military capabilities, however, the casualty statistics are also very asymmetric, in that the Iraqis suffered very considerably more casualties in the 1992 conflict.) Strategic thinking in military circles began to consider whether the post-Cold War conflicts could be very different affairs: increasingly mechanized and surgical.

Such an experience, in turn, informed NATO's thinking in 1995 when it considered how to tackle the Yugoslav conflicts, and led to a preference for surgical bombardment of Serb targets from the air rather than the insertion of ground troops into a potentially bloody and protracted conflict. As I will explore, these post-1991 developments reverberate to this day and complicate the whole question of national security strategy and policy. The NATO bombing campaign in Libya during 2011 raised not only the question of how best to tackle a military intervention in the twenty-first century, but also how well NATO can now undertake such an operation over a sustained period. It is also an element of the 'boots on the ground' debate, which I will explore in Chapter 8.

Returning to President Clinton's National Security Strategy in 1995, we note a subtle change in emphasis in the nature and scope of threats faced. The document notes that:

> The dangers we face today are more diverse. Ethnic conflict is spreading and rogue states pose a serious danger to regional stability in many corners of the globe. The proliferation of weapons of mass destruction represents a major challenge to our security. Large scale environmental degradation, exacerbated by rapid population growth, threatens to undermine political stability in many countries and regions.[22]

A question is begged in such an analysis as to whether issues such as rogue states, weapons proliferation, and problems arising from environmental degradation and political instability only became security issues worthy of note in the 1990s. The answer must surely be of course not, so it would appear that what was happening in the rhetorical shift at this time was a broadening and deepening of security considerations beyond the former leviathan threat of the Soviet Union and its expansionist intentions. Indeed, the academic response to the uncertain, postmodern world after the Cold War was, as Sheehan points out, to broaden conceptions of security beyond the primarily military conceptions that had held sway through most of the twentieth century and into other dimensions and sectors of security such as societal, environmental, and economic security.[23] As the vanguard of the Copenhagen School of security

---

[21] A. Leland and M.-J. Oboroceanu, 'American War and Military Operations Casualties: Lists and Statistics', Washington DC, Congressional Research Service, 26 February 2010, p 3.

[22] The White House, 'A National Security Strategy of Engagement and Enlargement', February 1995, p i.

[23] M. Sheehan, 'Military Security' in A. Collins (ed), *Contemporary Security Studies* (Oxford: Oxford University Press, 2010), 170.

scholars, Buzan, Waever, and de Wilde described in the 1990s, a broadening of security concepts is associated with a notion of the 'securitization' of certain issues. Much like the process of politicization, securitization places an issue (eg environmental degradation) newly on a security spectrum, and establishes a degree of existentiality of threat.[24] Many of these issues need to be considered not necessarily as direct security threats themselves (eg an extreme weather event is a very different situation from a military attack) but as 'force multipliers' in security threat. Thus, environmental degradation might force the movement of populations, which in turn leads to increased pressure on resources in certain areas, which in turn can lead to a conflict that spreads beyond the immediate region.

The other underpinning element of the Copenhagen School's thesis is that securitization happens as a 'speech act' by political leaders and governments.[25] By labelling an issue as a *security* issue, a political actor 'claims a need for and a right to treat it by extraordinary means'.[26] Issues become security issues through political leaders saying they are so, and this utterance naturally leads to the need to 'do something'. The essentially exceptionalist policy approach to security issues is part and parcel of a notion of national security. On grounds of national security, governments can impose emergency powers or martial law, or derogate from legal obligations that would normally apply, such as those relating to data protection, invasions of privacy or, sometimes, human rights protection.

In this way, we can see that the changes to security strategizing that happened in the Western world in the 1990s represented fairly complex notions and concepts. The modern-day conflict and reconstruction effort in Afghanistan, for example, is much more difficult to explain to a sceptical public in the West than was the need to fight Nazi Germany in the Second World War, or to amass nuclear weapons afterwards to balance the Soviet threat (even though some people were sceptical about that too). Part of the rationale for the change must surely be one of capability, resource, and priority. Issues such as threats arising from environmental degradation were not completely absent from the world during the Cold War, but the perceived size and danger of the Soviet threat and the size of the military response that was deemed appropriate trumped all other issues in terms of priority. With the removal of the Soviet threat, light can now usefully be shone on such other issues and resources allocated to mitigating the threats they represent. This is essentially the securitizing speech act that governments have undertaken in the post-Cold War era. There are risks to the speech act hypothesis, as Williams pointed out, in that it could be used to explain, in an essentially agnostic way, how authoritarian regimes also

---

[24] B. Buzan, O. Waever, and J. de Wilde, *Security: A New Framework for Analysis* (Boulder, CA: Lynne Rienner, 1998), 23–4.

[25] Ibid, 26.

[26] Ibid.

articulate their security policies.[27] Thus, a fascist regime or organization might claim that security threat revolves primarily around the presence of a particular ethnic or religious community. At the time of writing, the Syrian regime is claiming that the mass demonstrations in its towns and cities are the work of terrorists and armed thugs, rather than anti-government protestors, as the rest of the world is reporting. This shows how different actors will articulate security threat very differently depending on the circumstances, and will frame their security responses accordingly.

These examples also demonstrate the central importance of the media to the formulation and articulation of security threat and perception thereof, which, Williams suggests, was slightly overlooked in the Copenhagen School's speech act hypothesis.[28] Thus, it is impossible to examine the events of 11 September 2001, for example, without reference to the shocking and repeatedly transmitted images of the burning towers of the World Trade Center. In the UK, a television documentary entitled 'The Power of Nightmares',[29] first shown in late 2004, argued that the Islamist terror threat had been blown out of proportion by military-bureaucratic elites for whom a heightened security threat would be profitable. The impact of the message was slightly lost when, a few months after screening, Islamist terrorists did indeed carry out a suicide bombing in London which claimed the lives of 56 people and wounded hundreds more. Despite this, the importance of media to notions of security threat and articulation by various actors should clearly not be understated.

None of this is to suggest, however, that the transformations in national security articulation in Western states since the end of the Cold War are merely conspiratorial speech acts by power brokers, which belie the true nature of the threats. In accordance with more recent official national security statements in the West, it is arguably the case that some security threats *have* become more complex and nuanced than was previously the case, as globalization has delivered greater connectivity and integration between societies and states across the globe. The Cold War was not only a political gridlock, but it also affected international trade very adversely in many parts of the world. With the opening up of former Soviet bloc markets, coupled with changes in information and related technologies, globalization has accelerated. The implications of this for conceptions of security threat and strategizing are discussed in the next chapter.

By the beginning of the twenty-first century, national security strategies in the Western world very clearly reflect the process of broadening that has been underway since the 1990s, and the securitization of a wide range of issues.

---

[27] M.C. Williams, 'Words, Images, Enemies: Securitisation and International Politics', *International Studies Quarterly*, 47 (2003), 522.

[28] Ibid, 525.

[29] For a discussion of this documentary and the 'politics of fear', see A. Glees, 'UK Security Policy and the "Politics of Fear"' in P. Major and C.R. Moran (eds), *Spooked: Britain, Empire and Intelligence since 1945* (Newcastle upon Tyne: Cambridge Scholars Publishing, 2009), 156.

The UK's latest NSS, which forms the key framework of analysis for this book, notes in its introduction that, unlike the Cold War, Britain now faces a 'different and more complex range of threats from a myriad of sources'.[30] Such threats include 'terrorism, cyber attack, unconventional attacks using chemical, nuclear or biological weapons, as well as large scale accidents or natural hazards'.[31] The complexity lies not only in the range of threats themselves, however (many of which are identified as 'new threats'), but also in the nature of the originators of such threats. The strategy notes that:

> These new threats can emanate from states, but also from non state actors: terrorists, home-grown or overseas; insurgents; or criminals. The security of our energy supplies increasingly depends on fossil fuels located in some of the most unstable parts of the planet. Nuclear proliferation is a growing danger. Our security is vulnerable to the effects of climate change and its impact on food and water supply. So the concept of national security in 2010 is very different to what it was ten or twenty, let alone fifty or a hundred years ago.[32]

Leaving aside the question already discussed of whether such threats can really be described as new, rather than the way in which they have been securitized, the picture being painted here is very much one of complexity, breadth of threats and actors, and international interconnectedness. This, it seems, is the new conception of national security in the Western world.

Defining 'national security'

Having introduced a notion of national security, it is worth pausing for a moment to consider how we define this concept. I have established that security is, to a certain extent, a constructed concept for any given state at any given time. Factors such as political realities and priorities will play major roles in determining which issues are securitized, as will the media to a certain extent in certain situations. This hypothesis partly explains how and why the issues identified as key national security priorities in the West have changed and developed over time. In particular, the end of the Cold War and its perceived existential military threat of East versus West, have been replaced by a broader range of securitized issues and a deeper construction of security actors and dimensions that move far beyond the purely military sphere, and into civil and commercial dimensions. As with many issues, therefore, security it rather more complicated than it initially appears.

The other component of national security—the 'national' part—is no less complicated. In unravelling the definition of national security it is necessary to consider definitions of nations and states, and how they fit together.

---

[30] NSS, n 4, at 3.
[31] Ibid.
[32] Ibid.

Most importantly, it is worth noting that, while the terms 'nation' and 'state' are often used interchangeably (and sometimes together in the term 'nation-state'), they are not always the same thing. The UN was established in 1945 at the end of the Second World War. As Langhorne describes, the UN was the latest incarnation of earlier attempts to establish international alliances of states in the interests of forging peace, formed on the back of long and murderous conflicts in Europe.[33] The earlier episodes were the Concert of Europe, established in 1815 at the end of the Napoleonic wars, and the League of Nations, founded in 1920 at the end of the First World War. The UN has effectively become the pre-eminent club for states across the world, having presided over the period in history in which the traditional concept of a nation-state has come to define administration over every corner of the earth. By 2012, there were 193 member states in the United Nations General Assembly (and, at the time of writing, the Palestinian National Authority is bidding to become the 194th). This marks a considerable expansion from the 55 states that signed the original charter in 1945, and even the figure of 166 states that were members at the end of the Cold War, in 1991.[34]

Despite its name, the UN speaks of its members as 'states', and is effectively an organization for sovereign states which agree to abide by its charter.[35] A better and more accurate name for the organization would probably be United States, but that name had already been taken by 1945! The notion of a sovereign state, at least in modern times, is generally considered to originate with the Peace of Westphalia treaties, signed in Osnabrück and Münster in 1648, which established the end of the disastrous Thirty Years War in Europe. The treaties established the notion of the sovereignty of a ruler over a particular territorial area, within which he or she would have autonomy to establish the system of religion and administration, without interference from other sovereigns. The great political philosopher, Thomas Hobbes, whose work *Leviathan* appeared in 1651, developed this idea further with two key concepts: first, he emphasized the manner in which the sovereign of a state effectively gave life to a state as a distinct entity, effectively becoming the 'head of the body', without which neither component could function. Secondly, he suggested that states were the highest form of authority in the international order, and existed within an anarchic 'state of nature' in which their own interests prevailed, and over which no higher authority could rule.[36] With the establishment of the UN and its activities post-Cold War, an idealist vision of international authority that can truly challenge the supremacy of individual states is perhaps finding its feet for the first time since these developments in the seventeenth century.

---

[33] R. Langhorne, *Global Politics'* (London: Hodder Arnold, 2006), 82.

[34] UN, Member States, see <http://www.un.org/en/members/growth.shtml> (accessed 29 June 2011).

[35] See <http://www.un.org/en/documents/charter/chapter2.shtml> (accessed 29 June 2011).

[36] J.S. Nye and D.A. Welch, *Understanding Global Conflict and Cooperation* (Boston, MA: Longman, 2011), 3.

Much later, the great social scientist, Max Weber, described the central importance of security and coercion to the state, and the pre-eminence of military discipline within the institutions of the state.[37] Malešević describes this as a process over time of the 'cumulative bureaucratisation of coercion',[38] which was central to the manner in which modern states established processes and institutions that could raise armies and establish security in both defensive and offensive ways, with Napolean and his *levée en masse* of 1793 being a key development.

The notion of a 'Westphalian state' as it is often described now, is therefore a conception of an administrative unit of organization within a particular territory. It does not necessarily say anything about a connection to a 'nation' of people that underpins that state, only (in its original form) of allegiance to a particular sovereign. (Although the experience of Napoleon suggests that French nationalism was central to the cumulative bureaucratization of coercion, in the sense that citizens could be persuaded to fight for *la patrie*.) As constructivist theories of nationalism have suggested, nationality and nationalism are, like security, essentially constructed conceptions, based on a varying menu of cultural, social, and political factors, such as shared language, a history of territorial integrity and continuity, or a set of religious or ideological identifiers or 'values'. Benedict Anderson describes the nation as 'an imagined political community'.[39] The political component signifies that political leaders will mobilize nationalism for political gains, as Napoleon did in order to mobilize a very large army that could march across Europe.

This is important to the story of national security. First, it explains why nations and states are not always connected geographically or politically. In some cases, a set of people that might consider themselves to be a nation, can be spread across more than one state (the Germans during the Cold War, eg, who achieved 'reunification' of two states in 1989). In other cases, a nation may exist without a state, classic examples of which are perhaps currently the Palestinians (notwithstanding the status of the Palestinian National Authority), or the Kurds, for whom Kurdistan has not yet been achieved. A third category is a state which contains within itself a number of different nationalities, who may from time to time mobilize themselves around a secessionist movement to break away and form a new state (examples include the Tamils in Sri Lanka, Baluchis in Pakistan, or Igbos in Nigeria).

Perhaps of more significance in the UK example, which I will explore later in the book, is the question of how 'national values' are brought into the security debate by political leaders. The current UK government has stressed in its counter-terrorism strategy, for example, that problematic extremism is defined

---

[37] M. Weber, *Economy and Society* (New York: Bedminster Press, 1968), 1152.

[38] S. Malešević, *The Sociology of War and Violence* (Cambridge: Cambridge University Press, 2011), 5.

[39] B. Anderson, *Imagined Communities* (London: Verso, 2006), 6.

as 'active opposition to fundamental British values'.[40] This immediately brings into debate how we define the British nationality and its values, and when and how these relate to the citizens within the British state. Not everyone within that state will hold the same view of such issues.

With all these issues established, we can propose that 'national security' is defined as a particular articulation of security priorities and concerns put forward by the political leaders of a state, at a given time in its history. The manner in which the leaders will mobilize these concerns is constructed around the interests of a particular set of people, identified as the citizens of the state. This defines a notion of the 'national interest', the defence of which will define how states will act in particular circumstances. As Nye and Welch describe, the traditional Realist view of international relations defines national interest as a set of issues that revolve around the need to preserve and project power within the anarchic international system of states.[41] Liberals, idealists, and constructivists, on the other hand, whose theories have gained in currency since the end of the Cold War, will tend to suggest that the national interest can start to incorporate a much wider set of values and concerns than merely those of military and diplomatic power. This range of issues and concerns is not set in stone: perhaps more than ever before in history, agreement on what constitutes the national interest and national security is very much contested.[42] Ripsman and Paul encapsulate the debates by presenting different notions of what they describe as 'the national security state'.[43] Conceptions of such an institution will vary from purely military ideas around territorial integrity, to a wider range of 'interests', including economic, cultural, and political concerns. These wider issues begin to bring in the concept of 'human security', to rival national security, which Fukuda-Parr describes as focusing on 'the well-being and dignity of people rather than the protection of national borders'.[44] Here we can start to see the potential 'moral' dimension of foreign policy, as Blair articulated in his Chicago speech. Such issues are closely connected to processes of globalization, which I will explore in the next chapter.

Key points

- The 2010 NSS and SDSR in the UK were heralded as representing the first national security strategy in Britain based on a structured and objective

---

[40] HM Government, 'Prevent Strategy' (London: TSO, June 2011), p 34 n 38.

[41] Nye and Welch, n 36, at 45.

[42] Ibid, 46.

[43] N.M. Ripsman and T.V. Paul, *Globalization and the National Security State* (Oxford: Oxford University Press, 2010), 10–12.

[44] S. Fukuda-Parr, 'New Threats to Human Security in the Era of Globalization', *Journal of Human Development*, 4/2 (2003), 167.

risk assessment. The Coalition government also established a National Security Council process in the UK for the first time under that name.

- The NSS delivers a three-tier prioritization of risks facing the UK, based on a calculation of both likelihood and impact. Tier One comprises risks from terrorism, from cyber attack, from a major natural hazard or accident, and from an international military crisis which draws in the UK.
- During the Cold War, national security in the UK was framed squarely around the expansionist Soviet military and nuclear threat.
- The immediate post-Cold War period was dominated by increasingly 'culturalist' notions of security threat, such as the ethnic conflicts in the Balkans. Tony Blair expressed a new 'doctrine' in 1999 which described an interventionist role for Britain on moral and humanitarian grounds.
- Securitization during the 1990s increasingly 'broadened' the range of national security risks, taking in such issues as environmental and 'human security' factors.
- A notion of 'national security' also brings in the question of national values and national identity, namely the place that Britain wishes to occupy in the world.

2

Setting the Scene: The Threat Picture in a Globalized World

'Wider' security risks

The National Security Strategy (NSS) and associated Strategic Defence and Security Review (SDSR) of 2010 identify the threat picture in two main ways. The first, as outlined in the previous chapter, is to identify a three-tier priority list of specific 'priority risks' which emerged from a risk assessment exercise. The details of the risks thus identified in this process are the subject of the following three chapters.

The second way of looking at the national security threat picture and strategic response is to look at the set of risk dimensions across which the specific threat priorities have been allocated into tiers of priority. Under the title of 'wider security', the SDSR notes that the National Security Risk Assessment (NSRA) process, about which I will say more in the next chapter, identified eight 'wider security risks', which manifest themselves in different ways across the priority bands.[1] These are:

1. Terrorism
2. Instability and conflict overseas
3. Cyber security
4. Civil emergencies
5. Energy security
6. Organized crime
7. Border security
8. Counter proliferation and arms control.

---

[1] HM Government, 'Securing Britain in an Age of Uncertainty: The Strategic Defence and Security Review' (London: TSO, October 2010), 41.

From a response capability point of view, this is the framework around which planning needs to take place, since any one of these dimensions could contribute to a security risk in different ways and at different levels of priority. Analysts of security in the globalized world will recognize many of these issues as 'transnational threats', notably terrorism, crime, and proliferation. The point to note is that, while all these issues existed before 1991, two things have happened subsequently: first, processes of globalization, and particularly the transformations in social networking and business activity which the information revolution has enabled, have allowed such security threats to transmogrify themselves in new and dangerous ways. Secondly, governments have increasingly securitized a new set of issues, such as energy security, in ways that were not quite the same during the existential military preoccupations of the Cold War.

The political backdrop

The UK's NSS of 2010 is an interesting document politically as much as for its content. The Cameron and Clegg Coalition administration, installed in May 2010, made national security strategizing one of its highest priorities. This was evidenced by the announcement of the formation of the National Security Council (NSC) just a day after the new government took office. While such an institution is familiar to the United States and many other countries, the UK has not previously had a body of this name at the top of its security policy administration (although, as I will discuss later, the previous Gordon Brown administration had established a forerunner in the shape of the National Security, International Relations and Development (NSID) Committee in 2008). Previously, the role was conducted by the Prime Minister and key members of the Cabinet such as the Foreign and Defence Secretaries, with help from the Joint Intelligence Committee (JIC) in the Cabinet Office. The aim of the new NSC is to 'coordinate responses to the dangers we face, integrating at the highest level the work of the foreign, defence, home, energy and international development departments, and all other departments of government contributing to national security.'[2] This reflects, at an administrative level, the broadened and deepened conception of security that has taken place in countries such as the UK since the end of the Cold War.

The NSC sits in the Cabinet Office, just along the corridor from the JIC, with which it interacts closely. Policy is clearly not the job of the JIC (officials point out the important line to be maintained between 'assessment'

---

[2] 'David Cameron establishes National Security Council', ConservativeHome, available at <http://conservativehome.blogs.com/thetorydiary/2010/05/david-cameron-pledged-before-the-election-that-one-of-his-first-acts-as-prime-minister-would-be-to-create-a-national-secur.html> (accessed 25 June 2011).

and 'policy'),[3] but the question of which issues are securitized and placed within the governmental priority list for intelligence should fall across both committees to a certain extent. The political aspects of the NSC are first, perhaps inevitably with a new element of administration, that battle lines and areas of responsibility are not yet certain. These will always become sticks with which the Opposition can beat a government. The origins of thinking around the NSC in the UK are to be found in the planning that led up to the Iraq War in 2003. Dubbed in the media as 'sofa politics',[4] Tony Blair's style of government was perceived to be one in which many key decisions were often made by small, informal gatherings of ministers and other key officials, and including the Press Secretary, discussing issues directly with the Prime Minister, outside the more formal parliamentary and committee structures and processes. The totemic example of this process was the decision to join the United States in invading Iraq in 2003, around which there was widespread and damaging disagreement not only within the government, parliament, and the judiciary, but also across the electorate as a whole. Such momentous decisions in the foreign policy sphere in particular, it was argued, should not be made outside rigid parliamentary processes.

Cameron pledged to place such matters more firmly on an accountable administrative footing by establishing the NSC. One of the problems, inevitably, is that the degree to which the NSC can operate as a completely objective and depoliticized institution will constantly come under scrutiny. The political correspondent for *The Telegraph* noted in May 2011, for example, that the decision to withdraw British combat troops from Afghanistan by 2015, announced by the parliamentary Foreign Affairs Committee, appears not to have been made within the NSC, when this is exactly the type of foreign affairs policy question that probably should fall under its remit.[5] Whether this is little more than teething problems in establishing new decision-making processes within a new set of complex and sometimes overlapping institutions, or a more sinister example of certain highly political decisions (of which the withdrawal of troops from Afghanistan is certainly an example) continuing to be kept outside wider circles of discussion and scrutiny, remains to be seen.

The second way in which the NSS is highly political is the manner in which it betrays the key debates of the time of its formation, alongside the long-term strategic issues with which it is dealing. In particular, the need to get a grip on an adverse economic situation, which the strategy effectively securitizes,

---

[3] Interview with National Security Secretariat official, September 2011.

[4] M. Kavanagh, 'How to fix the National Security Council', *The Spectator*, 15 May 2011, available at <http://www.spectator.co.uk/coffeehouse/6947108/how-to-fix-the-national-security-council.thtml> (accessed 29 May 2011).

[5] J. Kirkup, 'What exactly is the point of David Cameron's National Security Council?', *The Telegraph*, 4 May 2011, available at <http://blogs.telegraph.co.uk/news/jameskirkup/100086387/what-is-the-point-of-david-camerons-national-security-council/> (accessed 15 May 2011).

runs as a strong thread throughout the document. It identifies the 'largest single challenge' affecting national security and 'all other areas of public policy', as the need to 'return our nation's finances to a sustainable footing and bring sense to the profligacy and lack of planning that we inherited.'[6] This is a thinly veiled reference to the types of issues that revolve particularly around very large and long-term defence contracts, which have shown a tendency to deliver considerable cost and delivery-time overruns. Classic examples in the past have included the Eurofighter Typhoon fighter jet and Nimrod surveillance aircraft. The Commons Public Accounts Committee suggested in 2010 that defence procurement overspend could be as much as £36 billion, a figure representing more than 97 per cent of the entire annual defence budget.[7]

The issue quickly becomes politicized, in that the Opposition at the time could accuse the then Labour government of poor management and 'profligacy' contributing to the overall economic crisis, and also pledge that they would themselves deliver much better management of the situation when in power. In addition to the political point, however, there is a genuine question raised about the appropriate nature of defence spending, both in size and substance. The types of projects that tend to overrun are those involving high-tech military capability, such as complex new aircraft, or naval vessels such as aircraft carriers, which require long development times. The problem often becomes a spiralling one. In its critical 2010 report on defence spending cited above, the Commons Public Accounts Committee noted the example of a government contract for new aircraft carriers signed in 2008. The government had to delay the project as it could not fund the £5.2 billion price tag within the originally agreed timescales, and this added to the overall cost. The incoming Coalition government claimed that it would have liked to scrap the project altogether, but that this would have increased the cost to the taxpayer by a further 5 per cent, and meant the closure of three shipyards, with a loss of 5,000 jobs.[8]

A project of this size represents a very considerable investment: this contract alone accounts for approximately 14 per cent of the entire annual defence budget. We can see the very obvious knock-on political aspects of the impact on British manufacturing and the consequent loss of jobs in affected constituencies. These are the factors that allow heavy politicization of such issues as defence spending and development, but the key security question is whether the broader and deeper security threat picture in a globalizing world identified by the strategy still calls for the types of high-tech equipment that were central to the Cold War. As the chief of the British Army

---

[6] HM Government, 'A Strong Britain in an Age of Uncertainty: The National Security Strategy' (London: TSO, October 2010), 14.

[7] 'MPs critical of Ministry of Defence Overspend', BBC News, 14 December 2010, available at <http://www.bbc.co.uk/news/uk-politics-11985266> (accessed 15 January 2011).

[8] Ibid.

at the time, and now Chief of Defence Staff, General Sir David Richards, said in 2010:

> Hi-tech weapons platforms are not a good way to help stabilise tottering states—nor might their cost leave us any money to help in any other way—any more than they impress opponents equipped with weapons costing a fraction.[9]

Thus, as we saw in 1974, the need for Britain to possess eight nuclear-powered submarines with the ability to launch long-range nuclear-armed ballistic missiles was generally accepted by many as an appropriate way in which to structure the defence budget in the face of the security threat picture at the time. In the twenty-first century, such equipment, which costs multiple billions of pounds of taxpayers' money to develop, does not gain much leverage against asymmetric targets such as Al Qaeda terrorists or the Taliban, who are generally armed either with home-made explosive devices or basic automatic rifles. Nor does it help to tackle such issues as environmental degradation or human security arising from climate change. The question has to be asked, therefore, especially in a time of financial stringency, whether such items should be appearing in the defence budget at all. This is a question I will explore.

Of course, in many ways, the question is not as simple as that. As the head of the army, General Sir David's remarks were interpreted by some as suggesting that he was merely fighting the army's corner by calling for 'more boots on the ground', and taking a swipe at the navy and the air force, who tend to own the type of high-tech military equipment in question. The Chief of the Naval Staff and First Sea Lord, Admiral Sir Mark Stanhope, countered the argument by claiming that the UK's influence and interests depend on it being able to project power across the globe, including a capability to conduct 'high intensity warfare'.[10] As is often the case in British debates on this subject, he invoked the Falklands factor, by reminding us that the Argentinian invasion of the Falklands and the British military response in 1982 (in which naval and air power were crucial) 'came from left field' and showed that strategic shocks cannot be predicted. He noted that it is dangerous to build long-term strategy around immediate security concerns such as Afghanistan, because the threat picture is dynamic and unpredictable.[11] The conundrum thus presented is central to the nature of post-Cold War security planning and strategizing. It is perhaps instructive that the very title of the 2010 NSS includes the phrase 'age of uncertainty'. As the early twentieth-century Danish physician, Niels Bohr, noted 'prediction is difficult, especially about the future'.[12] For military strategizing, the added problem is that the long and expensive development cycles for high-tech

---

[9] R. Norton-Taylor, 'UK military chiefs clash over future defence strategy', *The Guardian*, 18 January 2010, available at <http://www.guardian.co.uk/uk/2010/jan/18/military-defence-spending-army-navy> (accessed 15 February 2011).

[10] Ibid.

[11] Ibid.

[12] Cited in the *The Economist*, 'The perils of prediction', 15 July 2007, <http://www.economist.com/blogs/theinbox/2007/07/the_perils_of_prediction_june> (accessed 15 March 2011).

military equipment fit neither with shorter term political cycles, nor with the manner in which security threats and strategic shocks can unfold in a rapidly globalizing world.

What is clear, however, is that spending on defence by European countries has clearly declined since the end of the Cold War. NATO Secretary General, Anders Fogh Rassmussen, recently noted that the European component of NATO has reduced its defence spending by 20 per cent in this period, which has caused its contribution of the overall total of NATO expenditure to fall from 34 per cent in 1991 to 21 per cent in 2011.[13] Ripsman and Paul analyse this trend within the context of the proposition put forward by some analysts of globalization, that the change in the threat picture and particularly the reduction in state-on-state conflict since the twentieth century, will inevitably deliver greatly reduced defence expenditures, as security threats start to evolve into sectors outside the military sphere.[14] The picture that Ripsman and Paul find when looking at the global picture actually challenges this hypothesis, and suggests that Europe may be out of step with the world in general on this point. While global defence expenditure did decline sharply in the late 1980s (in step with the decline and eventual demise of the Cold War), it has since risen steadily again, and particularly so after the 9/11 attacks in the United States. Between 2001 and 2002, for example, global defence expenditure actually rose 6.2 per cent to $948 billion, and has continued rising steadily since.[15]

As ever, such issues can become highly political, and expenditure figures are always subject to conjecture. The UK Ministry of Defence claims that its defence expenditure, adjusted for inflation, has actually risen in the four years since 2007 by 1.5 per cent, to £37 billion.[16] As a proportion of GDP, however, the UK's defence expenditure fell steadily from 4.1 per cent in 1988, to 2.7 per cent in 2009, a figure roughly equivalent to that of France, and twice as much as Germany.[17] On the question of future defence spending, the Prime Minister confirmed that the defence budget would fall by 8 per cent in real terms over the four years after 2008.[18] Perhaps more importantly, US defence expenditure as a proportion of GDP over the same period dipped from 5.7 to 3 per cent between 1988 and 1999, but then rose steadily to 4.7 per cent in 2009.[19] The mismatch in these trends inside and outside Europe may be leading to a political crisis in NATO, as I will discuss later, as the United States finds itself

---

[13] A. Fogh Rassmussen, 'NATO after Libya', *Foreign Affairs*, 90/4 (2011), 4.

[14] N.M. Ripsman and T.V. Paul, *Globalization and the National Security State* (Oxford: Oxford University Press, 2010), 41.

[15] Ibid, 42.

[16] 'Defence spending', MOD, available at <http://www.mod.uk/DefenceInternet/About Defence/Organisation/KeyFactsAboutDefence/DefenceSpending.htm> (accessed 15 June 2011).

[17] Figures derived from Stockholm International Peace Research Institute (SIPRI), Military Expenditure Database, 2011, available at <http://www.sipri.org/databases> (accessed 10 June 2011).

[18] Cited in P. Cornish and A.M. Dorman, 'Dr Fox and the Philosopher's Stone: The Alchemy of National Defence in the Age of Austerity', *International Affairs*, 87/2 (2011), 341.

[19] SIPRI, n 17.

increasingly holding the purse strings for major NATO operations in the contemporary era.

The strategic context—globalization and transnational threats

In terms of a strategy to take on the post-Cold War world, the NSS claims to be a historic document in that it is purportedly the first to carry out a detailed view of all defence and security capabilities, and the first to do so by any government since the terrorist attacks of 11 September 2001.[20] If this bold claim is correct, then the NSS is a unique window on to the national security thinking of a major European state in the post-Cold War and post-Al Qaeda era. In its opening paragraphs, the NSS sets out the 'strategic context' in which the strategy is framed. Interestingly, the transnational dimension of the current security picture is described and scoped in terms of a number of factors. First, the strategy describes a situation which is neither passive nor wholly defensive against threats coming into the state, but rather one which incorporates a component of reaching out and pre-empting threats before they can develop. Evidence of this is encapsulated in the ambitious intention described in the strategy to 'shape a stable world',[21] which is less likely to incubate major transnational threats such as terrorism and crime.

Secondly, the NSS stresses the importance of international relationships in the UK's work on building and defending its national security, not only with traditional partners such as the United States, but potentially with a wider range of new partners as a more multipolar world takes shape and new powers emerge. This is the basic logic that transnational threats require transnational responses, and that states cannot act alone in a globalized world.

The NSS mentions globalization relatively early in its analysis, and describes this as a process that has 'made the world more interconnected' through technology, travel and migration, and trade. Since many of the security threats that the UK government articulates are closely connected to the phenomenon of globalization, it is worth exploring at this stage what exactly this process entails. Not least because the word tends to be used rather liberally in modern political debate. McGrew provides a useful conceptualization of globalization as 'a fundamental shift or transformation in the spatial scale of human social organisation that links distant communities and expands the reach of power relations across regions and continents.'[22] Some sceptics of the contemporary globalization process have remarked on the fact that international interconnectedness is

---

[20] NSS, n 6, at 9.

[21] Ibid, 10.

[22] A. McGrew, 'Globalization and Global Politics' in J. Baylis, S. Smith, and P. Owens (eds), *The Globalization of World Politics: An Introduction to International Relations* (Oxford: Oxford University Press, 2010), 19.

not a new phenomenon, and that the world was arguably more globalized in trade at earlier stages of history, but the counter argument is that what we are seeing now is a revolutionary transformation from 'internationalization' to 'globalism'. As Langhorne observes, globalization 'is not a replacement for the international politics of an earlier era but has joined them in a highly complicated and pluralistic world.'[23] In essence:

> The process and results of globalisation are changing the way we live our lives on a personal basis and they are changing the institutions which we collectively use to give form and predictability to our economic, social and political relationships.[24]

These comments stress the multidimensional elements of the current experience of globalization which are fundamentally changing the nature of power structures and articulations across the world in a complicated, and not necessarily very even, way. Running like a thread through the three critical dimensions of economic, social, and political transformations under globalization, the explosion of information technology since the latter stages of the twentieth century has accelerated and deepened the changes in a way that has never before been seen. These changes represent enormous opportunities for those who can benefit from them, but they also represent security risks to society at levels of complexity that require fundamentally new approaches.

On the economic front, increased trade flows across the world have been enabled by the enhancement of communications to a stage where they are instantaneous and very cheap. When calling a customer service helpline or placing an order over the phone, you are just as likely now to be speaking to someone in Bangalore as in Birmingham, and generally it makes no difference to the transaction. Technology has also enabled the ability to move capital and to trade almost instantaneously across the globe, as financial markets have become automated and linked together. The NSS notes the opportunities in such a situation for the UK, observing that 'our location and our time zone position us as a link between the economic centres of Asia and America, as well as forming part of the European single market.'[25] London's financial centre and its ability to trade in global markets has become one of the mainstays of the UK economy.

At the same time, the size of capital flows across the world (estimated to be $1.88 trillion per day in 2008) and their facility to change direction instantaneously represents an enormous risk to national economies. For an emerging economy, the effects can be very damaging. To name just one example, Indonesia suffered a potentially catastrophic outflow of $4.35 billion by investors from its central bank during the financial crisis in 2009, causing a serious

---

[23] R. Langhorne, *The Essentials of Global Politics* (New York: Hodder Arnold, 2006), 1.
[24] Ibid.
[25] NSS, n 6, at 21.

dent in its growth projections and placing many people in economic peril.[26] The World Bank estimated that the financial crisis would place 53 million more people below the poverty line in developing countries.[27] At the same time, as McGrew notes, even the most economically powerful countries are not immune from the effects of such enormous and dynamic flows of capital.[28] The security effects of this are multifaceted. First, evidence is clear that globalization is a process that delivers winners and losers, and which widens the gap between rich and poor. This, in turn, runs the risk of feeding into radical anti-globalization and anti-West ideologies. Indeed, in the Muslim world in particular, a notion of 'Westoxification' is often invoked to describe the type of societal ills that supposedly come from Western-style development, such as urbanization, unemployment, and the breakdown of traditional familial support networks.[29] Whether or not this is a simplification of the processes of globalization under-way (many of these issues are not necessarily Western in essence), they can be mobilized by radical movements both on the political left (picking up on the former threads of Marxism and anarchism) and within political Islam. There is a theory that Al Qaeda, for example, is essentially an anti-globalization move-ment at heart,[30] cloaked in selected Islamic ideology to give it some credibility among Muslim communities.

Socially, modern communications technology is allowing populations to link together in horizontal networks which transcend national borders and jurisdic-tions. Social networking, media, and communications facilities such as Facebook, YouTube, and Skype, allow individuals to communicate and share information either collectively or point-to-point, instantly and without any ref-erence to local or national identity. Such facilities essentially inhabit 'cyber-space' rather than any national networks. From a security point of view, this process delivers a number of effects. Particularly, but not only, for authoritarian regimes, it is becoming increasingly difficult to control information and to pre-vent details from becoming public where the state would rather they did not. The effects of this are being seen very clearly in the Arab Spring uprisings cur-rently underway across the Middle East, whereby social networking may be facilitating the spread of such information as police actions against protestors, within and between countries but also out to the international community. It is indicative that an important part of the security crackdown on protests in such countries as Iran and Syria has been the restriction of internet and social

---

[26] 'Indonesia plays down capital outflow concern', China Economic Net, available at <http://en.ce.cn/subject/financialcrisis/financialcrisiswr/201007/01/t20100701_21570582.shtml> (accessed 29 June 2011).

[27] I. Islam and A. Chowdhury, 'Global Economic Crisis and Indonesia', *Jakarta Post*, 5 May 2009), available at <http://www.thejakartapost.com/news/2009/05/05/global-economic-crisis-and-indonesia.html> (accessed 25 June 2011).

[28] McGrew, n 22, at 23.

[29] 'The curse of Westoxification', *The Economist*, 16 January 2003, available at <http://www.economist.com/node/1522110> (accessed 12 March 2011).

[30] J.L Gelvin, *The Modern Middle East: A History* (New York: Oxford University Press, 2007), 5.

media usage.[31] Meanwhile, the West has been rocked by the Wikileaks episode from 2010 onwards, whereby classified telegrams between US diplomats have been made available to the press, causing severe embarrassment in some cases. Questions are now being asked about whether secret information can truly remain so in the age of the internet.

Secondly, as with other dimensions of globalization, the enormous benefits of being able to construct instant social networks across the globe can also become risks, where the people doing the networking are doing so for nefarious reasons, such as organized crime groups and terrorists. Al Qaeda's ability to use the internet and social networking both to spread jihadist propaganda and to recruit new young radicals to the global cause, has been a revelation in many ways. The case of Younis Tsouli, who made himself available to Al Qaeda in Iraq over cyberspace from his bedroom in London, and offered his very considerable IT skills to the movement, is a striking example of how social networking can be a serious security threat.[32] Similarly, international hacking groups such as LulzSec and Anonymous—the former of which came to prominence in 2011 with the arrest of a 19-year-old alleged hacker in Essex, who had been breaking into international corporations and security agencies[33]—rely very much on an international web of skilled hackers who come together entirely over cyberspace. There is also evidence that some of the more state-centred attempts at hacking originating from such countries as China, may be in part conducted by politically motivated 'netizens' and non-state 'patriot hackers' rather than necessarily official employees of state security agencies.[34] To all of these processes, the binding together of individuals through social networking over the internet provides a new range of possibilities that were not previously present.

All the processes of communication over borders and social networking described above also provide a new set of political possibilities and developments. The NSS notes that 'new systems of influence' in international politics are starting to develop, which are 'outside the traditional international architecture'.[35] The strategy is referring particularly to broader governmental institutions such as the G20, which, the NSS notes, will potentially become much more significant than the old G8 as multipolarity develops and new powers emerge. Some of these new powers are as much economic as military powers. But the transformation potentially goes wider and deeper than this. Many 'Globalization School' advocates note that the post-Cold War period

---

[31] S. Tisdall, 'Iran helping Syrian regime crack down on protestors, say diplomats', *The Guardian*, 9 May 2011, available at <http://www.guardian.co.uk/world/2011/may/08/iran-helping-syrian-regime-protesters> (accessed 27 June 2011).

[32] J. Richards, *The Art and Science of Intelligence Analysis* (Oxford: Oxford University Press, 2010), 60–1.

[33] D. Meyer, 'Essex teenager arrested for hacking and DDoS', *ZDNet UK*, 21 June 2011, available at <http://www.zdnet.co.uk/news/security-threats/2011/06/21/essex-teenager-arrested-for-hacking-and-ddos-40093170/> (accessed 29 June 2011).

[34] A. Klimburg, 'Mobilising Cyber Power', *Survival*, 53/1 (2011), 44.

[35] NSS, n 6, at 15.

of globalization has seen a growing proliferation of, and influence by, non-governmental and international organizations. McGrew identifies the development as the emergence of an 'embryonic transnational society', whereby a range of international organizations, advocacy networks, and citizen's groups 'have come to play a significant role in mobilizing, organizing, and exercising political power across national boundaries'.[36] Non-governmental organizations (NGOs) such as Greenpeace, the World Wildlife Fund, and Amnesty International, to name but a few, which are essentially transnational organizations, are starting to play a significant role in some parts of international decision-making.

Again, the speed and ease of communications in the internet age is facilitating the growth and mobilization of such organizations and movements, as information and awareness about situations in different parts of the world can be made available much more readily. This leads to a new twist on the notion of cosmopolitanism, whereby citizens of the world can expect not only certain minimum standards of rights and protection, but other members of the international citizenry come under a certain moral obligation to resolve humanitarian issues when they become aware of them. As Bellamy notes, the former UK Prime Minister, Tony Blair, invoked what he called the 'doctrine of the international community' when he built the case for taking Serbia to task for its contraventions of human rights in the region of Kosovo in 1999.[37] This was a significant development, as it set a precedent for state-on-state military action in support of a minority group seeking secession from within a state, but also emphasized the need to intervene where such humanitarian issues come to the attention of the international community. One of the problems with this concept is that it can only ever be applied selectively, as intervention during 2011 in Libya but not in Syria has shown.

While the growth of 'people power' in this sense, which starts to mobilize horizontally across state boundaries and outside official channels using modern social networking techniques is clearly a significant element of modern politics in a globalizing world, there is some disagreement about just how far-reaching such a process will be. Ripsman and Paul argue that the influence of NGOs has actually been 'episodic and confined to specific issues'.[38] They argue that the rise of the NGO 'does not present a fundamental challenge to the nation-state'.[39] With this said, it would be a foolish government in the contemporary era, not least in a democratic system, which ignored public opinion on certain securitized issues and the degree to which civil society can organize and mobilize itself around these issues, either through formal organizational structures such as NGOs or merely using social networking in an open and horizontal way.

---

[36] McGrew, n 22, at 27.

[37] A.J. Bellamy, 'Humanitarian Intervention' A. Collins (ed), *Contemporary Security Studies* (Oxford: Oxford University Press, 2010), 363.

[38] Ripsman and Paul, n 14, at 164.

[39] Ibid.

In describing the security threats that emerge from this picture of globalization, the NSS unsurprisingly identifies international terrorism as the primary issue of concern in the post-Cold War scene. Al Qaeda is essentially a stateless movement, which speaks to an international community without reference to national borders and identities, and does so by using the internet for social networking, recruitment, propagandizing, and training. It is the ultimate non-state actor in security threat. Where this comes home to roost specifically in the UK, the NSS notes, is in the phenomenon of young radicalized foot soldiers for the movement travelling abroad with ease and relative anonymity to receive training in terrorist techniques, which they then bring back to the UK.[40] In some cases, radicalized recruits have not even had to travel abroad for their indoctrination and training, as they have been able to access instruction remotely over the internet, or through contact with other recruits.[41] The accelerating processes of globalization in such areas as international travel and mobility, and information and communications technology, are essential elements of this process. We should recall that the 9/11 attacks, which killed more people than the Japanese attack on Pearl Harbor in 1941, were conducted by civilians who had freely entered the United States to attack it from within.

The NSS also identifies 'a number of other transnational threats' which emerge from the same phenomenon of globalization.[42] These include international networks proliferating sensitive and prohibited technologies, organized crime groups of various types, and cyber activities such as hacking and espionage. In the case of the latter, while traditional espionage continues to be an issue for the security and intelligence agencies, the information revolution has opened up new opportunities not only to conduct espionage against commercial or governmental targets, but also to do so in a state of anonymity. This, in turn, 'makes the attribution of attacks more difficult, thus reducing the political risk associated with spying'.[43] Thus, while terrorists want their attacks to be noticed for reasons of political influence, spies positively want the opposite, yet both have been greatly enabled by the information revolution and the processes of globalization.

Such issues as international terrorism and cyberattack are identified within the NSS as being in the top tier of security threat. It is to the collection of issues identified in this tier of the strategy that we now turn in more detail.

Key points

- The NSS and SDSR's identification of risks was the result of an NSRA exercise, which identified a set of eight 'wider security risks': essentially risk headings

---

[40] NSS, n 6, at 14.
[41] Ibid.
[42] Ibid.
[43] Ibid.

under which the risk prioritization was established. Many of these are classic 'transnational threats'.

- The political backdrop to the establishment of the NSC by the new Coalition government in 2010 was an intention to end the 'sofa government' of the Blair years, and to transform NSID which had been established by the previous Brown government.
- The largest single challenge underpinning the whole new process was identified by the government as the grave economic situation, and the need to make cuts, especially in defence.
- European countries have been steadily spending less on defence in the post-Cold War years as a percentage of their overall GDP, leading to a potential political and operational crisis in NATO.
- The NSS takes globalization as an important starting point in understanding the way in which security threat has developed in transnational directions, and also in suggesting a policy response of risk management and 'resilience'.

3

Tier One Threats

Risk and resilience

We have mentioned that the National Security Strategy (NSS) aims to be a first in many ways in its treatment of the question of national security in the post-Cold War and, indeed, post-9/11 world. Another area in which it arguably breaks new ground is in its conception of 'risk and resilience' as central notions to the manner in which the threat is identified, and, just as importantly, in which strategy responses are framed. The strategy notes that 'we must do all we can, within the resources available, to predict, prevent and mitigate the risks to our security'.[1]

This statement encapsulates a number of interesting concepts which are worth exploring in more detail. First, national security threats are articulated in terms of 'risks to security', which could, as I have discussed, include any number of issues, both man-made and otherwise. The common currency is something which imperils security. Secondly, the language of 'predict, prevent and mitigate' is highly instructive, and is a collection of ideas which are increasingly defining strategy responses to security threats in the modern world.

As many scholars have noted, a security threat such as that from terrorism is not a simple equation or a zero-sum game, since there is a complex and symbiotic relationship between defensive security actions, and the plans and actions of the attackers. In this way, terrorism is, on the face of it, somewhat different from a threat such as that from environmental disasters, since these are not directly linked in likelihood or nature to the policy actions of human beings (notwithstanding disasters potentially arising from anthropogenic activities such as those purportedly causing climate change).[2] Consequently, many

---

[1] HM Government, 'A Strong Britain in an Age of Uncertainty: The National Security Strategy' (London: TSO, October 2010), 25.

[2] See eg J. Zhuang and V.M. Bier, 'Balancing Terrorism and Natural Disasters—Defensive Strategy with Endogenous Attacker Effort', *Operations Research*, 55/5 (2007), 976.

researchers of terrorism have used game theory to analyse the interactions, noting that 'actions are interdependent and, thus, cannot be analyzed as though one side is passive'.[3]

As the IRA noted in a message to the Thatcher government in 1984 after a bomb in the Grand Hotel in Brighton: 'remember we only have to be lucky once. You have to be lucky always.'[4] The chilling point being made was that the terrorists very often hold most of the cards, in terms of planning the next move. The government, in turn, can never completely protect itself and its citizens against a determined terrorist threat, and can never be absolutely sure it has complete penetration of the terrorist movement, so the calculation is one of risk management rather than absolute prevention. Minimizing the number of attacks and their severity may well be the best that can be done.

This brings in a notion that post-Cold War threats such as terrorism are different from the types of national security threat faced before. In protecting against an existential threat such as Soviet invasion or annihilation in nuclear conflict, a government could not aim for an 80 per cent solution: it would not be enough to catch most but not all of the incoming nuclear missiles. So the deterrent had to be absolute. With terrorism, on the other hand, aside from the inherent impracticality of catching every single terrorist who is moving around freely within a democratic state, there is the added risk that an absolute security response would destroy the very fabric of society in a free and democratic state and make life intolerable. In a sense, the government would run the risk of doing the terrorists' work for them.

As Sir David Omand, a strong advocate of the risk-management approach to modern security, has noted, tackling threats such as terrorism in the future 'is going to have to be guided by a security strategy that embodies these post-Cold War shifts in national security thinking towards focusing on the protection of the citizen, anticipation of risks and building enhanced societal resilience.'[5] He goes on to observe that 'there can be no absolute security, but fatalism or trusting to chance will expose the public to avoidable danger'.[6]

Resilience is another important concept here, which has increasingly found its way into the lexicon of national security. The dictionary definition of resilience suggests a certain elasticity in absorbing, and bouncing back from a blow or an attack. A society could not be resilient to nuclear annihilation, but in the face of a less existential event, particularly one which it is impossible completely to prevent, a society can think about how best to absorb the event and move on from it without major disturbance. This is a useful concept when thinking about many of the threats currently identified as national security

---

[3] T. Sandler and D.G Arce, 'Terrorism and Game Theory', *Simulation and Gaming*, 34 (2003), 319.

[4] 'The IRA campaigns in England', BBC News, 4 March 2001, available at <http://news.bbc.co.uk/1/hi/uk/1201738.stm> (accessed 12 March 2011).

[5] D. Omand, *Securing the State* (London: Hurst, 2010), 17.

[6] Ibid.

threats, such as environmental catastrophes or terrorist attacks. As the NSS notes:

> For those risks that we can predict, we must act both to reduce the likelihood of their occurring, and develop the resilience to reduce their impact.[7]

The element of prediction here is complicated. In these cases, the sense is not that individual events can necessarily be predicted beforehand, but just that the overall pattern of threat is predictable. It is widely foreseen, for example, that a terrorist attack in the UK is quite likely at the time of writing, since there have been attempted and successful attacks in the recent past, and there is no reason to suspect that the motivation for such attacks has disappeared. The successful prediction of individual attacks, however, will be a sporadic process. Sometimes good intelligence will allow this, but sometimes it will not, as the attacks of 7 July 2005 demonstrated. The British government, and many other administrations, express this in terms of the official 'terrorist threat level'. At the time of writing, this is set as 'Substantial' in the UK, which the Home Office interprets as meaning that 'a terrorist attack is a strong possibility'.[8]

Combining these dual concepts of potential severity, and likelihood of threat, is the essence of risk management. By comparing the results with available resources, a strategy of risk response can start to be assembled. The analysis that went into the production of the NSS was based on the foundation of a National Security Risk Assessment (NSRA), conducted in autumn 2010.[9] The NSRA measures threats on a graph of impact (in relation to the economy, casualties, and social/structural factors) against likelihood of occurrence. The measurements go from low to high, such that risks occupying the top right hand corner of the graph are the most worrying in that they are high likelihood and high impact. As we have already identified, some terrorist attacks would sit in this corner, as the government assesses the likelihood of such attacks to be high and the potential impact from them to be very high, especially if they were to deploy unconventional methods such as chemical or biological devices. Risks towards this corner of the graph are likely to find their way into the top tier of national security priorities, since there is an onus on the government to find ways to predict, prevent, and mitigate them wherever resources will allow. Risks in lower tiers of priority are not necessarily lower impact, should they happen, but might be much less likely. For example, the risk of 'a major release of radioactive material from a civil nuclear site within the UK' is placed in the tier 3 category, since it is potentially of very high disruptive impact but is considered reasonably unlikely at the present time.

---

[7] NSS, n 1, at 25.

[8] See <http://www.homeoffice.gov.uk/counter-terrorism/current-threat-level/> (accessed 12 June 2011).

[9] Cabinet Office, 'Fact Sheet 2: National Security Risk Assessment', available at <https://update.cabinetoffice.gov.uk/sites/default/files/resources/Factsheet2-National-Security-Risk-Assessment.pdf> (accessed 7 November 2011).

The outcome is shown in Figure 1.1 (see p 6). Those risks identified as being in the top tier of the strategy are:[10]

- international terrorism affecting the UK or its interests, including a chemical, biological, radiological, or nuclear attack by terrorists; and/or a significant increase in the levels of terrorism relating to Northern Ireland;
- hostile attacks upon UK cyberspace by other states, and large-scale cyber crime;
- a major accident or natural hazard which requires a national response, such as severe coastal flooding affecting three or more regions of the UK, or an influenza pandemic;
- an international military crisis between states, drawing in the UK and its allies, as well as other states and non-state actors.

When considering this range of threats, we can see an interesting combination of threats that could be said to be closely related to the process of globalization (international terrorism and cyber attack); threats relating to broader non-military spheres which would not necessarily have been securitized in the past (accidents and natural hazards); and more traditional military threats (an international military crisis which draws in the UK). All these are assessed to possess the combination of likelihood and impact which places them at the top of the government's national security strategizing and investment. It is worth exploring each of these in turn to consider how they are likely to constitute threats to a country such as the UK in the modern era.

Terrorism

The Terrorist Threat—Lord Alex Carlile, Independent Reviewer of the government's counter-terrorism legislation 2001–11

The contextual starting point is the current threat assessment, made independently by the multidisciplinary team of experts at the Joint Terrorism Analysis Centre (JTAC).

The threat level was changed on the 11 July 2011 from SEVERE to SUBSTANTIAL. The current threat level means that the threat of a terrorist attack remains a strong possibility and may occur without warning.

It means what it says.

Further, the impending Olympic and Paralympic Games mean that the threat level is most unlikely to be reduced until after that great festival is over.

What does the threat mean? It means that there is a strong possibility of a single or multiple suicide bombing attack occurring entirely unpredictably,

---

[10] NSS, n 1, at 27.

with consequent death and injury on at least the scale of the events in London in July 2005. We should not forget that in the 7/7 attacks 52 people were murdered and over 770 were injured, some extremely seriously.

Worryingly, violent Jihadist terrorism techniques have become more varied since 2005, including the technique of massacre by the use of automatic weapons as in Mumbai on the 26 November 2008.

The threat does not come only from violent Jihadists, though that remains the principal threat with as many as 2000 potential suspects under scrutiny. A smaller, but measurable threat comes from right-wing extremism; and from 'lone-wolf' terrorists with unpredictable behaviour patterns. A very real threat continues to be made by Irish dissident terrorist groups. They have murdered and bombed within Northern Ireland during the past year, and have ambitions to act in Great Britain.

Terrorism is clearly not a new threat to the state. As far as the UK is concerned, probably the oldest continuous terrorist movement in human history has now entered its third century of threat to the British state, in the form of Irish Republican terrorism. Despite the peace dividend that came with the Good Friday Agreement in 1998, leading to the main paramilitary organizations in Northern Ireland laying down their arms and the establishment of a devolved power-sharing assembly in the province, the early twenty-first century has seen a troubling re-emergence of dissident Irish Republican terrorism. To a certain extent, this development is not unusual in long-running nationalist terrorist movements which have failed to reach their original and ultimate goal of complete national sovereignty for the community they claim to be representing. The ETA movement in Spain has shown many similarities to the situation in Northern Ireland, including the continuance of the armed struggle by militant hardliners despite agreements on regional autonomy with the government and the waning of public support.

Militant hardliners on the fringes of such movements will always be suspicious of moves by the centre-ground in their organizations to strike political deals and compromises with the state foe, and will often aim to seize the initiative and restart the process of violence. In Irish Republicanism, we saw the Continuity Irish Republican Army (CIRA) split away from the Provisional IRA (PIRA) in 1987, when the latter commenced secret negotiations behind the scenes with the British and Irish governments. In 1997, there was a further splintering of the movement when the Real IRA (RIRA) broke away from the PIRA on the occasion of the second IRA ceasefire, which presaged the signing of the Good Friday Agreement the following year.

Both dissident movements, the CIRA and the RIRA, and a third maverick Republican movement in the shape of *Óglaigh na hÉireann* (Soldiers of Ireland) have recently announced their firm intention to continue the armed struggle with the British state. The NSS notes that there has been a steady increase in terrorist attacks on 'national security targets' in Northern Ireland (which means primarily police and military targets), from 22 during 2009 to 37 up to the publication of the NSS in October 2010.[11] Some of these have been deadly, notably the killing of two British soldiers at the Massereene Barracks in March 2009 by the RIRA, and the killing of a police officer in the same month by the CIRA. There are also indications that the RIRA wishes to extend its terrorist campaign to the British mainland, as noted above by Lord Carlile. The terrorist movement has not achieved this since it planted some bombs in London in 2000, which failed to detonate, and fired a rocket-propelled grenade at the headquarters of MI6.[12] For these reasons, JTAC has advised the Home Office to set the terrorist threat level at 'severe' for Northern Ireland itself, and 'substantial' for mainland UK, which indicates that an attack is 'a strong possibility'.[13]

For Northern Ireland itself, there is also the problem that increased terrorist activity tends to be associated with heightened sectarian violence between some members of the Catholic and Protestant communities in the province. In June 2011, serious sectarian rioting erupted in parts of Belfast, at a level not seen for several years. Hundreds of people were involved and live ammunition was fired, leaving two men with gunshot wounds. The police described the incident as 'major disorder', and deployed stun grenades in their efforts to quell the violence.[14] Such incidents remind us that the underlying causes of tension and violence buried deep within certain communities in Northern Ireland have not yet been resolved, and may be making a transition across generations.

Alongside the terrorist threat related to Northern Ireland, the ongoing threat from Al Qaeda-motivated groups and individuals is assessed to remain very serious, and arguably of much greater potential impact to British society than the threat posed by dissident Irish Republicans. These two strands of terrorism overlap in time, but are otherwise completely disconnected from one another in virtually all respects.

The growth of Al Qaeda (meaning the 'base' or 'foundation') through the latter half of the 1990s represents the emergence of a relatively unique strand of sub-state, internationalized, and largely ideologically driven terrorism. In many ways it is the epitome of the terrorist threat in the globalizing world, and, in fact, has been described as the vanguard of 'new terrorism' by leading scholars such as Walter Laqueur and Bruce Hoffman.[15] Evidence that such a shift was

---

[11] Ibid, 14.

[12] D. Sharrock, 'Real IRA may be planning fresh bombing campaign on the UK mainland', *The Times*, 24 April 2010, available at <http://www.timesonline.co.uk/tol/news/uk/crime/article7106899.ece> (accessed 30 April 2010).

[13] NSS, n 1.

[14] S. Malik, 'Sectarian violence erupts in Belfast', *The Guardian*, 21 June 2011, available at <http://www.guardian.co.uk/uk/2011/jun/21/police-attacked-belfast-sectarian-clashes> (accessed 7 July 2011).

[15] See eg M.J. Morgan, 'The Origins of the New Terrorism', *Parameters* (Spring 2004), 29–43; W. Laqueur, *The New Terrorism: Fanaticism and the Arms of Mass Destruction* (New York: Oxford University Press, 2000); B. Hoffman, *Inside Terrorism* (New York: Columbia University Press, 1998).

taking place was noted in the fact that, while terrorist attacks were declining in number through the latter part of the twentieth century, their deadliness in terms of the number of casualties was rising.[16] Such a phenomenon was demonstrated by the bombing of two American embassies in East Africa in 1998, and very comprehensively by the 9/11 attacks in the United States in September 2001, which were by far the most deadly terrorist attacks in history.

Under the tutelage of Osama Bin Laden and Ayman al Zawahiri, the latter of whom is assumed to have taken over as leader of the movement on Bin Laden's death in early 2011, Al Qaeda advocates a loosely articulated jihadist doctrine which sees members of the public as legitimate targets, and which can be picked up by anyone in the worldwide *umma* of Muslims willing to take the agenda forward. This makes the movement very different from more traditional nationalist terrorist movements such as the IRA, for example, which are generally more concerned with state targets (eg police, military, and government officials); more focused geographically and functionally in their target selection and their operations; and more structured in their membership and operational planning. Nationalist terrorist movements have essentially focused political agendas, and, as such, do not have much ideological resonance with those outside the immediate vicinity of their fight (notwithstanding support from diaspora communities, as was the case historically with members of the Irish community in the United States, for example).

Al Qaeda, on the other hand, is more of an idea and an ideology than a specific movement, although the raid on Bin Laden's lair in Pakistan in early 2011 showed that a core leadership with at least the intention of planning and strategizing for the movement as a whole did exist, even if those international operational capabilities had been severely degraded. The new Coalition government in the UK installed in 2010 has made a renewed attempt at grappling with a definition of the Al Qaeda-related terrorist threat and the policy responses that should flow from it, with its review and reissue of the Prevent strategy, which forms part of the overall Counter-Terrorism Strategy of the UK. I will examine this strategy in more detail in Chapter 10. The new Prevent strategy document notes that:

> We judge that radicalisation is driven by an ideology which sanctions the use of violence; by propagandists for that ideology here and overseas; and by personal vulnerabilities and specific local factors which, for a range of reasons, make that ideology seem both attractive and compelling.[17]

The policy review breaks from the logic of the previous Labour government which launched the first Prevent strategy, by reincorporating the term 'Islamist extremism', and suggesting a causal link between extremist ideologies and terrorism. This reintroduces the risks, from which the Labour government tried

---

[16] Morgan, n 15, at 29.
[17] HM Government, *Prevent Strategy* (London: TSO, June 2011), p 13.

in vain to distance itself, of implying that a strand of terrorism the ideology of which is derived from a selective reading of one religion, Islam, casts a shadow of suspicion over all adherents of that religion. This is one of the peculiarly complex issues in tackling the modern terrorist threat, an issue to which I will return later.

That said, the Prevent strategy notes that, of 115 offenders in custody for terrorism offences at the time of the strategy's publication, 79 (representing 69 per cent) were connected with the Al Qaeda threat. This serves to underline that this particular strand of terrorism still represents the highest threat within the overall picture of terrorist threats in Britain. Indeed, every year since the 9/11 attacks, there has been at least one serious Al Qaeda-related incident in the UK, whether the arrest of individuals purported to be plotting a major attack, or an actual attack itself, either successful or otherwise. It is interesting to note that these attacks and plots have taken a wide variety of forms, from suicide attacks, to remotely detonated devices. The personnel involved in the planning have also varied across several dimensions, from young and educated university students, to practising doctors in the case of the 2007 Glasgow airport attack, and to a young white convert with learning difficulties in the case of Nicky Reilly's attempted nail-bombing of a cafe in Exeter in 2008. One of the most recent attacks involved a radicalized female student of King's College in London, who took it upon herself in 2010 to attempt to assassinate an MP in his constituency office using a knife.[18] Finally, as Lord Carlile notes above, the threat of a 'Mumbai-style' attack using automatic weapons remains a serious risk. All in all, the picture is one of a full spectrum from organized and semi-organized groups of individuals, to what appear to be entirely self-starting personal attack plans in certain cases. Such developments perhaps emphasize the point made earlier, that terrorism and its security responses are part of a symbiotic and constantly evolving relationship with one another.

The Director-General of the Security Service (MI5), Jonathan Evans, claimed shortly after his appointment in 2007 that there were at least 2,000 people in the UK known to his service who posed a serious risk to national security through their active support of terrorism.[19] In 2010, he reiterated the warning, noting that there was 'a serious risk of a lethal attack taking place', and that he could 'see no reason to believe that the position will significantly improve in the immediate future'.[20] While he was speaking of the combination of threat from a resurgent Irish Republican terrorism and that from Al Qaeda-related

---

[18] V. Dodd, 'Profile: Roshonara Choudhury', *The Guardian*, 2 November 2010, available at <http://www.guardian.co.uk/uk/2010/nov/02/profile-roshonara-choudhry-stephen-timms> (accessed 16 June 2011).

[19] '"Thousands" pose terror threat', BBC News, 5 November 2007, available at <http://news.bbc.co.uk/1/hi/uk/7078712.stm> (accessed 2 July 2011).

[20] D. Gardham, 'Britain facing a new wave of terrorist attacks, MI5 warns', *The Telegraph*, 16 September 2010, available at <http://www.telegraph.co.uk/news/uknews/terrorism-in-the-uk/8008033/Britain-facing-a-new-wave-of-terrorist-attacks-MI5-warns.html> (accessed 25 February 2011).

activities, he also noted that significant numbers of young British Islamists were probably receiving training in the ungoverned spaces of Somalia, and that this would almost inevitably manifest itself later as an attack back in the UK.[21] Here, again, we see the link between processes of globalization and the modern international terrorist threat, whereby ease of movement and communications between countries shortens the distance between problematic conditions in states abroad and national security threats in the UK.

As the above-mentioned case of the knife attack on MP Steven Timms in 2010 showed, Al Qaeda-related terrorism can come from a variety of sources, and the threat is not a monolithic one. The NSS notes that there are essentially three levels to the Al Qaeda threat.[22] The first relates to the organization's core leadership in the Afghanistan/Pakistan region, which has been severely pressurized by counter-terrorism action (of which Bin Laden's death was an example) but not expunged altogether. The second threat comes from 'affiliates' around the world such as Al Qaeda in the Arabian Peninsula (AQAP), Al Qaeda in the Islamic Maghreb (AQIM), or more loosely connected extremist Islamist militant groups such as *Lashkar-e Toiba* (LeT) and *Tehrik-e Taliban-e Pakistan* (TTP). The third dimension of Al Qaeda-related threat is constituted by 'terrorists inspired by its ideology', of which the attacker of MP Steven Timms was a good example. She had not received any direct training or instruction from the organizational hierarchy of Al Qaeda or connected groups, as far as we can determine, but had simply decided to act on the central message of violent jihadism.

Some of the more recent serious terrorist incidents connected with Al Qaeda in the UK have not originated from the core Al Qaeda leadership in Afghanistan/Pakistan, but instead appear to point towards the tutelage of an affiliate, AQAP. This appears to have been the case in the examples of the attempt to detonate bombs hidden within printer toner cartridges being moved by freight airliners in 2010,[23] and the infamous 'underpants bomber', Umar Farouk Abdulmutallab, who failed to detonate an explosive device on a transatlantic flight in December 2009.[24] As well as again demonstrating the flexibility of the terrorists to choose new methodologies of attack, these cases also suggest that, as core Al Qaeda weakens, the other dimensions such as the affiliated groups outside the Afghanistan/Pakistan region may become more important.

---

[21] Ibid.

[22] NSS, n 1, at 28.

[23] 'Ink cartridge bomb reveals innovation of terrorist groups', *The Telegraph*, 30 October 2010, available at <http://www.telegraph.co.uk/news/uknews/terrorism-in-the-uk/8098587/Ink-cartridge-bomb-reveals-innovation-of-terrorist-groups.html> (accessed 6 July 2011).

[24] G. Whittell and A. Fresco, 'I'm the first of many, warns airline "bomber" Umar Farouk Abdulmutallab', *The Times*, 29 December 2009, available at <http://www.timesonline.co.uk/tol/news/world/us_and_americas/article6969645.ece> (accessed 16 May 2010).

Cyber threats

The Cyber Threat—Andy Dancer, Chief Technical Officer for the Encryption Group, TrendMicro

Virtualisation and Consumerisation provide increased efficiency for servers and people respectively, but at the price of rapid change and increased complications in IT security. Traditional wisdom says lock it down, keep it stable & consistent while minimising the attack surface—these drivers force the opposite. We are also connecting more and more systems together—again a triumph of operational efficiency over security.

In parallel we have seen cyber-crime truly becoming a crime with the shift away from individuals trying to prove how clever they are and into Organised Crime and more recently strong rumours of State Sponsorship. We have also seen the volume of threats increasing exponentially and the speed of latching onto new world events (poisoned search) and vulnerability exploit accelerating dramatically.

Squeezed from both sides, no longer is it sufficient to build an electronic fortress and hide inside it. There are now so many legitimate channels passing through the fortress walls it becomes easier for an enemy to masquerade as one. The push to cloud computing is forcing services together onto shared hardware and reducing the separation that has traditionally existed. Now we have to recognise that the true value is actually our data. We have to create multiple layers of protection locking tighter and tighter around that data so that a breach has limited reach and compromises the minimum volume of data possible.

Finally we have to plan to fail—assume that some of our defences will be breached and try to notice that as quickly as possible (defence in depth) and plan in advance for how to react to it. It's a little like servicing your car and joining a motoring organisation in case it breaks down. Work in advance to stop it failing but have a plan for what to do if it does because that way you get fixed quicker and for far less money!

Returning to the case of MP Steven Timms, it appears that his attacker obtained her inspiration for her actions from ideological radicalization over the internet, in the shape of jihadist sermons by the Yemen-based radical preacher, Anwar al-Awlaki. This is one of the ways in which the cyber domain represents a serious security threat dimension to the UK. The second Tier One threat to Britain's national security identified in the NSS is not so much that from internet radicalization, but the threat of 'hostile attacks upon UK cyber space by other states and large scale cyber crime'.[25] It is fair to say that the cyber-security issue has quickly moved to centre stage in the national security debate in many Western countries, and the UK is certainly no exception. As Neil Thompson,

---

[25] NSS, n 1, at 27.

the Director of the Office of Cyber Security and Information Security at the Cabinet Office recently said, 'Cyber is routinely on the National Security Council agenda, and we have a minister for cyber in the cabinet'.[26]

The first element of the heightened securitization of cyber threats is the exponential growth and penetration of networks into the daily fabric of state and society in the post-Cold War period. In a relatively short time—the first commercial web browser available to the public, Netscape, only became available in 1994—the degree of governmental, public, and corporate traffic and business on the internet has grown at a staggering rate. Looking globally, the NSS notes that in the 15 years from 1995, the number of users on the internet had increased more than a hundredfold, from 16 million to more than 1.7 billion.[27] Coupled with the growth of mobile phones over the same period, and the increasing 'convergence' between phone and internet technologies, the transformation in the way we communicate and do business in the post-Cold War period has been nothing short of breathtaking. More importantly, as noted earlier, it marks out the current phase of globalization from earlier periods of 'internationalization' in history, by coupling a growing interconnectedness of trade and social interaction with a fundamental revolution in technology and society.

In tandem with the enormous benefits that the internet can offer to individuals and to business, it is widely recognized that a growing dependence of critical systems on networked architecture also represents enormous security risks. The NSS identifies the range of risks as comprising enhanced opportunities for espionage, crime, and terrorism, and the use of the internet as a military weapon.[28] It is estimated that cyber crime, mostly manifesting itself as fraud and the theft of intellectual property, costs the global economy $1 trillion per year, with 'untold human cost'.[29]

The UK government, as is the case with most governments around the world, now faces a daily barrage of cyber attacks aimed at penetrating and compromising information and systems. As Andy Dancer notes above, the government is finding itself 'squeezed from both sides' in terms of individual and more organized attacks. The former Secretary of State for Defence, Dr Liam Fox, said in 2011 that the Ministry of Defence (MOD) blocked and investigated 'more than 1000 potentially serious cyber attacks' during 2010.[30] The attacks take a variety of forms, from denial-of-service attempts to penetration and information exfiltration attempts. In the technologically complex and murky world of cyber activities, the only certainties seem to be that precise attribution of attacks

---

[26] Neil Thompson (Director, Office of Cyber Security and Information Security, Office of Security and Counter Terrorism), 'The National Cyber Security Programme', presentation at National Security 2011 (GovNet Events), London, 5 July.

[27] NSS, n 1, at 29.

[28] Ibid.

[29] Ibid.

[30] 'More than 1000 cyber-attacks on MOD, says Liam Fox', The Guardian, 8 June 2011, available at <http://www.guardian.co.uk/government-computing-network/2011/jun/08/1-000-cyber-attacks-on-mod-says-liam-fox> (accessed 7 July 2011).

is virtually impossible, both in terms of countries of origin and whether the miscreants are state-sponsored or private. Motivations for attacks, furthermore, seem to be vague and overlapping. Commercial espionage is clearly at the root of many attacks but fraud, ideological motivation, and possibly even techno-logically advanced anarchism could be at the root of much of the activity. Occasionally, specific individuals will emerge from the mist, such as 19-year-old Ryan Cleary, a young hacker based in his parents' house in Essex, who was arrested in 2011 after breaking into and compromising a range of systems and sites, from governmental targets (such as the ill-chosen target of the Serious Organised Crime Agency (SOCA) in the UK, which may have precipitated his final fall from grace), to commercial targets such as Sony's PlayStation online system.[31] Reports suggested he was part of the shadowy hacking group 'LulzSec', although such groups are, by definition, as virtual as much as they are actual and can form and disband with ease.

On the state front, it is clear that a growing dependence on networks in gov-ernment and in sensitive sectors of the economy, such as arms, offers enormous new opportunities for espionage, and does so in a much more anonymized and difficult-to-trace way. Intelligence chiefs in the UK and elsewhere have repeat-edly pointed the finger at the Chinese and Russian governments for sponsoring 'cyber warfare' on Western governmental targets, and have even gone so far as to warn that commercial penetration by Chinese network companies such as Huawei provide the Chinese government with the capability to 'shut down Britain by crippling its telecoms and utilities'.[32] Why the Chinese government would wish to do so is not yet clear, and leads to the counter-argument that such fears may be irrational and blown out of proportion. However, evidence is mounting that a growing number of cyber attacks do appear to be emanating from Russia and China, whether they are officially sanctioned or merely using patriotic private resources, and this has to be considered a threat to national security and a suitable case for mitigation.

Part of the challenge posed by cyber threats is their conceptualization. In addition to offering specific new threat opportunities, the cyber realm should also be seen as merely an extension of other activities in the 'real world', which it can facilitate and enable. Fraud, for example, is as old as time, but the infor-mation revolution has offered it new methodologies. Similarly, terrorists might also seek to explore a cyber attack capability, either as a direct weapon (eg dis-abling a critical element of national infrastructure, causing death and injury) or as an adjunct to conventional attacks (eg by disabling military or emergency-response communications systems during an ongoing terrorist attack). At the

---

[31] V. Dodd and J. Halliday, 'Teenager arrested in Essex over Lulzsec hacking attacks', *The Guardian*, 21 June 2011, available at <http://www.guardian.co.uk/uk/2011/jun/21/hackers-lulzsec-arrest-essex-census> (accessed 30 June 2011).

[32] M. Smith, 'Spy chiefs fear Chinese cyber attack', *The Sunday Times*, 29 March 2009, avail-able at <http://www.timesonline.co.uk/tol/news/uk/article5993156.ece> (accessed 20 June 2010).

moment, Al Qaeda's intent to use cyber options is assessed to exceed their capability,[33] but this may not always be so and immunization might be better than treating the symptoms when they occur.

It is important to note that there are some sceptics within the debates on cyber threat, although they are a minority at present. The analyst Bruce Schneier, for example, has warned of over-hyping the threat when it is so little understood at present.[34] He notes that, 'if we frame the debate in terms of war, if we accept the military's expansive cyber-definition of "war", we feed our fears'.[35] This is partly the question of how a securitizing speech act can frame a threat in a particular way which is not necessarily appropriate to the reality. Such debates also exist in the arena of terrorism, and the threat of environmental disaster. In the case of cyber threats, there is a great deal of conjecture about what *could* happen, rather than good examples of what has actually happened. This is not to say that there are not very real threats out there which need to be treated, but it is also worth noting that knowledge and understanding about this particular threat are both somewhat embryonic at the current time.

Natural hazards and disasters

A very different type of threat, as we have discussed, is that posed by natural hazards and environmental disasters. A threat from this source shows fundamental differences in essence to that from human activities such as organized crime or terrorism, so it is reasonable to propose that it requires a different way of thinking. In academic circles within security studies and international relations, there has been much debate and disagreement about whether environmental issues really constitute 'national security' threats at all. Towards the latter half of the twentieth century, scholars such as Ullman began to suggest that the complete focus on military factors within security thinking was inappropriate. He wrote in the early 1980s that defining national security purely around military factors potentially 'conveys a profoundly false image of reality', and can 'ignore other and perhaps even more harmful dangers'.[36] The great seventeenth-century philosopher Thomas Hobbes had envisaged any number of threats to life in observing that life was 'solitary, poor, nasty, brutish and short'.[37]

---

[33] R. Westlake (Director, Prepare, Protect, CT Science and CBRNE, Office for Security and Counter Terrorism), 'Afternoon Keynote Address', presentation at National Security 2011 (GovNet Events), London, 5 July.

[34] B. Schneier, 'Threat of "cyber war" has been hugely hyped', CNN News, 7 July 2010, available at <http://edition.cnn.com/2010/OPINION/07/07/schneier.cyberwar.hyped/> (accessed 7 July 2011).

[35] Ibid.

[36] R.H. Ullman, 'Redefining Security', *International Security*, 8/1 (1983), 129.

[37] Ibid, 130.

This led to an 'existential' strand of thinking around environmental and 'human' security, which increasingly came to challenge traditional Realist thinking about military-centred security. A landmark document was the UN Development Programme's 1994 Human Development Report, which argued strongly for a new human security approach focused on development rather than military hard power. The summary document noted that:

it will not be possible for the community of nations to achieve any of its major goals—not peace, not environmental protection, not human rights or democratization, not fertility reduction, not social integration—except in the context of sustainable development that leads to human security.[38]

Here we can see environmental factors securitized within the overall umbrella of human, rather than national, security. By this time, a lively academic debate was underway about the inclusion of such issues as environmental threat within the arena of national security. In a robust presentation of the case against, Levy wrote in 1995 that the argument that environmental values are essentially national values, and thus degradation of the environment was a national security issue, 'has no basis except as a rhetorical device aimed as drumming up greater support for measures to protect the environment.'[39] The point that Levy was making was not that the environment should not be protected, but just that it should not necessarily be done under the rubric of national security. An opposing view had been offered by Peter Gleick, who argued in a 1991 paper that there were 'clear connections' between 'environmental and resource problems and international behaviour', which raised the question as to whether 'traditional means and institutions for resolving international political conflicts are adequate to address them'.[40] In a paper in the same journal edition, however, Daniel Deudney suggested that making such a connection between the environment and security reflected 'muddled thinking'.[41] He noted that traditionally militaristic national security thinking and environmentalism do not go well together, and, in fact, are often fundamentally opposed to one another. What was needed, in his view, was not to combine these issues in a potentially confusing way, but to 'challenge the tribal power of nationalism and the chronic militarization of public discourse'.[42]

In the ensuing years, a number of major natural catastrophes brought the issue more squarely into the security debate. The addition of the climate change issue over the same period added an extra impetus to the thinking. To name but

---

[38] UNDP, 'An Agenda for the Social Summit', UNDP Report 1994, p 1, available at <http://hdr.undp.org/en/media/hdr_1994_en_overview.pdf> (accessed 20 June 2011).

[39] M.A. Levy, 'Is the Environment a National Security Issue?', *International Security*, 20/2 (1995), 36.

[40] P.H. Gleick, 'Environment and Security: The Clear Connections', *Bulletin of Atomic Scientists* (April 1991), 17.

[41] D. Deudney, 'Environment and Security: Muddled Thinking', *Bulletin of Atomic Scientists* (April 1991), 22.

[42] Ibid, 28.

a few incidents, the Indian Ocean tsunami in 2004, the Katrina hurricane and flooding in New Orleans in 2005, the flooding in Pakistan in 2010, and the combined massive earthquake, tsunami, and nuclear incident in Japan in 2011, all served to demonstrate that a major natural catastrophe could hit a developed or developing state alike and cause untold death and destruction at levels far greater than any terrorist could envisage. The effects in all these regions and countries were far-reaching, ultimately having a profound effect on the economy and politics in the affected countries as much as on the individuals unfortunate enough to be hit. The Japan case was also interesting in that it showed the potential linkage between incidents in a disaster which can compound the security impact, in this case moving from a strong earthquake to the flooding and meltdown of a nuclear reactor.

The climate change debate has been, and will continue to be, the subject of many books in its own right. Suffice it to say that the normative thinking at the time of writing is that climate change is happening, that it is greatly affected by anthropogenic processes such as carbon emissions, and that it will increasingly be the trigger for major natural disasters. These, in turn, have the potential to cause major security issues for local, regional, and international communities. In July 2011, a group of international scientists announced that they were ending their 'equivocal' stance on the connection between extreme weather events and climate change, and that the potential link between the two 'could no longer be ignored'.[43]

The way to conceptualize the link between environmental issues and security seems to be to think of such issues as 'catalytic', as the World Commission on Environment and Development described them in 1987.[44] The NSS-11 uses the term 'risk multiplier' to describe how the effects of climate change, for example, can be responsible for 'exacerbating existing tensions around the world'.[45] The example of the Darfur crisis is raised, to show how, in the UN's analysis, a marginalization of agricultural land due to sustained drought from climate change in the region, has forced nomadic herders into settled agricultural lands, where they have come into conflict with local farmers over grazing land.[46] This local crisis can, in turn, develop into a much larger crisis which brings in the international community. The causal link between all these factors is actually debatable—it is difficult to say with certainty that ploughing resources into tackling climate change will prevent such conflicts from happening—but, in a sense, this is immaterial. What has happened is that a local conflict over marginal resources has conflated into a much larger crisis, which has brought in the

---

[43] S. Connor, 'Extreme weather link "can no longer be ignored"', *The Independent*, 1 July 2011, available at <http://www.independent.co.uk/environment/climate-change/extreme-weather-link-can-no-longer-be-ignored-2305181.html> (accessed 6 July 2011).

[44] Cited in J. Barnett, 'Environmental Security' in A. Collins (ed), *Contemporary Security Studies* (Oxford: Oxford University Press, 2010), 221.

[45] NSS, n 1, at 17.

[46] Ibid.

international community. The fact is that development support to help such marginal agricultural communities to become more resilient in the face of environmental pressures should not be at issue, whatever the reason for those pressures in the first place.

On the local and national fronts, the NSS points out that the floods across many parts of the UK in summer 2007 necessitated the 'largest ever civil emergency response since the Second World War'.[47] Going further back, to 1953, a serious episode of coastal flooding in the east of the country left 307 people dead and caused damage that would be worth £5 billion at today's rates.[48]

Clearly, the UK is in the fortunate position that it is not likely to face the types of natural disasters than many other parts of the world would need to factor into their security strategies. In the United States, for example, serious risks include tropical storms (as was the case with Hurricane Katrina), tornadoes, and winter storms, and the prospect of a major earthquake along the San Andreas fault, to name just a few threats. Many countries around the Pacific Rim have suffered major earthquakes in recent years which have caused very considerable death and destruction, including Japan, New Zealand, and Chile, for example, and destructive tsunamis have followed in some cases. Following the disaster of Hurricane Katrina in the New Orleans district in 2005, and the Japanese earthquake and tsunami of 2011, these states have a very valid and appropriate reason for factoring natural disasters into their national security strategies.

As for the UK, one of the highest risks in this category is identified as that from human pandemic disease.[49] The most notable cases in recent years have comprised strains of influenza, such as the 'Spanish flu' outbreak in 1918–19, which caused an estimated 228,000 additional deaths in the UK alone, and the more recent and thankfully less serious swine flu outbreak in 2009.[50] The risk of another influenza outbreak is assessed as of 'high probability', and likely to cause not only additional deaths, but considerable disruption and impact to the economy in terms of staff taking time off work.[51] The risk from pandemics is, again, another factor in which risk may have been heightened by the effects of globalization. Rapid and widespread international travel means that strains of disease from far afield can quickly end up back in the UK, and can spread rapidly before they are properly identified.

On the international front, current thinking about the manner in which environmental problems become security threats relates to the 'force multiplier' effect described earlier, which, in turn, feeds into the factor of 'ungoverned

---

[47] Ibid, 17. The author can attest to the disruption caused, as our own family were among 420,000 people left without tap water for several days when a water treatment works was overrun with flood water and the water supply polluted!

[48] Ibid.

[49] Ibid, 30.

[50] Ibid, 30–1.

[51] Ibid.

spaces' and 'failed states', and the security risks they can pose to the West in an interconnected world. It is conceivable that climate change or other environmental stresses could feed into a general failure of a state's structures and viability, and this, in turn, could provide ungoverned spaces in which terrorists and criminals could flourish. This could arguably be said to be one of the stresses in East Africa for example, including Sudan and Somalia, although it is also the case that issues of politics and economic management could be just as important in those examples. Such problems in failed and failing states could also force migrations of people away from stricken areas and towards the West, potentially posing further more direct security stresses on the system. In this sense, the basic logic that a globalizing world connects together these processes into potential scenarios of cumulative security threat, is sound, though somewhat untested.

There is also a potential ideological factor to consider, in that climate change and environmental stress are seen in some quarters as another example of imbalance between the rich North and poor South. The former, it is argued, consumes most of the resources and produces most of the carbon emissions, while the global South is much more likely to suffer the deleterious effects of environmental degradation and marginalization of agricultural land. This could, conceivably, feed into radical anti-West ideologies. Before his death, for example, Osama Bin Laden occasionally blamed American and industrialized world industries for global warming, and urged action against them.[52] In this way, radical movements such as Al Qaeda show credentials as fundamentally anti-West and anti-globalization movements. This may be another convoluted way in which environmental issues can feed into national security concerns, and connects to the cyber-related threat of the manner in which terrorist groups such as Al Qaeda can mobilize supporters around the world through their use of radicalization over the internet.

International military crisis

The final area of threat identified as being in the top tier in the NSS is the threat of an international military crisis. The document states that no state is perceived to pose a direct military threat to the territory of the UK at present, but that more of an immediate issue is the likelihood that UK forces will continue to be deployed in military conflicts overseas. This seems a sensible prediction, since, in the period after the Cold War, UK forces have been involved substantially in conflicts in the Balkans, Iraq, Afghanistan, Sierra Leone, and latterly in the NATO intervention in Libya.

---

[52] '"Bin Laden" blames US for global warming', BBC News, 29 January 2010, available at <http://news.bbc.co.uk/1/hi/8487030.stm> (accessed 28 June 2011).

Interestingly, the NSS states that the reasons for judging that forces should be deployed in these cases was because 'our national interests or our national responsibilities were at stake'.[53] These responsibilities are further identified as humanitarian interventions, which was ostensibly the case in the 2011 campaign in Libya, for example. This identifies a complex addition to the basically defensive notion of national security, and goes slightly beyond the extended notion of undertaking operations abroad because of internationally interconnected risk factors which obliquely affect national security at home. The idea that operations may be undertaken entirely for humanitarian purposes brings in an essentially Idealistic notion of playing a role in the international community for the greater good of peace between and within nations: in a sense, the 'moral' dimension that Blair described in his Chicago speech of 1999. In this sense, national security and national interests cannot be seen solely as myopic self-interest and self-defence issues, as the essence of the Realist notion of anarchy between nation-states would have implied.

Immediate questions arise as to when and how such interventions should be undertaken. We have seen that a sense of realpolitik will often determine whether an intervention is considered appropriate. The classic current example was the decision to undertake robust military intervention in Libya to deter a humanitarian catastrophe at the hands of General Gaddafi, but not to do the same in Syria, despite clear indications that the government there is committing the most appalling human rights abuses against anti-government protestors. The rationale in the latter case is ostensibly because the Syrian region involves a much more complicated web of interests and complexities, such as those concerning Iran, Israel, and the Middle East Peace Process. Intervention here would run the risk of turning into a much more complicated and wider regional conflict, and probably one involving Iran. The NSS acknowledges the difficulties here in a slightly opaque way, noting that 'each situation will be different and these judgements will not necessarily be easy'.[54]

An oblique reference is made to Iran in the NSS in the form of an observation that 'the ambitions of states to acquire nuclear weapons capabilities could trigger international crises and armed conflict'.[55] The programme to try to disrupt Iran's efforts to develop an offensive nuclear capability has certainly lurched towards international crisis on more than one occasion in recent years. The United States has already warned Iran of unspecified 'consequences' if it continues to fail to meet its obligations in agreements aimed at defusing the crisis,[56] which can be interpreted as leaving the door open to punitive military action.

---

[53] NSS, n 1, at 30.

[54] Ibid.

[55] Ibid.

[56] 'US warns Iran over nuclear standoff', Al Jazeera, 19 November 2009, available at <http://english.aljazeera.net/news/middleeast/2009/11/2009111962711262687.html> (accessed 26 June 2011).

Given that the UK has supported its most important ally in other military operations in the region, it seems reasonable to assume that it may seek to do so
again if a military option emerged over Iran. (This would be a most interesting
test for the new National Security Council process.)

Ripsman and Paul, in their analysis of globalization's effect on the 'national
security state', explored the hypothesis put forward by supporters of the benefits of globalization, that a greater interconnectedness in the post-Cold War
world would radically reduce the instance of state-on-state conflicts in favour of
low-intensity and internal conflicts.[57] While this is true in global statistical
terms (interstate conflict has reduced substantially since the turn of the century,
while intrastate conflict has risen in its place), the picture is patchy across the
world. In particular, the United States itself has been involved in both low-
intensity conflicts (LICs) since the 1990s, and in more traditional interstate
conflicts (in Afghanistan, and twice in Iraq, although both conflicts have quickly evolved into more complex counter-insurgencies). Thus, in Ripsman and
Paul's assessment, 'there is no evidence that the United States has abandoned
traditional warfare in favour of LICs'.[58]

European countries are categorized in Ripsman and Paul's analysis as being
'states in stable regions', where many of the predicted beneficial effects of globalization on national security postures have been seen.[59] Thus, as we have
noted, defence expenditure in many European states has gradually fallen in the
post-Cold War period (at least in terms of its percentage proportion of GDP),
and national security rhetoric and strategizing have broadened to include a
range of non-traditional and newly securitized issues such as the environment.
To some extent, the UK fits this picture, but it could be argued that it falls
slightly between stools in Ripsman and Paul's analysis. In particular, through
our close alliance with the United States, we have been much more heavily
involved in conflicts in Iraq and Afghanistan than many of our European neighbours. In this way, the UK has also continued to be involved in state-on-state
conflicts in the post-Cold War period, and it is perhaps reasonable to assume, as
does the NSS, that these will remain an important part of our national security
posture for the foreseeable future.

Key points

- Three of the four risks identified in Tier One of the NSS are transnational
  threats which require an approach of 'risk and resilience' rather than necessarily
  complete risk mitigation, as was necessary during the Cold War.

---

[57] N.M Ripsman and T.V. Paul, *Globalization and the National Security State* (Oxford: Oxford
University Press, 2010), 29.

[58] Ibid, 55.

[59] Ibid, 83.

- Terrorist threats to the UK are headed by a resurgence of Irish Republican terrorism, and the ongoing threat from Al Qaeda-related terrorism. In the case of the latter, AQAP may now be more dangerous than the core Al Qaeda leadership.
- Cyber threats have increased with the exponential rise in the number of internet users around the globe, and the increasing networking and connectivity of government and infrastructure systems. Experts suggest that we have to protect ourselves as best we can, but also 'plan to fail'.
- Natural hazards and environmental threats were increasingly securitized through the end of the twentieth century, and have gained greater prominence through a series of cataclysmic disasters in the early twenty-first century affecting both developing and developed countries. In the UK, the risk of a pandemic is assessed to be the most significant risk.
- The post-Cold War period has shown that international military crises involving the UK, contrary to 'Globalization School' expectations, have not disappeared. It is reasonable to assume that these will remain a risk for the UK's national security strategizing in the foreseeable future.

4

Tier Two Threats

Overlapping risks and capabilities

The top tier of identified security risks thus covers four main areas: terrorism, cyber attack, environmental threats, and the risk of becoming involved in international military crises. These are identified as the areas in which most resources will be allocated. Below Tier One, a range of other risks are identified, which are connected tangentially to the higher priority risks and overlap with them. The National Security Strategy (NSS) identifies that the Strategic Defence and Security Review (SDSR), which was published in conjunction with the NSS, outlines the range of capabilities and approaches that are to be taken in responding to risks across the priority spectrum. In this way, a picture starts to be painted of how an uncertain, complex, and overlapping security threat picture cannot necessarily be seen as a discrete set of separate threats. The cyber dimension, for example, cuts across many of the other threats as a type of modality rather than necessarily as a threat in itself. Terrorists, criminals, and militaries may all use cyber techniques to enhance their objectives, in addition to a range of other more conventional methodologies. On the military front, as I will discuss, any number of scenarios could develop in which military forces might be needed, ranging from low-intensity conflicts (LICs), to limited and minor peacekeeping operations, and up to major military campaigns such as Afghanistan or Iraq. It is difficult to predict which are more likely and how many there will be, hence the process of prioritizing risks can never be an exact science and should always be seen as a dynamic picture.

The response, as I will discuss in later chapters, is to think about flexible capabilities which can be mobilized in response to any number of situations, and which can deal with unpredictable situations as they emerge. A nuclear emergency, for example, could develop as a result either of a conventional terrorist attack, or from a cyber attack—whether terrorist or otherwise—or from an accident or a natural catastrophe such as flooding. In a sense, the trigger for the situation is one consideration, but the main strategic implication will be having in place a rapid response capability which can deal with the results of the crisis. This is why the SDSR refers to a list of eight cross-cutting 'wider security risks' (outlined in Chapter 2) in addition to the three tiers of priority risks, since capabilities and strategies will need to be structured in ways that can be built up over time while being able to respond to a dynamic and unpredictable picture.

In the second tier of priority risks identified by the National Security Risk Assessment (NSRA) are the following:

- an attack on the UK or overseas territories by another state or proxy using chemical, biological, radiological, or nuclear (CBRN) weapons;
- a risk of major instability, insurgency, or civil war overseas, which creates an environment that terrorists can exploit to threaten the UK;
- a significant increase in the level of organized crime affecting the UK;
- severe disruption to information received, transmitted, or collected by satellites, possibly as a result of deliberate attack by another state.

An attack using 'unconventional' weapons

The first risk focuses on the technological aspects of CBRN and the risks it poses in the modern era. Rudimentary chemical and biological weapons have been developed by some states—by the United States and Soviet Union during the Cold War, for example—for some years. Some states have used such munitions in combat situations. During the First World War, the use of chlorine and mustard gases on the battlefield is estimated to have accounted for 4 per cent of the casualties.[1] The Iran–Iraq war of 1980–8 saw extensive use of blistering and nerve agents, primarily by Saddam Hussein's Iraqi regime, resulting in thousands of casualties. The same regime used these chemical munitions against civilian Kurdish targets in March 1988, killing an estimated 10,000 residents of the village of Halabja.[2]

With the advent of the era of 'new terrorism' from the 1990s onwards, substate actors also started to consider the use of such 'unconventional' weaponry in their arsenal. In 1995, the fanatic Aum Shinrikyo cult in Japan deployed the nerve agent Sarin on the Tokyo subway, killing 15 people and injuring hundreds more.[3] In the immediate aftermath of the 9/11 attacks in the United States, a wave of anthrax attacks delivered through the post caused many to consider that Al Qaeda, which had just set a new benchmark in civilian casualties from a terrorist attack, would be very happy to use such unconventional weapons against civilians. As is transpired, the anthrax was not the work of

---

[1] J.W. Wirtz, 'Weapons of Mass Destruction' in A. Collins (ed), *Contemporary Security Studies* (Oxford: Oxford University Press, 2010), 327.

[2] Ibid, 328.

[3] J.S. Nye and D.A. Welch, *Understanding Global Conflict and Cooperation*, 8th edn (Boston, MA: Longman, 2009), 309.

Al Qaeda, but it is clear that Al Qaeda's terrorist organization has expressed an interest in using such weaponry from an early stage. Bin Laden even suggested that it was a religious duty for his followers to acquire CBRN capability.[4] With such fanatic organizations for whom civilians are legitimate targets and mass casualties and disruption are the desired aim, CBRN makes perfect sense alongside conventional attacks.

The increasing proliferation of weapons of mass destruction (WMD) technology in the latter half of the twentieth century connects with the fear that terrorists may be successful in attempts to acquire the appropriate materials and know-how to deploy a CBRN attack. The episode of Abdul Qadeer Khan caused Western governments to see the issue in a new light. Khan, who was head of Pakistan's nuclear programme for a quarter of a century, was found to have assisted Pakistan's development of a nuclear capability in the 1970s by stealing designs and contacts from his period working at a nuclear engineering establishment in the Netherlands. Intelligence began to suggest that Khan had acquired much of the technology and materials that Pakistan needed through proliferation networks possibly involving China, and also that he started to proliferate the same technology to other countries seeking to develop nuclear capabilities.[5] In 2004, an internal investigation in Pakistan concluded that Khan had proliferated sensitive nuclear technology to Iran and Libya using black market contacts.[6]

At the same time, the end of the Cold War and collapse of the Soviet Union led to serious fears that WMD materials and equipment from the very considerable arsenal that had been developed by the Soviets, could easily be spirited away from crumbling and poorly guarded facilities by organized criminals or simply by opportunists. A 2004 National Intelligence Council assessment of the problem in the United States judged it 'highly unlikely that Russian authorities would have been able to recover all the material reportedly stolen'. The assessment was that undetected smuggling had occurred, although the volume and destinations of such smuggling were unknown.[7]

The fact of the matter is that, over the course of the twentieth century, the know-how and capability of states in the WMD field has gradually extended beyond the small number of nuclear weapons states to a wider range of states, including India, Pakistan, Israel, North Korea, and—possibly—Iran. Others have shown definite intentions of acquiring nuclear capabilities, such as Libya, Iraq,

---

[4] C. Quillen, 'Three explanations for al-Qaeda's lack of a CBRN attack', The Jamestown Foundation, 21 February 2007, available at <http://www.jamestown.org/programs/gta/single/?tx_ttnews%5Btt_news%5D=1015&tx_ttnews%5BbackPid%5D=182&no_cache=1> (accessed 21 June 2010).

[5] 'Weapons of Mass Destruction—A.Q. Khan', GlobalSecurity.org, available at <http://www.globalsecurity.org/wmd/world/pakistan/khan.htm> (accessed 20 June 2011).

[6] Ibid.

[7] 'Annual Report to Congress on the Safety and Security of Russian Nuclear Facilities and Military Forces', National Intelligence Council, December 2004, available at <http://www.dni.gov/nic/special_russiannuke04.html> (accessed 15 May 2010).

and Syria, even if they were ultimately unable to do so or otherwise abandoned their programmes. The general trend has to be one in which such proliferation is increasingly possible, especially if more capable organized crime networks choose to act as facilitators.

It is now reasonable to assume that a potential nexus exists in the pursuit for WMD technology between certain 'rogue states', which George W. Bush famously described as an 'axis of evil' in early 2002, and certain sub-state actors, whether they be criminals looking to make money or terrorist organizations. Rogue states, in this context, mean states that have a track history of supporting terrorist and proxy organizations in the pursuit of their foreign policy objectives, and are not averse to proliferating sensitive technology. This was essentially the rationale for the hugely controversial campaign in Iraq in 2003. Tony Blair described the calculation as a change in the 'balance of risk' which meant that simply containing Iraq and its obfuscation over its WMD intentions was no longer good enough in a post-9/11 world.[8] He later spoke about the 'calculus of risk' having changed with the 9/11 attacks, whereby a threat that was potentially containable took on a new level of risk in a world where terrorists appeared to be hell-bent on causing as many casualties as possible and were not averse to using WMD capability in doing so.[9] Thus, we can see in this rationale how certain developments in the globalizing world can come together to act as force multipliers of risk and threat, in ways which require new approaches.

Within the UK, there have been a few cases of Al Qaeda-inspired terrorists attempting to use unconventional munitions, or at least thinking seriously about how to do so. Significant examples include the 'ricin plot' of 2003, in which Kamel Bourgass was convicted of offences in relation to the preparation and planned spreading of the deadly ricin poison in London. A year later, Dhiren Bharot was arrested and subsequently convicted of planning mass-casualty attacks in the UK and the United States, including plans for a radiological dispersal device.[10] At around the time that the ricin plot was being wound up, the Director General of the Security Service, MI5, Baroness Eliza Manningham-Buller, was warning that it was only 'a matter of time' before a 'crude version of a CBRN is launched on a major Western city'.[11]

---

[8] 'Blair terror speech in full', BBC News, 5 March 2004, available at <http://news.bbc.co.uk/1/hi/3536131.stm> (accessed 12 March 2010).

[9] T.A. Peter, 'Blair Iraq war enquiry: Calculus of risk on WMD changed after 9/11, *The Christian Science Monitor*, 29 January 2010, available at <http://www.csmonitor.com/World/terrorism-security/2010/0129/Blair-Iraq-war-inquiry-Calculus-of-risk-on-WMD-changed-after-9-11> (accessed 2 July 2011).

[10] D. Gardham, 'Muslim was planning dirty bomb attack in UK', *The Telegraph*, 13 October 2006, available at <http://www.telegraph.co.uk/news/uknews/1531326/Muslim-was-planning-dirty-bomb-attack-in-UK.html> (accessed 13 October 2010).

[11] P. Johnston, 'Dirty bomb attack only a matter of time, says MI5 chief', *The Telegraph*, 18 June 2003, available at <http://www.telegraph.co.uk/news/uknews/1433291/Dirty-bomb-attack-only-a-matter-of-time-says-MI5-chief.html> (accessed 20 February 2010).

Thankfully, Baroness Eliza's prediction has not as yet come to pass, possibly due to a combination of luck and good counter-terrorism policy, but it has to be the case that a risk of such an attack remains a very real threat. The NSS-11 identifies the threat as coming from 'another state or proxy',[12] which captures the potential connection between 'rogue states' such as Iran (which has a history of supporting terrorist proxy groups and militias such as Hezbollah in Lebanon and Jaish al-Mahdi in Iraq), and terrorist movements such as Al Qaeda. In actual fact, any connections between these entities are speculative and, in some ways, objectives are not shared between the anti-Shia sectarian Al Qaeda and Shia Iran.[13] On the other hand, Iran has shown that it is not averse to dealing with Al Qaeda's bedfellow in Afghanistan, the Taliban, where a common enemy of Western nations is present, according to Western intelligence assessments.[14] If this is correct, it suggests that regional and political calculations by a state such as Iran could make the connection between a state capability in WMD and the sponsoring of a sub-state or proxy terrorist group.

Unstable and failed states

The second identified risk on the second tier of priority concerns situations of instability in states abroad, and the manner in which this instability can affect security back in the West. If the war in Iraq concerned the perceived risk of rogue states developing WMD and making them available to other groups, then the war in Afghanistan has become—after its initial focus specifically on rooting out Al Qaeda training camps—a campaign to address a situation in which a failing state has become a haven for terrorists. The Afghanistan campaign is now a comprehensive campaign of reconstruction of a state following decades of civil war and state decay. The NSS describes the risk as follows:

> Fragile, failing and failed states around the world provide the environment for terrorists to operate as they look to exploit ungoverned or ill-governed space.[15]

We saw in Chapter 1 how a notion of a strong state developed historically in Europe around the concept of strong security, and the Weberian premise that a state is defined by a 'monopoly of the legitimate use of physical force in the enforcement of its order' within a given territory.[16] This internal and

---

[12] HM Government, 'Securing Britain in an Age of Uncertainty: The Strategic Defence and Security Review' (London: TSO, October 2010), 27.

[13] A. Hameed Bakier, 'Jihadis Speculate on Secret Cooperation between Iran and Al Qaeda', The Jamestown Foundation, *Terrorism Focus*, 6/6 (26 February 2009).

[14] US Department of State, Office of the Coordinator for Counterterrorism, 'Country Reports on Terrorism 2009', available at <http://www.state.gov/s/ct/rls/crt/2009/> (accessed 6 July 2011).

[15] SDSR, n 12, at 28.

[16] M. Weber, *Max Weber: Essays in Sociology* (Abingdon: Routledge, 1991 [1946]), 78.

external military strength was consolidated, argues Malešević, with a 'cumulative bureaucratisation of coercion'.[17] By extension, a breakdown in security capability should be a defining characteristic of a failed state. Rotberg described the examples of Afghanistan, Somalia, and Sierra Leone as states which 'are incapable of projecting power and asserting authority within their own borders, leaving their territories governmentally empty'.[18] (It is fair to say that Sierra Leone may since have climbed out of this category, at least for the time being.) Again, in the past, this would not necessarily be a problem for anyone other than the state itself, but the interconnectedness of the world under globalization means that 'these states pose dangers not only to themselves and to their neighbours but also to peoples around the globe'.[19]

The mountainous areas between Pakistan and Afghanistan in the tribal Pashtun belt have a very long history of ungovernability, and a very antagonistic relationship with the succession of invading forces that have attempted to bring them within the orbit of centralized state structures, from Alexander the Great, to the British, and the Soviets. Under the Frontier Crimes Regulations during the British Empire in India, the Pashtun tribal areas were given autonomy to operate tribal law in their districts with minimal oversight from the centre, providing they ensured peaceful coexistence with their imperial overseer. With the birth of Pakistan, the same degree of legal and administrative autonomy to these tribal areas was continued in the shape of the Federally Administered Tribal Areas (FATA), which are much more loosely connected to the Pakistani state than are other settled areas.

The outcome of this historical process is that the Pashtun areas, occupying as they do a particularly challenging terrain, and divided between the states of Pakistan and Afghanistan around the very loosely defined Durand Line (which local tribes ignore and cross at will in many areas) is one of the most ungoverned and underdeveloped regions in the world.

It is clear that the complete lack of central authority in this area made it a good place to which Al Qaeda could relocate when they were forced to leave Sudan in 1995, and for them to set up training camps and operate with relative impunity. The same conditions clearly also exist in such places as Somalia—where decades of civil war have left large tracts of the country in little more than tribal and militia control—and the vast and empty Maghreb region of north Africa. However, weak state authority in such areas is not enough in itself: in all these cases, an ideological affinity with local tribes and groups was also essential. In the case of Afghanistan and parts of Somalia, an extreme fundamentalist and obscurantist form of Sunni Islam means that Al Qaeda, while not necessarily accepted with open arms, are tolerated as guests in the region. In Afghanistan, Al Qaeda's war with the West fitted with centuries of bellicose

---

[17] S. Malešević, *The Sociology of War and Violence* (Cambridge: Cambridge University Press, 2010), 5.

[18] R.I. Rotberg, 'Failed States in a World of Terror', *Foreign Affairs*, 81/4 (2002), 128.

[19] Ibid, 127.

tribal fanaticism and opposition to external influences, which had culminated in the Taliban regime in the latter half of the 1990s.

Secondly, in times past, extreme remoteness and lack of communications would have been a double-edged sword for a movement with global aspirations. With globalization's technological developments, however, and particularly the advent of satellite phones and remote internet access, an organization such as Al Qaeda can physically locate to extremely remote and hard-to-reach areas, and still communicate and relay plans to foot soldiers in the back streets of Western cities. In this sense, the infrastructural frailties of a weak or failing state can be leapfrogged to a certain degree, at least in the area of communications technology. Thus, it took nearly ten years to find Osama Bin Laden after the 9/11 attacks in the United States, and some of his key lieutenants are still at large, but his organization was able, albeit to an increasingly limited degree, to communicate, plan, and place propaganda messages on to the worldwide web throughout this period.

In addition to the communications links with remote areas enabled by globalization, the physical ease and volume of movement in the modern world mean that individuals can travel back and forth to terrorist training camps in remote and ungoverned regions with relative ease. Individuals in Britain and elsewhere can now consider attending terrorist training camps in such failed states, or indeed gain combat experience in insurgencies, and then readily bring back the knowledge they have gained to conduct operations at home. Spotting and intercepting such movements of individuals in the massive flow of human traffic between countries is no easy task, and many will slip through the net. The NSS notes that the two individuals who conducted a suicide attack on Glasgow airport in 2007 'had undergone such experiences' of exposure to violence and conflict in Iraq.[20] It also notes that the Al-Shabaab insurgency in Somalia, which is clearly inspired by if not actually franchised by Al Qaeda, may offer similar opportunities for certain members of the British community.[21]

In addition to the physical connections and risks arising from weak and failing states, there are ideological factors also. In all counter-insurgency doctrines (about which I will say more later) the importance of 'winning hearts and minds' is paramount. The aim of an intervening army is not to cause local people to think of them as neo-imperialists, but for a wedge to be driven between the locals and insurgents and to turn the tables on the latter. (Where this backfires and the opposite effect happens, is central to David Kilcullen's 'accidental guerrilla' thesis.[22]) There is also a need to challenge ideological

---

[20] HM Government, 'A Strong Britain in an Age of Uncertainty: The National Security Strategy' (London: TSO, October 2010), 28.

[21] Ibid.

[22] See D. Kilcullen, *The Accidental Guerrilla: Fighting Small Wars in the Midst of a Big One* (London: Hurst, 2009).

rhetoric which suggests that the very reason a failed state is in such a situation is due to historical imperialism, exploitation, and subjugation by the global North.

Key to the intervention operation in such situations is development and infrastructure support, to show that the invaders are actually intending to lift the country out of its structural weakness and leave it a better place. This is how and why the Afghanistan operation becomes much more than simply about chasing down terrorists, but is also about restructuring and rebuilding a state. In the language of the NSS and the SDSR, this is the essence of the twin national security objectives of 'ensuring a secure and resilient United Kingdom; and shaping a stable world'.[23] The logic is a preventative one of addressing not only immediate threats, but trying to 'drain the swamp' in which they might fester again in the future.

Of course, in the Afghanistan situation there is also an ideological objective for the West in spreading democracy and establishing an essentially Westphalian state structure, seen as central components of the new state that must be built. This runs into direct ideological conflict with the Taliban's *Salafist* Islamic view of the world, in which Western democracy is seen as a recipe for corruption and anathema to Muslim peoples. As an editorial in *Le Monde* discussed in January 2011, the conundrum is encapsulated in the phrase 'democratic state', where this is applied to Afghanistan.[24] The country obtained independence as a state in 1921 under Amanullah Khan, but the political basis of that state has never been clear or agreed upon. Communism failed largely because it came up against cultural and religious barriers, but Islam has so far only brought further conflict and failed to unite different ethnic factions. As for democracy, that has never been present and arguably still is not, despite the attempts to establish an electoral process in the country. Is part of the problem the fact that the Western democratic model that International Stabilisation and Assistance Force (ISAF) is attempting to establish in Afghanistan is fundamentally at odds with the existing landscape of tribal chiefs, ethnic leaders, and mullahs? Perhaps the plan is far too ambitious to work in a state as fractured and complex as Afghanistan.

More importantly, it is not clear whether the immense complexities of the UK's strategic objectives of 'shaping a stable world' have been fully understood, even after ten years in Afghanistan. These are issues that will have to be learned, with new scenarios such as post-conflict Libya looming on the horizon. These are issues to which I will return. For now, the NSS usefully recognizes the risks arising from failed states in an interconnected world.

---

[23] SDSR, n 12, at 33.

[24] 'Où en sommes-nous en Afghanistan?', *Le Monde*, 14 January 2011, available at <http://www.lemonde.fr/idees/article/2011/01/14/ou-en-sommes-nous-en-afghanistan_1465293_3232.html> (accessed 30 January 2011).

Organized crime

The Threat from Organised Crime—Sir Ian Andrews, Chair of the Serious Organised Crime Agency (SOCA)

Organised crime is entrepreneurial, agile and resilient. It does not respect boundaries and is already globalised. Ruining lives and targeting the most vulnerable individuals, businesses and communities, it is directly or indirectly responsible for much low-level crime on our streets. Like any business, it will exploit opportunities in the market and it prospers in ungoverned and inadequately regulated spaces where it corrupts and undermines fragile states, societies and governments.

This trend is accelerating exponentially with the increasing dependence of society on the internet. Most organised crime will very soon either be enabled by, or take place in, cyberspace. It will also be fuelled by demographic pressures, resource shortages and the consequences of climate change. Criminal groups may specialise in certain commodities, but they all specialise in money, and the power and lifestyle it buys.

Organised crime must be an integral part of national security strategies. The UK National Security Strategy has placed it centre stage in the collective consciousness across government. How the country will respond to the threat is set out in the Government's Organised Crime Strategy, published in July 2011.

Since it was formed in 2006, SOCA has greatly improved its understanding of the drivers and enablers of organised crime and how to disrupt them. We now have a much better appreciation of how organised crime operates, who is involved, and which interventions work, and which do not. The government's new National Crime Agency will build upon this knowledge to take the response to organised and other criminality to the next level.

One of the myriad problems that Afghanistan faces is that its formal economy, shattered by years of insecurity and lacking infrastructural development, has become dominated by organized crime in the shape of an opium economy controlled by warlords. The Asian Development Bank estimates that opium was a major source of income for more than 80 per cent of the rural population of Afghanistan by 2009.[25] Afghan opium accounts for 90 per cent of the world's supply, and represents up to 30 per cent of the economy in the country.[26] Aside from the structural weaknesses this represents for Afghanistan's economy and future development, this also means that society and politics in the country are

---

[25] M.I. Sarwari, *Asian Development Outlook: South Asia* (Manila: Asian Development Bank, 2009), 185, available at <http://www.adb.org/documents/books/ado/2009/south-asia.pdf> (accessed 20 March 2011).

[26] Ibid.

gripped by the corrupting force of warlords, which stifles the development of democratic and accountable institutions. These processes run into direct conflict with the attempts to stabilize and reshape the state of Afghanistan and to ensure that it does not continue to be a source of problems regionally and internationally.

Giraldo and Trinkunas argue that organized crime, particularly around the international trade in illegal narcotics, arms, and people, has undoubtedly risen considerably since the 1980s in conjunction with the rise of modern globalization, although its effects around the globe are uneven.[27] For some countries, such as Afghanistan, it is certainly the case that the illegal trade in such commodities can rise to a level where it can subvert and threaten the very fabric of the state. Other narcotics-producing countries, notably Colombia, have experienced a similarly existential struggle between cocaine-producing cartels and the establishment of democratic and accountable state structures, with the wholesale murder and corruption of the police and judiciary a persistent problem for many years. In some cases, successful counter-crime strategies in such regions merely have the effect of displacing the problem to other states. There is evidence that Mexico, for example, currently in the grip of a bitter war with cocaine trafficking cartels that has claimed the lives of 28,000 people in violent confrontation since 2006,[28] is suffering the effects of a concentration of trafficking routes through Central America as maritime trafficking through the Caribbean becomes more difficult.[29] Similarly, interdiction of trans-Atlantic trafficking of drugs from Latin America to Europe may be leading to the opening up of new overland routes through West Africa,[30] highlighting the risks posed by organized crime to fragile states, as identified by Sir Ian Andrews in the box above. Indeed, the very attraction of such countries and regions to the traffickers are that states are weaker, large areas are less governed, and counter-crime security structures, where they exist at all, are less effective and more open to corruption. This, in turn, leads to serious and persistent developmental problems for such countries in the grip of such criminal trade.

The UK's Serious and Organised Crime Agency (SOCA), which will become part of the National Crime Agency (NCA) from 2013, assesses the threat picture from organized crime under its UK periodic Threat Assessment (UKTA) process.

---

[27] J. Giraldo and H. Trinkunas, 'Transnational Crime' in A. Collins (ed), *Contemporary Security Studies* (Oxford: Oxford University Press, 2010), 429.

[28] R. Carroll, 'Mexico drug war: the new killing fields', *The Guardian*, 3 September 2010, available at <http://www.guardian.co.uk/world/2010/sep/03/mexico-drug-war-killing-fields> (accessed 4 July 2011).

[29] C.R Seelke, L.S. Wyler, J.S. Beittel, and M.P. Sullivan, *Latin America and the Caribbean: Illicit Drug Trafficking and US Counter-Drug Programmes* (Washington DC: Congressional Research Service, 12 May 2011), 2.

[30] Ibid.

The latest published UKTA, for 2009–10, identifies the following issues as the key organized crime threats facing the UK:[31]

- Drugs trafficking
- Fraud
- Organized crime groups
- Human trafficking
- People smuggling
- Money laundering
- Identity crime
- Firearms
- Vehicle crime
- Threats to the 2012 Olympics in London
- Armed robbery
- Intellectual property crime
- Counterfeit currency

Within this long list, the assessment notes that 'as far as the scale and relative significance of the threats, it is still the case that most of those identified as involved in organised crime are engaged in drugs trafficking and distribution.'[32] That said, the report also notes that more is known about this particular threat than is the case with newer and more sophisticated criminal threats, such as complex financial fraud. Overall, the UKTA notes that 'the overall threat to the UK from organised crime is high'. It also places a figure of £20 billion a year on the costs to the country from organized crime (including the costs of combating it),[33] while the NSS suggests the annual tariff is somewhere between £20–40 billion.[34] The latter also suggests that there are 'around 38,000 individuals' involved in organized crime affecting the UK.[35] As discussed in the previous chapter and identified by Sir Ian above, the cyber dimension to contemporary organized crime seems to be causing particular anxiety, with an estimate of its annual cost to UK companies—confusingly—identified as being 25 times higher than the top-end figure above, at £1 trillion.[36] A specific concern revolves around opportunities for fraud presented by hosting the Olympics in London in 2012.

It is reasonable to assume that the process of globalization will allow serious and organized crime to develop and mutate in new directions, much as it allows business and social interaction generally to do so. Willetts notes that, in addition to the ongoing threats associated with the trafficking of drugs, a 'new slave

---

[31] 'The United Kingdom Threat Assessment of Organised Crime: 2009/10', SOCA, available at <http://www.soca.gov.uk/threats> (accessed 17 January 2011).

[32] Ibid, 5.

[33] Ibid, 6.

[34] NSS, n 20, at 14.

[35] Ibid.

[36] Ibid, 29.

trade' has developed in recent years, focused primarily on the sexual exploit-ation of women.[37] As Langhorne noted, 'a rising tide raises all boats, whether innocent or criminal'.[38] This will include new opportunities for fraud and theft afforded by the information revolution. Yet again, how such issues are quanti-fied and securitized in a national security context, and in a country such as the UK, is open to some debate.

As Giraldo and Trinkunas described, a renewed focus on the threat of organ-ized crime in the media and in academia coincided with the end of the Cold War, as new security preoccupations took shape.[39] In the UK, the Intelligence Services Act of 1994 placed the two overseas intelligence agencies, the Secret Intelligence Service (MI6) and Government Communications Headquarters (GCHQ) on the statute books for the first time, and specified that their remit was to gather intelligence not only on issues of national security, but also on those affecting the 'economic well-being' of the UK, and on the prevention and detection of serious crime. This reflected the shift—indeed the broadening—of focus since the Cold War. Interestingly, the domestic intelligence agency, MI5, had been placed on the statute books in 1989, and in 1996 the Security Service Act was amended to allow it, too, to collect intelligence on serious crime groups. This reflected a shift in focus partially away from the Cold War preoccupations of Communist-bloc espionage. Just as interestingly, with the rise of the terrorist threat through the late 1990s, the Security Service announced in 2006 that it was withdrawing again from work on serious crime targets.[40] While these devel-opments probably reflect very real shifts in security threats, they also reflect the re-securitization and relative prioritization of issues in the intelligence and security domain following the Cold War.

Notions of organized crime can be problematic, much as traditional notions of a well-structured terrorist organization become questionable when one looks at a phenomenon such as Al Qaeda. Much transnational crime is not necessar-ily organized in the hierarchical way that the Cali or Medellin cartels in Colombia were organized, but can more accurately be described as flexible, networked, and entrepreneurial.[41] SOCA's UKTA recognizes these nuances, noting that 'many groups are in practice loose networks of criminals that come together for the duration of a criminal activity, acting in different roles depending on their skills and expertise.'[42] In this way, modern serious crime in a globalized world might reflect many of the best practices of business—and of

[37] P. Willetts, 'Transnational Actors and International Organizations in Global Politics' in J. Baylis, S. Smith, and P. Owens (eds), *The Globalization of World Politics: An Introduction to International Relations*, 5th edn (Oxford: Oxford University Press, 2010), 337.
[38] R. Langhorne, *The Essentials of Global Politics* (New York: Hodder Arnold, 2006), 164.
[39] Giraldo and Trinkunas, n 27, at 429.
[40] 'Security Service Work on Organised Crime', Security Service, 2006, available at <https://www.mi5.gov.uk/output/news/security-service-work-on-serious-crime.html> (accessed 5 July 2011).
[41] Giraldo and Trinkunas, n 27, at 432.
[42] SOCA, n 31.

other threat dimensions such as terrorism—in the contemporary globalized and networked world. Such complexities are important to understand and to research, not least so that the public and businesses can fully understand, prioritize, and mitigate the threats they are facing. The addition of the highly complex cyber realm to the world of crime means that we may be only at the beginning of our understanding of what such modern threats mean and how they will develop.

Properly conceptualizing the risk from organized crime is a difficult business, and one around which there is not complete consensus. Some have pointed out how crime is a deeply politicized issue and a big media factor in a country such as the UK, which can cause the paradox that perceptions of crime become out of step with crime statistics. (Indications are that instances of violent crime in the UK, for example, have been declining in recent years, but the general public perception is that they have been rising.[43]) The NSS states the risk, in Tier Two of priority, as arising from 'a significant increase in the level or organised crime affecting the UK'. It would be reasonable to suggest that the UK's state structures are, at present, robust enough to withstand an existential threat from organized crime. Such dangers have been experienced in weaker states such as Afghanistan or Colombia, or indeed in post-Soviet states such as Russia, where organized crime took a real grip on the institutions of the state during the transition from centralized communism to capitalism. That said, the increasing mutation and development of entrepreneurial transnational organized crime is starting to generate and launder sums of money sufficiently large to threaten the integrity of the banking system.[44] With the growth of new criminal opportunities in the cyber dimension, the future, as ever, is unpredictable, and should be part of the calculations around security and resilience.

Disruption to satellite communications

The final area of risk identified in the Tier Two priorities is that of 'severe disruption to information received, transmitted or collected by satellites, possibly as a result of a deliberate attack by another state.'[45] This is essentially a resilience issue, arising from the networked nature of modern states, and again marks out this period of globalization from earlier periods of internationalization.

Interestingly, while the NSS flags this up as a specific risk in the Tier Two box, it does not provide any detail on the nature of the threat elsewhere in the document. The SDSR says slightly more, noting a certain degree of 'dependence on

---

[43] E. Duncan, 'Let's be tough on the perception of crime', *The Times*, 11 July 2011, p 21.

[44] Willetts, n 37.

[45] NSS, n 20, at 27.

space' in both military and civil spheres, and that certain satellites and their ground stations are 'critical to our security and the economy'.[46]

Since the 1960s, satellite technology has grown to become a key technology in a range of spheres. During the Cold War, its military capabilities were increasingly critical in terms of imagery intelligence (IMINT) delivered from behind enemy lines, where other forms of intelligence were unable to operate. Satellites also delivered critical command-and-control capabilities, and latterly missile defence systems in the shape of 'Star Wars' technology. In the civil sphere, developments were no less significant with the rise of satellite television broadcasting through the 1960s and 1970s, which began to make the transmission of news and events global and almost immediate. By the 1990s, the 'first CNN war' in the shape of the 1991 campaign to eject Iraqi forces from Kuwait underlined how far such news technology had come, and its potential to revolutionize global perceptions of politics and conflict.

In telecommunications, satellites were initially critical to the bulk international market, although their importance waned somewhat with the advent of fibre optic cables, which could carry much greater data volumes at higher transmission rates. With the post-Cold War information revolution and the sort of convergence between telephony and internet communications described earlier, however, the importance of satellites has surged ahead again. In military spheres, as well as continuing to provide critical IMINT at ever-greater resolutions, satellites continue to be central to command-and-control, providing the type of capability, for example, that allows unmanned aerial drones (UAVs) to be remotely operated from thousands of miles away. In this way, satellites have been central to the Revolution in Military Affairs (RMA) since the end of the Cold War, which makes modern conflict, as Gregory describes, 'a-geographical' and radically 'compresses the kill chain'.[47]

In the civilian sphere, meanwhile, the growth of geolocational facilities and their growing importance to commerce and social networking, including Global Positioning Satellite (GPS)-based services and applications such as in-car satellite navigation, in addition to expanding and improving satellite television services, have also given this area of technology a further shot in the arm. In these ways, satellite technology is becoming critical to modern business and commerce.

Meanwhile, there is evidence that certain states are working on capabilities to intercept and disrupt satellites. In January 2007, China appeared to conduct a successful test in which it destroyed a weather satellite using a ground-based medium-range ballistic missile (MRBM).[48] A Foreign Ministry spokesman in China claimed that the test, which was the first known of its type in 20 years, should not be seen as threatening, and that 'China has never, and will never

---

[46] SDSR, n 12, at 65.

[47] D. Gregory, 'War and Peace', *Transactions of the Institute of British Geographers*, 35 (2010), 160.

[48] 'China confirms satellite downed', BBC News, 23 January 2007, available at <http://news.bbc.co.uk/1/hi/world/asia-pacific/6289519.stm> (accessed 16 October 2010).

participate in any form of space arms race'.[49] Others beg to differ, however, notably the Taiwanese, for whom US military satellites provide an invaluable monitoring and warning capability against any Chinese military move in the region. These tests by the Chinese rather suggest that they recognize very well the strategic significance of certain satellites, and the disruption that can be effected if they can be taken out of the picture, either using direct missile strikes as demonstrated in this case, or by using other methods such as electromagnetic pulse technology or even possibly cyber attacks. In a military context, taking out satellites is becoming the equivalent to taking out radar and radio-relay stations in degrading the enemy's command-and-control capabilities. This applies to the UK as much as to any other advanced industrial state, and should properly be considered an infrastructural security risk in the contemporary context.

Key points

- Tier Two threats overlap and connect with those in Tier One, and this means that the threat response cannot be seen in discrete categories.
- The risk of an attack using unconventional weapons has increased since the Cold War, through a combination of terrorists and other groups showing an intention to use such weaponry; the general trend towards increasing global proliferation of WMDs; and the lack of security in establishments in the former Soviet Union holding sensitive materials.
- Failed and fragile states can become a risk through their attractiveness to terrorists and organized crime groups which flourish in ungoverned spaces.
- Global organized crime continues to grow through the opportunities offered by the growth of the internet and the general interconnectedness of societies and markets. Narcotics trafficking is still at the heart of much of this crime, but new opportunities are emerging all the time.
- A resurgent dependence on satellite communications, in both civil and military spheres, has made disruption to such communications a critical national infrastructure issue. Some countries, such as China, have shown that they are developing mechanisms for disrupting and even destroying satellites in orbit, which could be seen as a hostile defence capability.

---

[49] Ibid.

5

Tier Three Risks

Backdrop—security in Europe

The risks identified as being in the third tier of priority in the National Security Strategy (NSS) overlap with those of higher priority to a certain extent, but also introduce specific threats in the areas of border security, energy security, and military commitments, in part relating to alliances with partners overseas, primarily NATO. The set of risks identified in Tier Three are:[1]

- a large-scale conventional military attack on the UK by another state (not involving the use of chemical, biological, radiological, or nuclear (CBRN) weapons) resulting in fatalities and damage to infrastructure within the UK;
- a significant increase in the level of terrorists, organized criminals, illegal immigrants, and illicit goods trying to enter the UK;
- disruption to oil or gas supplies to the UK, or price instability, as a result of war, accident, major political upheaval, or deliberate manipulation of supply by producers;
- a major release of radioactive material from a civil nuclear site within the UK which affects one or more regions;
- a conventional attack by a state on another NATO or EU member state to which the UK would have to respond;
- an attack on a UK overseas territory as the result of a sovereignty dispute or a wider regional conflict;
- short- to medium-term disruption to international supplies of resources (eg food, minerals) essential to the UK.

The first risk identified here seems anathema to Britain's position in the post-Cold War, EU era of existence. At the time of writing, the UK is celebrating the

---

[1] HM Government, 'A Strong Britain in an Age of Uncertainty: The National Security Strategy' (London: TSO, October 2010), 27.

remarkable achievements of the codebreakers at Bletchley Park who, most analysts suggest, made a pivotal difference to the Second World War.[2] At this time, we have to look around in Britain and consider that no risk is foreseeable that could be compared to the threat of invasion and domination by a European neighbour. Even the more recent Cold War, where, as I discussed in Chapter 1, the existential threat of invasion and domination by the Soviets and the installation of communism was considered a real threat and the one of highest priority to national security, such risks to national security already seem a distant memory. While the organization highlighted at the beginning of this book, NATO, has clearly played a pivotal part in both protecting and binding together European (and North American) states in security, the EU process has also been pivotal. The EU was initially a primarily economic union, taking full shape with the signing of the Treaty of Rome in 1957 that established the European Economic Community (EEC). This had emerged from the European Coal and Steel Community (ECSC), launched in 1951, which had bound together the key continental West European states, including West Germany, France, and Italy, in a way that envisaged that mutual security would be assured through the deep integration of key industrial linkages. With the Maastricht Treaty of 1993, which deepened the social and political elements of union alongside the economic dimensions, the Community became the European Community (EC), and later the European Union with the signing of the Lisbon Treaty in 2009. The UK joined the EEC in 1973, and has remained one of the largest and most significant members of the Union ever since (if not always the least controversial), despite electing not to join the single currency when it was launched fully in 2002.

The notion behind the EU was that mutual peace in Europe, which had proved elusive for centuries and had culminated with the most murderous war in world history, could be achieved through the twin dimensions of economic integration and a shared system of political values based around freedom and democracy. The initial economic spur was the very specific strategic factor of the coal and steel industries in the Alsace region between France and Germany, which had been central to conflict between those nations for many years, and which had changed hands between the two repeatedly in history. The establishment of Economic and Monetary Union (EMU) between the bulk of the EU's member states, which led to the common euro currency replacing national currencies fully in 2002, has further underlined the very deep integration of European economies.

The security outcome is that, in a relatively short time (essentially within one generation), the countries of Western Europe have gone from a situation of total war to one in which conflict between them seems unthinkable. Ripsman and Paul describe the states of the EU as being states in a 'stable region', which

---

[2] 'Queen unveils Bletchley tribute', BBC News, 15 July 2011, available at <http://www.bbc.co.uk/news/uk-14164529> (accessed 15 July 2011).

has become 'ensconced in unprecedented peace, stability and security'.[3] They go on to examine the specific examples of France and the UK, which, by extension of their position within the EU, ought to be the most willing of any states 'to depart from traditional security practices and doctrine, because the costs of relinquishing tight state control and scaling back preparation for interstate warfare are likely to be low', given the lack of military threat.[4] This is interesting in the context of the defence agreement signed between these two states at the end of 2010, about which I will say more later.

The results of this analysis are mixed. First, the NSS notes that the UK is currently 'more secure [than at any stage in its history], in the sense that we do not currently face, as we have so often in the past, a conventional threat of attack on our territory by a hostile power.'[5] At the same time, because of the nature of the 'age of uncertainty' in which we live, it is pointed out in the Strategic Defence and Security Review (SDSR) that Britain 'will continue to be one of very few countries able to deploy a self-sustaining, properly equipped brigade-sized force anywhere around the world and sustain it indefinitely.'[6] In this sense, the UK in particular has remained involved in essentially traditional interstate wars in the post-Cold War period, albeit overseas in such locations as Iraq and Afghanistan. (The latter is a slightly complex case in that it has become more of a counter-insurgency than an interstate war, but many of the military factors are the same.) France has also been involved in a number of military campaigns since the Cold War, albeit a fewer number than the UK, including the NATO action against Libya. So, while the immediate threat of defending the homeland may have receded for the time being in these two European states, this has not meant that they have removed any need for their military capabilities to the extent that might have been expected.[7]

Indeed, the twin factors put forward in security strategizing which determine that military capabilities remain on the agenda for certain European states, are the need to remain vigilant and prepared in an uncertain world where threats are unpredictable, and the element of 'new terrorism' since 9/11 which has, to a large extent, provided a new military security focus in the post-Cold War world. We saw in Chapter 2 how this latter factor has contributed to a gradual increase in US defence spending as a proportion of GDP since the end of the 1990s, after a brief post-Cold War period in which spending had been decreasing for the first time in many years. For the UK, one of the most significant elements of strategy in which these factors have been significant is in the much-debated decision to retain a nuclear deterrent, which the UK government

---

[3] N.M. Ripsman and T.V. Paul, *Globalization and the National Security State* (Oxford: Oxford University Press, 2010), 83.

[4] Ibid.

[5] NSS, n 1, at 3.

[6] HM Government, 'Securing Britain in an Age of Uncertainty: The Strategic Defence and Security Review' (London: TSO, October 2010), 4.

[7] Ripsman and Paul, n 3, at 87.

describes as the 'ultimate insurance policy in this age of uncertainty'.[8] Thus, while the nuclear capability is being further reduced in scale and size, it is seen as still required. Till notes that neither of the main political parties in the UK seems currently of a mind to scrap the nuclear capability, despite what would, presumably, be considerable cost-savings in so doing, as 'a nuclear deterrent is seen to offer protection through retaliatory punishment at least against a state-based threat'. How effective it would be against a threat from a sub-state terrorist group is somewhat uncertain.[9]

Similarly, the NATO alliance, about which I will say more later, is seen as central to the 'territorial defence of the UK',[10] by virtue of binding us together with our immediate European neighbours under the Article 5 agreement of the NATO Treaty. This means that the UK's own defence is not necessarily something that it must tackle alone, but it also means that the UK might itself become drawn into a conflict initiated by an attack on an alliance partner country. Thus, another Tier Three risk identified in the NSS is outlined as 'a conventional attack by a state on another NATO or EU member to which the UK would have to respond' under its treaty obligations.[11]

Wider regional conflict

In addition to the risk of being drawn into a conflict involving another NATO country, Tier Three also identifies the risk of 'an attack on an overseas territory as the result of a sovereignty dispute or a wider regional conflict'. This is a thinly veiled reference very largely to the case of the Falklands Islands, which caused the UK to become involved in an interstate conflict with Argentina in 1982 over the latter's military claim to sovereignty of the islands.

This overseas UK territory in the far-flung South Atlantic is a particularly salient factor in the debates that accompanied the NSS and SDSR, since many analysts have suggested that cutbacks and restructuring of the UK military under the latest SDSR mean that we would not now be able to launch a 1982-style unilateral military campaign to recover the Falklands, should they be seized again. In a letter to *The Telegraph* in June 2011, Admiral Sir John 'Sandy' Woodward, who led the task force that retook the Falkland Islands in 1982 following the Argentinian invasion, claimed that lacking support from the United States, a reduced navy following the defence review, and over-commitment of British forces in other military theatres, meant that Britain would be powerless to prevent another Argentinian invasion and would have to

---

[8] SDSR, n 6, at 5.
[9] G. Till, 'British Strategy after Afghanistan' in M. Codner and M. Clarke (eds), *A Question of Security: The British Defence Review in an Age of Austerity* (London: I.B. Tauris, 2011), 138.
[10] SDSR, n 6, at 12.
[11] NSS, n 1, at 27.

sue for peace diplomatically.[12] In many ways, the Falklands campaign of 1982 has become something of a bellwether for many analysts, and for many in the military, who are uncomfortable about the level of cuts in military capability under the 2010 defence review. This is particularly so as the Falklands campaign entailed the use of expensive, high-tech military hardware, and particularly naval and associated air force capabilities, which are now seen by many as relics of the Cold War and unsuitable to the types of threats that the UK faces. A particularly poignant development in which the ghost of 1982 appeared is the decision, under the SDSR, to axe the Harrier jump jet, which was in many ways one of the most iconic capabilities in the successful campaign to retake the Falklands. The decision was made on the basis that the Harriers were becoming dated technology, and that a situation in which a completely sea-based launch pad for air power was required, is seen as unlikely.

Tension over the Falklands has increased in recent years, however, with the discovery of oil reserves in the region, which Britain plans to exploit. Argentina is hotly disputing Britain's sovereignty over the relevant waters, however, and is ratcheting up the diplomatic pressure and bringing the whole sovereignty dispute back onto the table.[13] If the conflict were to escalate, the UK would have to think how to respond to protect its citizens. Interestingly, this could be an example not only of a conflict arising over a sovereignty dispute, but might also be a conflict over energy security, which I come to in more detail below.

In many ways, this part of the NSS reflects classic state-centric notions of national security. Here is reference to the UK's territory, and to the sovereignty of its lands, which were central tenets in the Peace of Westphalia in 1648 which established the modern nation-state. Under this Westphalian conception of state power, the need for military security to protect territory and sovereignty is without question and has to be part of national security strategy. For those proponents of more human-oriented security and the benefits of soft power, such state-based notions of security strategy should be robustly challenged in the twenty-first century.[14] Similarly, the notion that a credible risk is that of another state attacking the UK's home territory does seem to be a very problematic concept at the present time. As Simon Jenkins observed, 'absolutely no one is threatening to attack us now or in the foreseeable, indeed conceivable, future'.[15]

---

[12] T. Harding, 'Britain can do "nothing" to prevent Argentina retaking Falkland Islands', *The Telegraph*, 12 June 2011, available at <http://www.telegraph.co.uk/news/worldnews/southamerica/falklandislands/8571442/Britain-can-do-nothing-to-prevent-Argentina-retaking-Falkland-Islands.html> (accessed 17 June 2011).

[13] See eg R. Carroll, 'Argentina blocks ship in Falklands oil dispute', *The Guardian*, 12 February 2010, available at <http://www.guardian.co.uk/uk/2010/feb/12/argentina-falklands-supply-ship-oil-dispute> (accessed 28 March 2010).

[14] See eg N. Ritchie, 'Rethinking Security: A Critical Analysis of the Strategic Defence and Security Review', *International Affairs*, 87/2 (2011), 356–76.

[15] S. Jenkins, 'Does Britain really need the military?', *The Guardian*, 5 November 2010, available at <http://www.guardian.co.uk/politics/2010/nov/05/does-britain-need-the-military-army-navy-raf> (accessed 16 July 2011).

Even that such an attack would be assessed as low probability seems to be stretching the case somewhat; it seems very hard to imagine any scenario in which a conventional attack of this nature could happen. More likely are threats of attacks on the UK from terrorists, whether state-sponsored or independent, using a variety of possibilities ranging from CBRN to cyber attacks. Also reasonably likely are the types of state-based and treaty obligations-based military requirements, such as the need to protect citizens from attack in an overseas dependent territory such as the Falklands (with the possible exception of Gibraltar and the Sovereign Base Areas in Cyprus, it is hard to see diplomatic disputes arising over any other British Overseas Territories at present[16]) or the need to become involved in conflict in support of a NATO partner country. Yet, as Ritchie argues, even these types of operations are 'operations of political choice' relating to 'state-centric notions of security, interest and status'.[17] This is a hard human-security perspective on the issue in which any notion of military action becomes potentially questionable, one with which I would not necessarily agree. The point, as I will argue later, is that required military responses and postures do not necessarily map neatly to threats: it may be unlikely that an attack on the UK homeland is going to happen at any time soon, but that does not mean that we do not need a military at all (as Jenkins suggests[18]). Arguably, we will require some type of military capability for other scenarios.

Energy security

The current dispute over oil exploration in the Falklands region raises the issue of energy and resource security, which is identified as a set of risks in Tier Three of the NSS. Here, it manifests itself in two ways. First, in the risk of 'disruption to oil or gas supplies to the UK, or price instability, as a result of war, accident, major political upheaval or deliberate manipulation of supply by producers. Secondly, there is a risk of 'short to medium term disruption to international supplies of resources (eg food, minerals) essential to the UK'.[19]

Energy security is, in many ways, the classic example of a new security paradigm. This is so through its complex interconnectedness with other issues, such as economic and human security, and with broader issues such as climate change and development. It is entirely conceivable that energy security could increasingly become a military issue, as tension over access to key resources and energy supplies increases. Many analysts of international relations have already promoted the 'oil wars' thesis, which suggests that Western military interest in the Middle East, whatever might be said by the politicians, has really been about

---

[16] For a list of such territories, see <http://www.fco.gov.uk/en/publications-and-documents/treaties/uk-overseas-territories/browse-by-overseas-territory/> (accessed 16 July 2011).
[17] Ritchie, n 14, at 366.
[18] Jenkins, n 15.
[19] NSS, n 1, at 27.

maintaining access to oil.[20] Energy security is also a factor which, like many others, is felt unevenly through the world and is being affected in different ways through the processes of globalization. The essence of energy security, that is, an expectation that energy to supply our daily needs is always there and in a form that is affordable and accessible, is part and parcel of daily life in the industrialized world. In the global South, however, disruptions to energy supply and lack of easy availability to it are daily features of life, and can be very detrimental to social and economic activities. Concepts such as 'load-shedding' (rolling blackouts), which are frustratingly very familiar to anyone who lives in a large developing-world city, are simply never considered in London, Paris, or New York.

The normative conceptions of energy security are that, in a world in which the population is continuing to grow, and in which large states are industrializing at a rapid rate (notably India and China), a continued reliance on finite fossil fuels will start to become a problem as the exponential growth of energy demand starts to outstrip supply. Additionally, a rising graph of carbon emissions from exploitation of fossil fuels will exacerbate climate change, and this, in turn, will lead to a host of other security problems around the world.

As Froggatt and Levi identify, many of the security issues in this area are bound up in other strategic concerns in a complicated way. For example, biofuels are considered one of the key areas in which countries may be able to develop greener forms of energy supply, while reducing their dependence on oil. In this way, biofuels are an important part of strategy to counter climate change and reduce emissions. But the production process for biofuels at present is itself energy-intensive, and, in particular, tends to require large quantities of natural gas, which has the effect of increasing security dependence on gas-producing countries[21] such as Russia. An additional factor is that a large shift in agriculture globally away from food production and towards production of biofuels could push food prices up to dangerous levels. Global food prices rose by as much as 40 per cent in 2011, causing severe economic stress and instability in some parts of the world.[22] While much of the pressure was caused by drought and poor harvests, shifts in land usage in some parts of the world for energy-production reasons could exacerbate the situation.

Aside from showing that the security issues are complex and interconnected, this example also provides indications for how governments need to work more effectively across different areas of strategy and policy, as I will examine later.

---

[20] See eg M.T. Klare, *Blood and Oil: The Dangers and Consequences of America's Growing Petroleum Dependency* (London: Penguin, 2005); and S.C. Pelletière, *America's Oil Wars* (Westport, CT: Praeger, 2004).

[21] A. Froggatt and M.A. Levi, 'Climate and Energy Security Policies and Measures: Synergies and Conflicts', *International Affairs*, 85/6 (2009), 1135.

[22] R. Neate, 'Food price explosion will "devastate the world's poor"', *The Guardian*, 17 June 2011, available at <http://www.guardian.co.uk/environment/2011/jun/17/global-food-prices-increase-united-nations> (accessed 20 June 2011).

The SDSR estimates that the UK's energy security risks revolve around instability in key producer countries, lacking investment in certain supplier states, and 'imperfections in the functioning of global and UK markets'.[23] Such risks are likely to increase through a growing UK dependence on imports of oil and gas, and a generally growing global demand. Within the general picture of dependence, a lack of diversity of supply is always a risk, both from the perspective of stable pricing and from the danger of being held to ransom. The growing dependence of Western Europe in general on the supply of natural gas from Russia, for example, was shown to be a potentially serious problem in 2006 and 2009, when Russia entered into serious disagreements with Ukraine, through which most of the westbound gas passes, and supplies were severely curtailed.[24]

Within this picture, certain strategic parts of the globe may become increasingly important, and the likelihood of tension in such areas may become greater. Exploitation of oil and gas from the Caspian region, for example, which is attractive in that it potentially reduces oil dependency on suppliers in the Middle East, runs into geopolitical problems in the Caucasus region, through which key extraction pipelines such as the BTC line (Baku-Tblisi-Ceyhan) must pass. Some have suggested that Russia's conflicts with Georgia are in large part connected with these geopolitical concerns and the need for Russia to maintain political and economic power in this strategically critical region.[25] Asmus assesses the 2008 Russian conflict with Georgia as a throwback to previous confrontations with NATO, and the need to send a message to former Soviet states such as Georgia which want to move westwards in their political and military alliances.[26] This raises the spectre of traditional interstate conflict over key resources in the future.

Similarly, the NATO operation in Libya in 2011 was perhaps a case in point. As *The Economist* noted in February 2011, 'economies need oil and it is idle to suppose otherwise. The question raised by the wave of protests spreading across the Middle East is not whether to deal with autocrats, but how to deal with them.'[27] For Western nations, the strategy on how to respond to events in the Middle East will be driven partly by the need for ensuring stability of oil supplies in the region (a lack of which, as we have seen, is identified as a key element of energy security risk) while also considering human rights issues and the possible need for intervention. This is a simple, essentially realist, calculation of the situation for economies heavily dependent on Middle Eastern oil.

---

[23] SDSR, n 6, at 50.

[24] Froggatt and Levi, n 21, at 1131.

[25] P.E. Thomann, 'Russia-Georgia: the multipolar world's first war', *La revue géopolitique*, 10 October 2008, available at <http://www.diploweb.com/Russia-Georgia-the-multipolar.html> (accessed 28 December 2009).

[26] R. Asmus, *A Little War that Shook the World* (New York: Palgrave Macmillan, 2010), 5–6.

[27] 'Blood and oil', *The Economist*, 24 February 2011, available at <http://www.economist.com/node/18231320> (accessed 16 September 2011).

In the case of Libya, there was clearly an immediate risk to human rights on Europe's doorstep in Gaddafi's pledge to hunt down the 'greasy rats' from house to house, without mercy.[28] At the same time, it has to be significant that the two NATO members which were most enthusiastic about military action against Gaddafi's regime, Italy and France, were respectively the second and fifth largest importers of Libyan crude oil in 2010.[29] The United States, on the other hand, was only the 14th largest importer, representing just 0.5 per cent of Libyan exports.[30] This may explain the United State's relative ambivalence about the action in Libya. In the same way, the clearly muted Western diplomatic stance towards Saudi Arabia in most cases, despite their clear flouting of Western liberal ideals such as freedom, democracy, and gender equality, very obviously reflects the extreme strategic significance of maintaining a stable and friendly Saudi regime, the importance of which is built firmly on its position as one of the world's most important producers of oil (its position as number one was eclipsed only recently by Russia).

Because of the central importance of maintaining stable and affordable energy supplies from key areas, the geopolitical situation in such regions as the Middle East and Caspian will determine that the full range of tools will need to be deployed to ensure security. And the toolbox may need to include military options where necessary, as the SDSR notes.[31] The prospect of conflict may not only relate to a need to ensure stability of supply in regions such as the Middle East, which may undergo disruptive revolutions, but could also involve direct conflicts with other nations also seeking to expand and secure their own energy supplies in contested areas. In 2007, a Russian submarine planted a flag on the Lomonosov Ridge on the seabed under the North Pole, symbolically claiming Russian sovereignty over the area and the right to extract natural resources such as oil and gas.[32] The planting of a flag again reflects classic state-centric Westphalian principles of sovereignty and territory, but also raises the prospect of conflict. Russia is one of five states with disputed economic claims over coastal zones in the Arctic region, which have ironically become potentially more open to resource extraction through the process of global warming.[33] The other four are all NATO members (Canada, the United States, Norway, and Denmark through its ownership of Greenland), and it is not inconceivable that some form of conflict over the issue of access to lucrative oil and gas deposits could develop in the future.

---

[28] 'Endgame in Tripoli', *The Economist*, 24 February 2011, available at <http://www.economist.com/node/18239888> (accessed 29 March 2011).

[29] 'Facts on Libya: oil and gas', IEA/OECD, 21 February 2011, available at <http://www.iea.org/files/facts_libya.pdf> (accessed 16 July 2011).

[30] Ibid.

[31] SDSR, n 6, at 51.

[32] T. Parfitt, 'Russia plants flag on North Pole seabed', *The Guardian*, 2 August 2007, available at <http://www.guardian.co.uk/world/2007/aug/02/russia.arctic> (accessed 20 November 2010).

[33] Ibid.

The same issues could potentially apply to access to critical minerals and other resources, in addition to fossil fuels. A good example is that of rare earth metals, which are critical to the production of certain modern technologies such as fuel cells, mobile phones, and wind turbines for electricity generation. As states seek to improve their energy security by investing in the manufacture of green energy alternatives, the requirement for specific resources such as rare earth metals becomes an issue of energy and economic security. However, more than 95 per cent of current rare earth metal exports originate in China,[34] which provides that country with an enormous economic lever over world markets. As with dependence on oil and gas, such a high dependence on a critical resource originating from one country could be the catalyst for serious dispute in the future, and remains a potential issue of energy and economic security outside China.

The issue of energy security clearly reflects the highly complex policy overlaps and connections that any contemporary government needs to consider. Policy on developing green and sustainable energy supplies, for example, while addressing the issue of climate change, could also directly contribute to energy security through reducing dependence on fossil fuel imports from other states. As I will explore, the NSS process has recognized the important policy connections at play in this area, thus showing how contemporary conceptions of national security are more complex and more multi-faceted than was the case with primarily military preoccupations in history.

The risk of a nuclear emergency

A further specific risk identified as being in Tier Three of priorities is that of 'a major release of radioactive material from a civil nuclear site within the UK which affects one or more regions',[35] and also highlights these complicated linkages across policy areas. In part, this risk is a basic resilience issue. The former Intelligence and Security Coordinator, David Omand, describes the inclusion of resilience within national security strategizing as the third major shift in post-Cold War thinking; the first two being a shift from 'secret to protecting state' and 'an emphasis on the value of anticipation'.[36] He notes that:

> The third shift in national security thinking has . . . been to see the value in investing in national resilience, so that the impact of disruptive events on the public can as far as possible be minimized, for example through better training and equipping of the emergency services. Resilience is an increasingly important element of any sound security strategy, since advanced societies are

---

[34] J. Lifton, 'The Battle over Rare Earth Metals', *Journal of Energy Security* (January 2010), available at <http://www.ensec.org/index.php?option=com_content&view=article&id=228:the-battle-over-rare-earth-metals&catid=102:issuecontent&Itemid=355> (accessed 16 July 2011).
[35] NSS, n 1, at 27.
[36] D. Omand, *Securing the State* (London: Hurst, 2010), 9–13.

more vulnerable to disruption, especially as they become more network and IT dependent.[37]

The SDSR notes in its 'National Security tasks and planning guidelines' a need to be 'prepared for all types of emergencies, able to recover from shocks and to maintain essential services'.[38]

A radioactive leak would certainly be highly disruptive in that it would necessitate the evacuation of the nearby population and the restriction of travel within certain areas. In a country as small and crowded as the UK, this could cause very considerable disruption. The NSS was produced before the terrible earthquake and tsunami of early 2011 in Japan, which culminated in a nuclear emergency at Fukushima nuclear power plant in the north-east of the country. This event will have served only to underline the disruption that such an event can cause, and the manner in which catastrophes can chain together to cause unexpected and serious consequences (notwithstanding the fact that, as discussed in Chapter 3, the UK does not face the same propensity for natural catastrophes as does Japan).

The UK currently has 18 nuclear power plants, which generate 18 per cent of its energy. While most of these are due to be retired, a further 19 new generation plants are planned to be online by 2018.[39] Again, there is a complicated linkage between security at these plants and energy policy. Nuclear power production is seen as one of the potential solutions both to curbing greenhouse gas emissions, and to ensuring sustainable and independent energy supplies which reduce dependence on fossil fuel imports. The latest Draft National Policy Statement for Nuclear Power Generation produced by the Department of Energy and Climate Change (DECC) states that 'new nuclear power stations consented under the Planning Act 2008 will play a vitally important role in providing reliable electricity supplies and a secure and diverse energy mix as the UK makes the transition to a low carbon economy.'[40] While the logic here is clear from an energy diversity and security point of view, the strategy in this area introduces potential new risks of nuclear accidents and the need to prepare for such eventualities. It is interesting that Germany has gone in the opposite direction from the UK, deciding to retire all its 17 nuclear power plants by 2022 in response to the Fukushima disaster.[41]

---

[37] Ibid, 13.

[38] SDSR, n 6, at 12.

[39] 'Nuclear Power in the United Kingdom', World Nuclear Association, 7 July 2011, available at <http://www.world-nuclear.org/info/inf84.html> (accessed 16 July 2011).

[40] DECC, 'Revised Draft National Policy Statement for Nuclear Power Generation (EN-6)', vol 1 (London: TSO, October 2010), 1.

[41] 'Germany pledges nuclear shutdown by 2022', *The Guardian*, 30 May 2011, available at <http://www.guardian.co.uk/world/2011/may/30/germany-pledges-nuclear-shutdown-2022> (accessed 1 June 2011).

Border security

A specific aspect of the threat from organized crime identified in Tier Three is 'a significant increase in the level of terrorists, organised criminals, illegal immigrants and illicit goods trying to cross the border to enter the UK.'[42] As we have indentified in the discussions about the effects of globalization, people can increasingly move across the globe more easily, but they can also remain in contact with individuals and organizations overseas having done so thanks to improved modern communications.[43] The 9/11 attacks showed that a democracy with free movement is particularly vulnerable to the actions of those with malicious intent, but also that it is impossible and probably undesirable to tighten border security to such an extent that cross-border travel becomes extremely difficult and time-consuming. One of the key dilemmas of physical security is the drive to use technology to make cross-border travel more efficient and easy while, at the same time, improving surveillance of passengers passing through borders.

The calculation for national security strategists is one that entails a combination of 'upstream' and 'downstream' initiatives. It is not enough to tackle organized crime once it has landed and is operating within the UK: every effort should also be undertaken to disrupt and interdict criminals as they pass the border, and preferably, before they embark on journeys to the UK.

The formation of the UK Border Agency (UKBA), an agency of the Home Office, was announced in 2007, bringing together immigration, visa checking, and HM Revenue and Customs anti-smuggling activities. In addition to operating at the borders, the UKBA has approximately 270 risk liaison officers overseas, located in 130 countries, and cooperating with foreign crime and visa agencies.[44] This represents the critical upstream work of the agency, which has included the detection of 16,000 'clandestines' (ie, potential illegal immigrants) in northern France.[45] In the last year, the agency claims to have dealt with passenger movements of 100 million people across the UK's borders, seizing over 3.5 tonnes of Class A drugs and removing more than 40,000 people from the country.[46] At the airports, one of the critical capabilities has been the 'e-Borders' system, which automatically screens passengers against watch-lists prior to their travel. The system has been gradually enhanced in recent years, to a stage where it screens more than half of all passenger movements through UK air borders, and 92 per cent of all passengers on non-EU flights travelling into and out of the UK.[47]

---

[42] NSS, n 1, at 27.

[43] J. Giraldo and H. Trinkunas, 'Transnational Crime' in A. Collins (ed), *Contemporary Security Studies* (Oxford: Oxford University Press, 2010), 434–5.

[44] Brodie Clark (then head of the UKBA), 'Securing the UK border and controlling migration', presentation at National Security 2011 (GovNet Events), London, 5 July.

[45] Ibid.

[46] UKBA, 'Annual Report and Accounts, 2010–11' (London: TSO, 13 July 2011), 4.

[47] Brodie Clark, n 44.

Technological capabilities such as this will be increasingly critical, and will include such developments as biometric screening devices, and systems for automatically spotting illicit goods and people in freight and luggage. A whole industry has been spawned in such areas on the back of these security threats. Additionally, legislative and regulatory issues will be important in terms of the degree of passenger name information that should be made available to authorities, and the degree to which such information should or could be shared between agencies. The case of Umar Farouk Abdulmutallab, discussed in Chapter 3, is perhaps a case in point. He had been able to board a flight in Amsterdam bound for Detroit, having initially travelled from Accra in Ghana, despite being on a US terrorist watch-list and banned from entering the UK.[48] The balance will constantly need to be struck between greasing the wheels of globalization in the area of free movements of goods and individuals, and ensuring that border security is strong and has not been surrendered. There will also be a need to ensure, through cooperation with partner countries, that any gaps in the system cannot be exploited by terrorists and criminals.

The securitization of issues concerning migration has always been a complex and politically fraught one. In the public consciousness, and fuelled by media representations of the issue, security threats arising from migration have often been conflated with several different issues at once: from crime, to terrorism, to drains on economic well-being and even cultural and ethnic dilution and tension. We saw in Chapter 1 how one of the criticisms of the 'speech act' hypothesis of securitization, is that all manner of political actors can securitize issues in ways that are not necessarily always desirable.[49] Parties and movements on the radical right of politics, for example, especially in Europe, tend to take anti-immigrant policies as their defining rhetoric.[50] In the UK, the ultra-nationalist British National Party (BNP) undoubtedly capitalized on a sense that the Labour administration of the 1990s had been unwilling to be honest about the rising levels of immigration into the country.[51] In this way, the incoming Coalition government of 2010 has also been keen to place some distance between itself and the former government by being politically robust about the need to tackle the threats and risks that come from immigration, including that from an increase in the number of criminals and terrorists coming into the country. Whether there is a serious risk of a significant increase in the volume of undesirables entering the UK is difficult to determine, but officials claim that the general trend is for the traffic in humans and goods entering the UK to increase

---

[48] G. Whittell and A. Fresco, 'I'm the first of many, warns airline "bomber" Umar Farouk Abdulmutallab', *The Times*, 29 December 2009, available at <http://www.timesonline.co.uk/tol/news/world/us_and_americas/article6969645.ece> (accessed 16 May 2010).

[49] M.C. Williams, 'Words, Images, Enemies: Securitisation and International Politics', *International Studies Quarterly*, 47 (2003), 522.

[50] D. Art, *Inside the Radical Right: The Development of Anti-Immigrant Parties in Western Europe* (Cambridge: Cambridge University Press, 2011), 24.

[51] J. Richards, 'Reactive community mobilisation in Europe: the case of the English Defence League', *Behavioral Sciences of Terrorism and Political Aggression* (12 May 2011), 10.

year on year.[52] If the balances cannot be struck with better monitoring and technological advances in weeding out the undesirables from the flow of movements, then such risks will hold some water.

Key points

- Tier Three risks also overlap with those in higher tiers, but introduce new risks in the areas of border security and energy security.
- The risk of a military attack on the UK itself is considered as highly unlikely at present, not least as the UK is situated within the 'stable region' of the EU. But uncertainty means that such an eventuality cannot be forgotten completely. A conflict involving a British Dependent Territory, such as the Falklands, for example, is more likely.
- Considerations of energy security are increasing as the population increases, new states are developing and consuming ever-larger quantities of energy, and finite fossil fuel resources become more pressurized. Conflict over areas containing key resources, such as the Arctic, is not inconceivable.
- The risk of disruption from a radioactive leak has been underlined with the Fukushima nuclear power plant disaster in Japan in 2011, following the tsunami. The UK is continuing to invest in nuclear power, while other countries, such as Germany, are turning away from nuclear power.
- Border security faces the conflicting pressures of easing the flow of people and business across borders, while ensuring security and mitigating the movement of undesirable individuals such as criminals, terrorists, or illegal immigrants. Evidence suggests that such flows of people into the UK are increasing annually.

---

[52] Brodie Clark, n 44. Recent reporting suggests that the UK effectively 'lost control of its borders' at the turn of the century, and that the UKBA is unable to cope with current rates of immigration. Brodie Clark has, at the time of writing, been suspended by the Home Secretary. See R. Ford, 'Rebranding has done little to improve agency's reputation', *The Times*, 5 November 2011, p 7.

PART TWO

Responses

6

Responses

The response framework

Having outlined the threat picture, the 2010 National Security Strategy (NSS) and Strategic Defence and Security Review (SDSR) provide a great deal of information about the UK government's proposed responses to the situation. Some critics of the strategy claim that it is little more than a shopping list of threats, or a 'smorgasbord of horrors' as the head of Chatham House's International Security Programme, Paul Cornish, described it, without necessarily providing much in the way of 'strategy' with which to deal with the threats.[1] Krause noted that a broadened, human security-approach can risk simply being a 'list of bad things that can happen', which can lose 'all utility to policymakers'.[2] If everything is a risk, it is hard for governments to provide a sensible strategy that prioritizes and deals effectively with the key threats. Officials involved with the process, however, will claim that the 2010 NSS is, for the first time, a 'strategy' worthy of the name, since it is based on a structured risk assessment which clearly determines where the priorities are to be found and how the money should be spent by government. Previous processes calling themselves strategies have been closer to a subjective description of the perceived risks, with little connection to the policy that flows out of them.[3]

---

[1] P. Cornish, 'The National Security Strategy of the United Kingdom', Chatham House (Media—Expert comment, 26 March 2008).

[2] K. Krause, 'The Key to a Powerful Agenda, if Properly Delimited', *Security Dialogue*, 35/3 (2004), 367–8.

[3] Interview with National Security Secretariat official, August 2011.

The NSS and SDSR make it clear that the principal framework for responding to the contemporary threat picture is comprised by two 'objectives', as follows:[4]

  (i) to ensure a secure and resilient UK by protecting our people, economy, infrastructure, territory and ways of life from all major risks that can affect us directly; and
  (ii) to shape a stable world, by acting to reduce the likelihood of risks affecting the UK or our interests overseas, and applying our instruments of power and influence to shape the global environment and tackle potential risks at source.

These two objectives are then further split into eight 'National Security tasks', which I will describe below. Within this framework, the strategy makes a valiant attempt, I would argue, at going beyond the criticism of simply presenting a shopping list of threats by enshrining a number of key principles within the process of strategizing. The first of these principles is a notion, across all areas of risk-mitigation strategy, that places anticipation and possible prevention of threats alongside confronting and extinguishing them. This was an idea that manifested itself particularly with the UK's Counter Terrorism Strategy (CONTEST) after 2005, which saw that trying to prevent people becoming terrorists in the first place had to sit alongside, and was as equally important as, finding and catching fully-fledged terrorists when they were about to strike. With both policies acting in unison, the chances of success are improved. Part of this policy is about 'spotting emerging risks and dealing with them before they become crises'.[5] The process for so doing is identified as a biennial updating of the National Security Risk Assessment (NSRA) process, facilitated by 'horizon-scanning and early warning'.[6] This line of thinking now imbues the UK's national security strategy in a number of areas, and particularly those in which threats are complex and multifaceted, and against which the chances of total success are probably limited.

The second key principle is related to the first, and is enshrined in the notion of 'risk and resilience'. Accepting that not all contemporary risks can be totally mitigated all of the time, or certainly not without enormous cost in expenditure and possibly curbs on freedom, anticipatory and preventative action also need to be coupled with making society as resilient as possible in the face of risks being realized. Again, CONTEST provides an example of how this can work with its Protect and Prepare strands (the other two 'P's alongside Prevent and Pursue). Protect means hardening targets against attack as far as possible,

---

[4] HM Government, 'Securing Britain in an Age of Uncertainty: The Strategic Defence and Security Review' (London: TSO, October 2010), 9.

[5] HM Government, 'A Strong Britain in an Age of Uncertainty: The National Security Strategy' (London: TSO, October 2010), 5.

[6] Ibid, 34.

whether in physical security terms or in cyber-defences (from bollards in front of key buildings to anti-virus software), while Prepare means making sure emergency services are ready to deal with an incident when it happens as best they can. The essence of 'bouncing back' in resilience is captured in this principle, and applies equally to threats such as environmental disasters or accidents.

The third key principle is that of a 'whole government approach', which sees that the modern national security threat picture tends to cut across the way in which government departments are organized. Complex and interconnected threats require a similarly complex and collaborative response across several areas of government at once. In a sense, this is the central rationale of the National Security Council (NSC) itself, which aims to bind together individual ministers and think about—and coordinate responses to—security threats in a more holistic way. This is a new departure for the UK which has shied away from an NSC before now, seeing the Prime Minister and the Cabinet as sufficient executive power and decision-making capability in themselves. (In times of particular crisis, the temporary Cabinet Office Briefing Room (COBR) committee is assembled to act much as the NSC will act on a regular basis, in terms of gathering the key stakeholders together and driving the policy collaboratively.) Bringing the two principles together in terms of preventative action alongside proactive action, and coordinating across government departments, means, for example, that the question of stability and conflict overseas is tackled not only by the Ministry of Defence (MOD) in a military posture, but also by the Department for International Development (DfID) in terms of investing in conflict prevention activities in the longer term. The principles of such breadth of policy action are sound, even if the practice of making it happen seamlessly is far from easy in all cases.

The final theme in the new strategies is not so much a guiding principle, but rather a reflection of a new government trying to break new policy ground. It has to be said that, in examining the NSS and SDSR, there is the promise of a blizzard of strategy papers and processes in the various areas of threat, which, a critic might argue, provide a strong impression of a government busying itself in tackling the new threat picture without necessarily delivering tangible changes immediately. A good example which illustrates this point can be found in the Building Stability Overseas Strategy (BSOS), a joint DfID, Foreign and Commonwealth Office (FCO), and MOD strategy document, which notes that:

> The BSOS, which the Strategic Defence and Security Review committed the Government to produce, is one of several strategies stemming from the National Security Strategy. In implementing the strategy we will ensure that it is aligned with related strategies, notably the CONTEST Counter Terrorism Strategy, the Organised Crime Strategy, the Cyber Crime Strategy and the Defence Engagement strategy. It will take into account the Government's

strategies in areas such as proliferation and arms control, energy security, and climate change and resource competition, which it complements.[7]

The picture described here at once reveals the sheer number of strategy documents that seem to be spawning across the various areas of government dealing with different aspects of security threat, and also the complexity of dealing with security in the context of building stability in overseas countries, as just one example area. An overly cynical reading of the situation might suggest that documents are being delivered rather than concrete action on the ground, but this would probably be unfair, since there is nothing inherently wrong with rigorously planning and articulating what action needs to be taken and how it will be managed. It is far better to do this than to make policy 'on the fly' without any reference points. The situation also appears to reflect a government at an early stage of a new chapter in its security planning, whereby the first task is to scope and understand the size and nature of the problem before plans can be put into action, particularly in areas where comprehensive planning does not already exist. Much further work will need to be carried out in the coming years to make the plans a reality.

Administrative organization

Allied with the risks of a glut of strategy documents, the NSS and SDSR—again not necessarily surprisingly—talk a fair amount about organizational factors in discussing how to respond to the threat picture. Certain areas of government, particularly in the aftermath of failures or 'strategic shocks', will often have a light shone upon them and changes suggested. The creation of the new Department of Homeland Security in the United States after the 9/11 attacks is a good example. In the UK, the area of serious and organized crime policy has been a particular area of change and development in the post-Cold War period,[8] with the formation of the National Criminal Intelligence Service (NCIS) in 1992 evolving into the Serious and Organised Crime Agency (SOCA) in 2006, which in turn feeds into the National Crime Agency (NCA) which will come into effect in 2013. In specific 'cross-cutting' areas such as tackling cyber crime, a great many organizational considerations are on the table, and the final disposition of agencies and committees has probably not yet been established. While, on the one hand, such changes are necessary in the face of changing priorities and threat pictures, there is a risk that reorganization of departments creates an illusion of action being taken. It can also be extraordinarily resource-consuming and distracting for the civil servants who have to reorient and respond to the changed administrative structures. As Schweber identified in the commercial

---

[7] DfID/FCO/MOD, 'Building Stability Overseas Strategy' (London: TSO, 2011), 5.

[8] J. Richards, *The Art and Science of Intelligence Analysis* (Oxford: Oxford University Press, 2010), 43.

world, a natural first instinct in the face of uncertainty can be to reorganize,[9] when actually what might be needed is to think and work differently within existing structures. I explore these organizational issues in more depth, in Chapter 7.

As mentioned, the formation of the NSC itself is an important new administrative structure at the heart of the new policy on national security threat mitigation. The principles are that the NSC will set priorities for policy on security threats and will consider specific issues through coordinating and expert committees and secretariats, such as the existing Civil Contingencies Secretariat (CCS) in the Cabinet Office, and specific committees such as one to deal with weapons of mass destruction (WMD) proliferation issues. Work priorities are driven by the annual NSRA process. I will return to how the NSC drives the administration of national security policy and action in more detail in Chapter 7.

The resultant response strategy can be seen in two ways. First, Figure 6.1 shows how some of the various strategies and activities mentioned in the NSS and SDSR map to the risks identified in the three-tier matrix. In this figure the items in italics are the strategy areas relevant to each line of identified risk. This is not necessarily an exhaustive list, and does not necessarily identify all the overlaps between different parts of the strategy, but is intended to be broadly indicative of those activities and processes identified in the NSS and SDSR.

From this roundup, we can see a complex mixture of proposed new strategies; the activities of new and existing departments and organizations; 'pursue' work in such areas as military responses and intelligence activities, coupled with strategic and diplomatic work in such areas as conflict prevention and development assistance; national and supranational legislative and advisory work (comprising EU, G8, and UN levels); scientific activities in developing new capabilities and systems; and awareness-raising and preparedness campaigns such as the 'Get Safe Online' programme, or the 'Watermark' flood disaster response exercise. The actors involved are many and varied, from government ministers and departments, to foreign partners such as NATO and the EU, the corporate sector (especially in cyber, space, and energy realms) and the public, not least under the Big Society objectives of the Coalition government with which groups such as the Local Resilience Forums are an important vehicle. This is certainly a complex menu of responses to a complex threat picture.

We can also see areas of particularly intense cross-departmental working, notably in the area of cyber threat and in the issue of threats arising from instability overseas, to name but two. The strategies make valiant efforts to navigate pathways through the mapping of such complex and broad-reaching threats to the work of government and other stakeholders, and the results are nothing if not highly complicated.

---

[9] B. Schweber, 'Look out for that swinging pendulum', EDN, 17 December 1998, available at <http://www.edn.com/article/508177-Look_out_for_that_swinging_pendulum.php> (accessed 20 July 2011).

Figure 6.1 National security risks, and mapping of response activities

---

Tier One: The National Security Council considered the following groups of risks to be those of highest priority for UK national security looking ahead, taking account of both likelihood and impact.

- International terrorism affecting the UK or its interests, including a chemical, biological, radiological or nuclear attack by terrorists; and/or a significant increase in the levels of terrorism relating to Northern Ireland.

Counter-Terrorism Strategy (CONTEST); intelligence capabilities; upgrade of UK Border Agency (UKBA) capabilities including 'e-Borders'; the INSTINCT programme (Innovative Science and Technology in Counter Terrorism)

- Hostile attacks upon UK cyberspace by other states and large-scale cyber crime.

National Cyber Security Programme; National Cyber Crime Strategy; activities of the: Office for Cyber Security and Information Assurance (OCSIA) in the Cabinet Office (the main policy coordination body), MOD Cyber Operations Group, Cyber Security Operations Centre (located at GCHQ), Centre for the Protection of National Infrastructure (CPNI), Department for Business, Innovation and Skills (BIS) in the guise of the BIS Cyber Infrastructure Team, and campaigns such as 'Get Safe Online'; work with partners such as deliberations over the European Network and Information Security Agency (ENISA)

- A major accident or natural hazard which requires a national response, such as severe coastal flooding affecting three or more regions of the UK, or an influenza pandemic.

Coordination activities by Civil Contingencies Secretariat in Cabinet Office (part of NSS Secretariat); National Flood Emergency Framework; major exercises such as 'Watermark'; the National Resilience Capabilities programme; activities of the new Infrastructure Security and Resilience Advisory Council; the new National Maritime Information Centre; and Local Resilience Forums (reflecting Big Society policy objectives)

- An international military crisis between states, drawing in the UK, and its allies as well as other states and non-state actors.

Strategic defence reforms; alliances with multilateral partners such as NATO, 2010 bilateral defence agreement with France, and other potential bilateral operations with the United States

---

Tier Two: The National Security Council considered the following groups of risks to be the next highest priority looking ahead, taking account of both likelihood and impact. (For example, a CBRN attack on the UK by a state was judged to be low likelihood, but high impact.)

- An attack on the UK or its overseas territories by another state or proxy using chemical, biological, radiological,or nuclear (CBRN) weapons.

Coordination activities by Civil Contingencies Secretariat; Strategic defence reforms; alliances with multilateral partners such as NATO especially in areas of specific CBRN expertise and exercising; preventative work in the activities of the NSC committee on WMD proliferation; the Critical Capabilities Pool; diplomatic work towards the Nuclear Non-Proliferation Treaty (NPT), Biological and Toxins Weapons Convention (BTWC), and Chemical Weapons Convention (CWC); partnership working with the International Atomic Energy Agency (IAEA) and Organisation for the Prohibition of Chemical Weapons (OPCW); Global Threat Reduction Programme activities (led by DECC)

- Risk of major instability, insurgency, or civil war overseas which creates an environment that terrorists can exploit to threaten the UK.

Building Stability Overseas Strategyand the activities of the Joint Stabilisation Unit (FCO, MOD, DfID); Conflict Pool; work focusing on Millennium Development Goals; the activities of Provincial Reconstruction Teams in such places as Afghanistan; Official Development Assistance (ODA); Stabilisation Response Teams; and work towards supporting the Arms Trade Treaty

- A significant increase in the level of organized crime affecting the UK.

The formation of the new National Crime Agency (NCA); upgrading UKBA capabilities including 'e-Borders'

- Severe disruption to information received, transmitted, or collected by satellites, possibly as the result of a deliberate attack by another state.

The National Space Security Policy; activities of the Security Resilience Unit (SRU) at the Space Innovation Centre

---

Tier Three: The National Security Council considered the following groups of risks to be the next highest priority after taking account of both likelihood and impact.

- A large-scale conventional military attack on the UK by another state (not involving the use of CBRN weapons) resulting in fatalities and damage to infrastructure within the UK.

Strategic defence reforms; alliances with multilateral partners such as NATO, and with bilateral partners such as France and the United States

- A significant increase in the level of terrorists, organized criminals, illegal immigrants, and illicit goods trying to enter the UK.

NCA and Border Police Command; UKBA capabilities including 'e-Borders'; deliberations over the EU Passenger Name Record Directive; the new National Maritime Information Centre

- Disruption to oil or gas supplies to the UK, or price instability, as a result of war, accident, major political upheaval, or deliberate manipulation of supply by producers.

Deliberations over EU Energy Strategy for Europe; the International Energy Forum Charter; the National Maritime Information Centre; upgrading Ofgem capabilities under the Energy Bill; strategic infrastructure developments such as Green Deal and smart grid; the activities of the DECC

- A major release of radioactive material from a civil nuclear site within the UK which affects one or more regions.

Activities of Civil Contingencies Secretariat—see Tier One

- A conventional attack by a state on another NATO or EU member to which the UK would have to respond.

Strategic defence reforms; alliances with multilateral partners such as NATO and bilateral partners—see Tier One

- An attack on a UK overseas territory as the result of a sovereignty dispute or a wider regional conflict.

Strategic defence reforms; alliances with multilateral partners such as NATO—see Tier One

- Short- to medium-term disruption to international supplies of resources (eg food, minerals) essential to the UK.

Cross-government working, probably led by the Civil Contingencies Secretariat and relevant government departments

Response capability—an 'adaptable posture'

In an effort to summarize and focus thinking on the threat responses, the NSS and SDSR both note that the top four threat areas are terrorism, cyber threats, natural hazards, and international military crises. The policy response is enshrined in something called 'an adaptable posture',[10] the watchwords for which are deterrence and flexibility. The NSS encapsulates the response strategy in the four priority areas of risk as follows:[11]

> Building on the risk assessment . . . our main priorities for resources and capabilities will be to:
> - protect operational counter-terrorist capabilities in intelligence and policing, and the necessary technologies to support them, while still delivering some efficiency gains in these areas
> - develop a transformative programme for cyber security, which addresses threats from states, criminals and terrorists; and seizes the opportunities which cyber space provides for our future prosperity and for advancing our security interests
> - focus cross-government effort on natural hazards, including major flooding and pandemics, and on building corporate and community resilience
> - focus and integrate diplomatic, intelligence, defence and other capabilities on preventing the threat of international military crises, while retaining the ability to respond should they nevertheless materialise.

On the lower priority risks in Tiers Two and Three, the SDSR notes that 'lower probability does not automatically mean less resource, because some capabilities are inherently more costly than others.'[12] In making this statement, the strategy makes two important points. First, the strategy response to the low-probability but high-impact risk such as an attack on the UK by another state, is one of deterrence. The chief capability in this regard is a continued nuclear deterrent capability. This, of course, is enormously expensive to develop, update, and maintain. So a lower probability risk does not necessarily mean a cheaper response strategy (even though savings are being made in the shape of reduced numbers of warheads carried by each submarine and a reduced warhead stockpile, calculated to reduce costs by £3.2 billion).[13]

Secondly, much thinking has gone into restructuring and essentially cutting back the military in such a way that parts of it could be reconstituted if necessary, within acceptable timescales; a process described as 'ensuring, in partnership with allies, the ability to regenerate capabilities given sufficient strategic notice'.[14] This process, described as central to something called 'Future Force 2020' (of which I will say more in Chapter 8) is one constituting a spectrum of

---

[10] SDSR, n 4, at 9.
[11] NSS, n 5, at 34.
[12] SDSR, n 4, at 10.
[13] Ibid, 38.
[14] Ibid, 10.

'readiness' from low to high.[15] The central tenets of this plan are four 'R's and a 'D', namely: Readiness, Reconstitution, Reinforcement, Regeneration, and Dependency.[16] The dimension of partnerships in the strategy is discussed further in Chapter 11.

The process of transforming the military into a more flexible force is a key element in the third part of the 'adaptable posture', aimed at developing an ability better to respond to future uncertainty in the threat picture. The SDSR identifies this part of the strategy as comprising:[17]

- conflict prevention and capacity-building work overseas which will anticipate and stifle threats before they affect the UK;
- maintaining a 'broad spectrum of defence and other capabilities' which can work 'on the ground' to tackle emerging threats, and ensuring those capabilities are sufficiently flexible to be able to reconfigure to face new threats as they emerge;
- strengthening security partnerships and alliances;
- coordinating responses across government, combining 'defence, development, diplomatic, intelligence', and other capabilities.

National security 'tasks'

Beneath these principles, the strategy goes into a little more detail on how security and resilience are going to be delivered under the framework of a further set of eight 'National Security tasks'. These are identified as follows:[18]

1. Identify and monitor national security risks and opportunities.
2. Tackle at root the causes of instability.
3. Exert influence to exploit opportunities and manage risks.
4. Enforce domestic law and strengthen international norms to help tackle those who threaten the UK and our interests.
5. Protect the UK and our interests at home, at our borders, and internationally, in order to address physical and electronic threats from state and non-state sources.
6. Help resolve conflicts and contribute to stability. Where necessary, intervene overseas, including the legal use of coercive force in support of the UK's vital interests, and to protect our overseas territories and people.
7. Provide resilience for the UK by being prepared for all kinds of emergencies, able to recover from shocks and to maintain essential services.
8. Work in alliances and partnerships wherever possible to generate stronger responses.

---

[15] Ibid, 20.
[16] Ibid.
[17] Ibid, 10.
[18] NSS, n 5, at 33.

The SDSR goes into some detail as to what these eight tasks mean. The extra information varies between quite specific and tangible factors, such as the need for 'a military ability to help evacuate UK citizens from crises overseas', and much vaguer, amorphous notions, such as 'coordinated analysis and assessment of the highest priorities'.[19] As with any such list of activities, furthermore, it is not always clear which things are genuinely new approaches and which already happen to an acceptable level and will not be particularly changed. This delineation is not necessarily a requirement for any strategy of this nature, although it does make it potentially harder to identify which things are going to develop and be newly instituted and which are essentially just 'business as usual'. In this way, the 'grand strategy' approach can run the risk of being more rhetoric than new action on the ground. In this particular case, I would argue that there is some genuinely new thinking and intention in places, particularly in the realm of defence reforms.

It is worth briefly summarizing the points raised under each of the eight National Security tasks. *Task one* is about horizon-scanning and monitoring of the threat picture, and the emphasis here is very much on intelligence. This is identified in relatively general terms, such as the need for 'coordinated analysis and assessment' identified above, and also some slightly more specific factors, such as 'investment in technologies to support the gathering of communications data vital for national security and law enforcement'. This latter point reflects the fact that the intelligence sector has been one of the few in the security realm that has received more money under the Coalition government's strategy rather than a cut in funds, albeit specifically in relation to enhancing cyber capabilities.[20] We will return to the question of intelligence in more detail in the next chapter.

The *second* task is about 'tackling at root the causes of instability'.[21] This comprises three broad processes, with an international and a domestic focus. On the international front, the first two processes comprise work primarily by DfID on long-term development and conflict-prevention activities in 'fragile states'. The reconstruction work currently being undertaken in Afghanistan, not only in terms of standard development projects but also in such areas as Security Sector Reform (SSR) is a good example of activity in this area, although similar projects will be undertaken in many other countries also. Secondly, supporting this work is a commitment to deploy 'stabilization capabilities' early in a crisis situation, which comprise both civilian and military components. These capabilities range from military intervention in conflicts, to humanitarian aid and civilian reconstruction projects. Thirdly, on the domestic front, the second task also involves the terrorism-prevention work enshrined within the 'Prevent' strand of the counter-terrorism strategy, CONTEST. (Prevent does also have an

---

[19] SDSR, n 4, at 11–12.
[20] Ibid, 47.
[21] Ibid, 11.

international component, in terms of working with countries overseas where terrorist radicalization may be a problem and where it can be effectively confronted with programmes such as de- and counter-radicalization initiatives.) I will say much more about this in a domestic context in Chapter 10.

The *third* national security task, which is about 'exerting influence' internationally to reduce and mitigate risks, describes the classic interplay between 'soft' and 'hard' power. The latter involves the traditional approach of hard military power to establish an aim or enforce a position, or even to back-up diplomatic initiatives by hinting at the consequences of failing to comply with a particular recommended course of action. Soft power encapsulates the notion that 'it can be just as important to set the agenda and attract others in world politics as it is to force others to change in particular situations,'[22] The SDSR describes how the FCO and Diplomatic Service will work overseas to ensure our national security objectives, in part through the UK's commitments as a key member of the UN Security Council, EU, and NATO. There will also be a coordinated cross-government approach to assist fragile states in taking 'responsibility for their own security'.[23] Here, again, we see reference to such work as the SSR initiatives in Afghanistan, within which the UK has a particular responsibility for the reform of the counter-narcotics programme.

The *fourth* national security task is a mix of legal and technical expertise issues. On the legal front, the objective again has domestic and international dimensions. Regarding the former, the aim is to develop an effective law-enforcement capability able to tackle serious and organized crime and terrorism affecting the UK, and to be able to bring to justice its perpetrators 'where possible'. This is an oblique reference to some of the complex legal issues around being able to amass sufficient and appropriate evidential material on criminals and terrorists that can stand up in a court of law and secure convictions, and having an appropriate framework of legal instruments which does not compromise our values as a liberal democracy. Some of these issues in a terrorism context will be examined in Chapter 10. On the international front, the aim is the 'continuous development of a rules-based' system. This is where the UK commits itself to challenging and working with overseas partners, particularly in the counter-terrorism context, to evolve systems of law and justice which do not contravene human rights. Such work can be fraught where the UK's own intelligence and security agencies are having to work with partners whose flagrant abuse of a rules-based system of law and justice can implicate the UK's agencies in malpractice. The forthcoming Gibson Inquiry, announced by the Prime Minister in July 2010, will aim to examine the question of alleged

---

[22] J. Nye and D.A. Welch, *Understanding Global Conflict and Cooperation* (Boston, MA: Longman, 2011), 40.
[23] SDSR, n 4, at 11.

complicity in the torture of terrorist detainees by foreign partners with whom the UK agencies are working.[24]

A second component to the international dimension of the fourth national security task is that of working with international partners on securing fissile material and the prevention of proliferation of sensitive technologies. Given the nature of this task, as outlined in Chapter 4, it is essential that a multilateral approach is taken to tackle this most global of modern threats. This means continuing to work within international treaties and frameworks such as the Nuclear Non-Proliferation Treaty (NPT) and Chemical Weapons Convention (CWC), but also working bilaterally and through the EU with specific partner countries such as Russia, where the threats of fissile smuggling may be particularly acute. Closely allied to this activity is the need, identified in the fourth national security task, to retain the specific technical and scientific expertise within the UK in such areas as nuclear physics, so that the UK can properly identify risk and establish counter-measures.

The *fifth* national security task concerns protecting the UK and its interests, at home and abroad, defined in terms of both physical and electronic dimensions. There are several elements to this capability, including a 'minimum effective nuclear deterrent'; effective border forces; security and intelligence, and police capabilities able to tackle the terrorist threat; military capabilities aimed at protecting the UK's borders and dependent territories overseas; and 'investment in new and capable capabilities' such as those in the cyber realm, to ensure electronic as well as physical defence. This task encapsulates the thinking about modern conflict, which Gregory has outlined in his critique of today's warfare, as 'fluid formations through multiple theatres of war that are simultaneously virtual and physical'.[25] In this way, it no longer makes sense to decouple physical military and other threats from the cyber dimension, and counter-capabilities need to be structured accordingly.

The fifth national security task also flows into the *sixth* task, which concerns resolving conflicts and 'contributing to stability' overseas. This involves establishing an appropriate military capability which can intervene in conflicts overseas where UK interests are directly or indirectly threatened, including such capabilities as that required for evacuating UK citizens. Clearly, this range of military tasks, from protecting the UK's borders to intervening overseas, needs to be seen in the round, and to inform the appropriate disposition of military capabilities across the board. We will look at questions of defence structure and restructuring in Chapter 8. Alongside military capability, there is a further mention in the sixth national security task of 'an integrated approach to building

---

[24] 'Campaigners to shun UK inquiry into detainee "torture"', BBC News, 4 August 2011, available at <http://www.bbc.co.uk/news/uk-14397601> (accessed 22 August 2011).

[25] D. Gregory, 'War and Peace', *Transactions of the Institute of British Geographers*, 35 (2010), 160.

stability overseas',[26] whereby any military action is taken alongside activities in the diplomatic and developmental sectors.

The *seventh* task is about ensuring resilience of the UK, both in terms of being able to respond to disasters and attacks effectively, and protecting critical elements of the UK's infrastructure such as nuclear plants. This task again involves both physical and electronic components (in the case of the latter, in terms of ensuring cyber defences for elements of the Critical National Infrastructure (CNI)), and also national and local dimensions in the administration of responses to attacks. At the central level there is a need to ensure that military and other response capabilities are appropriately coordinated, in part through the activities of the CCS in the Cabinet Office, and through such processes as the gold-silver-bronze command structure for major operations and disaster responses. At the top of this structure, where an incident reaches a certain threshold of national significance and central government policy impact, the COBR can be assembled to ensure top-level management of the situation.[27] However, under the Coalition government's 'Big Society' aspirations, the local level is also important to the picture of emergency response and relief. In this way, Local Resilience Forums (LRFs) have been retained across England and Wales to coordinate disaster preparedness. (Arrangements are slightly different in Scotland and Northern Ireland.[28]) Interestingly, there is some evidence at the local level that the LRFs are particularly subject to the whims of news agendas (ie, they will be in the spotlight and be endowed with resources when a major incident has happened, but will gradually be denuded as time passes before the next incident). They are also often top of the list when it comes to local authority cuts, given that they are a largely preventative resource: a state of affairs that was found to be problematic in some areas when a wave of riots hit parts of England in summer 2011.[29] Care will need to be taken that this part of the strategy does not fall between the cracks, and that the grand strategy pronouncements are not at odds with realities on the ground.

The *eighth* and final national security task emphasizes the importance of maintaining and developing partnerships and alliances in pursuing national security goals. NATO and an 'outward facing' EU[30] are identified as the key groupings in which we will operate militarily and diplomatically, but specific partners and alliances such as those with the United States and with our immediate European neighbour, France, are also flagged as being of particular importance. There is both continuity and new direction in this area. The continuity

---

[26] SDSR, n 4, at 12.

[27] The COBR (Cabinet Office Briefing Room) is often erroneously described as the 'COBRA' in the UK media.

[28] Details are outlined on the Cabinet Office website at <http://www.cabinetoffice.gov.uk/content/local-resilience-forums#east> (accessed 22 August 2011).

[29] Interview with LRF chair, south-west England, August 2011.

[30] SDSR, n 4, at 12.

is reflected in the 'special relationship' with the United States, which, while not described in the NSS as such, clearly remains central to the UK government's strategic thinking, especially in the realms of defence and intelligence. Despite difficulties likely to arise from differing political outlooks and from budget cuts in defence across Europe, Aronsson concludes that the transatlantic defence relationship 'continues to be essential to the security of both the US and the UK', and has 'functioned as a backbone for NATO since the early days of the Cold War'.[31] The new direction, meanwhile, is represented in the Anglo-French alliance. While not completely new (de Durand describes the defence relationship between the two countries as one of 'an almost constant alliance' since 1945[32]), the 2010 NSS and SDSR in the UK reflects a new dose of reality in deepening and strengthening specific military integration between the two states, in which a 'meeting of minds has perhaps finally emerged'.[33] I will discuss this agreement further in later chapters.

Finally, alliance and partnership are not only international but also sectoral, in that a relationship between government and industry is also specified as being central to the eighth national security task. Another area of strategy, that of the Defence Industrial and Technology policy, will work in such areas as promoting UK defence exports, and considering appropriate levels of 'off-the-shelf' commercial purchases of defence capabilities rather than bespoke development where this is more cost-effective. Such approaches reflect new commercial realities—which are very much at the centre of the Coalition government's strategizing—as much as politico-military calculations.

Key points

- The twin pillars of the response strategy in the 2010 NSS are identified as ensuring a 'secure and resilient UK' and 'shaping a stable world'.
- Prevention and 'upstream' work is seen as a growing part of the strategy, to reduce risks before they can develop. This is particularly important in the tri-departmental Building Stability Overseas Strategy (involving DfID, the FCO, and the MOD).
- A blizzard of strategies at present reflects the early stage of the new NSC process, and care will need to be taken that this does not obscure real progress and action.
- Response strategies are multifaceted and generally very cross-cutting in government, particularly (but not only) in the area of cyber security. The aim has

---

[31] L. Aronsson, 'Strategic Considerations for the Anglo-American Alliance' in M. Codner and M. Clarke (eds), *A Question of Security: The British Defence Review in an Age of Austerity* (London: I.B. Tauris, 2011), 89.

[32] E. de Durand, 'Entente or Oblivion: Franco-British Defence Co-operation' in Codner and Clarke (eds), ibid, 91.

[33] Ibid, 116.

been not so much to build new departments and structures, but to coordinate activity across government under the National Security Secretariat.

- The overall response strategy is described as delivering an 'adaptable posture', stressing flexibility in the face of uncertainty, and a framework of eight 'National Security tasks' are identified in the NSS and SDSR. These include a range of generic response activities, from working upstream to reduce threats, to using diplomatic levers, and enhancing partnerships.

PART THREE

Strategies

7

Administering National Security: Governmental Strategies and Structures

The political origins of the National Security Council

The UK Prime Minister at the time of writing, David Cameron, had started to talk publicly about an intention to create a National Security Council (NSC) as early as 2007, when he was Leader of the Opposition. The proposal, he claimed, was 'substantial' and 'thought through' and 'would really make a difference'.[1] A Green Paper report called 'Unquiet World' which had been submitted to the shadow cabinet by the National and International Security Policy Group, chaired by Dame Pauline Neville-Jones, had noted that 'the machinery of government is not currently well organised to achieve' appropriate responses to the threat picture of 'complex issues', encompassing a broad range of threats from political turmoil, the proliferation of weapons of mass destruction (WMD), and energy security, to name but a few.[2] It reiterated a proposal made the previous year that an NSC should be created within the Cabinet Office. It also suggested that the Foreign and Commonwealth Office (FCO) be 'brought back from the sidelines'. On budgets, it suggested that:

> The method of budgeting for spending on the external aspects of national security by relevant departments (FCO, MOD, DfID) including cross

---

[1] T. Branigan, 'Embattled Cameron open new front with national security plan'. *The Guardian*, 27 July 2007, available at <http://www.guardian.co.uk/politics/2007/jul/27/uk.conservatives> (accessed 28 August 2010).

[2] National and International Security Policy Group (NISPG), 'An Unquiet World: Submission to the Shadow Cabinet', July 2007, at 9, available at <http://www.conservatives.com/pdf/securityreportfinal.pdf> (accessed 27 August 2011).

departmental spending pools should be adapted to support a national security approach and spending patterns altered to fund more adequately reform and nation building programmes relevant to the establishment of open societies.[3]

This latter point is particularly interesting, as it hints at the area in which the new National Security Strategy (NSS) could be a genuine step forward, and in which many countries have struggled to make progress with their own national security strategizing. First, one of the intentions of the concept of a 'national security approach' is that planning and strategizing should be considered thematically, across government, rather than within specific departmental stovepipes or categories. The key reference point should be those issues and values (presuming they can be defined to everyone's satisfaction) that constitute the national interest, rather than more specific military or political objectives. This approach inevitably—given the complexity and cross-cutting nature of contemporary transnational threats—means that risks and responses to them will not necessarily neatly map to departmental organization and boundaries. This, in turn, means that planning needs to be undertaken in a much more flexible and collegiate way than perhaps has been the case before. The idea of the NSC, in this context, is that it provides the cross-cutting senior policy-maker executive which can think about threats in this more joined-up way.

Secondly, the close linkage of national security strategizing to budgets is, as noted earlier, a key step forward and a linkage that is usually not present in many countries' processes in this area. It is one thing to list an array of complex modern threats to national security and express a desire to deliver a flexible and cross-cutting response; it is quite another to translate that clearly and promptly into specific government spending plans in various departments, including in the thorny area of defence. Usually there is a disconnect between these two processes, which can mean that the strategy is more rhetoric than actual 'strategy'.

David Cameron's statement above was made at the point at which Gordon Brown succeeded Tony Blair as Prime Minister. Shortly after his assumption of power, Brown made a substantial change to the Cabinet Defence and Overseas Policy Committee (DOPC), replacing it with a new National Security, International Relations and Development Committee (NSID). The DOPC had dated at least back to 1963 (Cabinet committees were usually secret at that time), when the combined Ministry of Defence (MOD) was formed, and probably was ready for a change, at least in spirit. The very name of the new NSID certainly captured the cross-government interplay of issues at the centre of post-Cold War national security, combining hard security concepts with diplomatic functions and longer term preventative development work. Whether, as Davies suggests, politics was at work in the sense that the formation of the NSID

---

[3] Ibid, 9.

was to 'steal a march' on the Opposition,[4] which had earlier boasted about 'setting the agenda on the vital issues of security',[5] is a moot point. An inevitable outcome, however, when Cameron became Prime Minister in 2010 and formed the NSC, was that some suggested it was little more than a cosmetic re-badging of Brown's NSID.[6]

One aspect that has arguably changed with the creation of the NSC is the former Opposition's promise to regenerate the FCO's power at the centre of foreign policy; a position which it had gradually lost over the years in favour of the Cabinet, MOD, and Department for International Development (DfID) in particular. The FCO had also chaired the Joint Intelligence Committee (JIC) until 1983, when the Franks Report following the Falklands War suggested that this had caused a structural weakness in intelligence assessment, and the chairmanship was subsequently passed to the Cabinet Office.[7] We saw in Chapter 6 how the intention of the new strategy is to place the FCO as the government lead in 'integrated strategies' on all national security issues which encompass an international dimension.[8] This particularly includes, although is not confined to, the 'Building Stability Overseas Strategy'. It is also notable that the first National Security Adviser and head of the NSC was Sir Peter Ricketts, a career diplomat from the FCO, who will move in 2012 to become UK Ambassador to France, being replaced by Sir Kim Darroch. It has also been very notable how the Foreign Secretary, William Hague, has been very much at the forefront of government statements and policy announcements on issues of national security, and that he visited Afghanistan within a few weeks of the Coalition government being installed alongside the ministers for Defence and International Development.

Why an NSC?

Whatever the substance of the charge of re-launching essentially existing structures, the debate raises the question of what an NSC is, exactly, and why a government decides to put one in place. For the UK, the notion of an NSC is a new thing—at least under that name—and is generally considered to be something more akin to the US political system, which has had an NSC since just after the Second World War. (The US NSC was purportedly influenced by

---

[4] P. Davies, 'Twilight of Britain's Joint Intelligence Committee?', *International Journal of Intelligence and Counterintelligence*, 24/3 (2011), 434.

[5] Branigan, n 1.

[6] D. Korski, 'Organising for national security'. *The Spectator*, 29 May 2010, available at <http://www.spectator.co.uk/coffeehouse/6041573/organising-for-national-security.thtml> (accessed 26 August 2011).

[7] J. Hughes-Wilson, *Military Blunders and Cover-Ups* (London: Robinson, 2004), 287.

[8] HM Government, 'Securing Britain in an Age of Uncertainty: The Strategic Defence and Security Review' (London: TSO, October 2010), 66.

Britain's Committee of Imperial Defence of the time.[9]) Many countries have an NSC, or something of a similar name performing the same functions. As Bruneau, Matei, and Sakoda observe, NSCs can be a critical element of 'civil–military relations' in democratic societies, and generally aim to perform some or all of a range of important functions within government. These can be broadly categorized as coordination functions (between different elements of government involved in national security issues; between the executive and the legislature; between the government and foreign partners; or between different intelligence and security agencies); information functions (producing a National Security Strategy; or producing all-source intelligence assessments on national security issues); or policy functions (mandating components of government to provide information when needed and providing an oversight and accountability function to security agencies and departments).[10]

Of course, political systems across countries are very variable in nature, and this leads to 'little commonality of experience from one country to another' in terms of how their NSCs function.[11] On the question of producing an NSS worthy of the name, which was one of the first major projects of the UK's new NSC, there are usually good reasons why a government will sidestep this task. Chief among these is the fact that a detailed strategy becomes a yardstick against which to measure an NSC's—and a government's—performance on difficult and complex issues.[12] This may be something that comes back to haunt the UK's Coalition government. Indeed, politics and political systems are crucial to the story. As Bruneau et al concluded, 'politics must be at the centre of any analysis of how institutions are adopted and allowed to function, or not function, to enhance national security.'[13] Numerous examples exist of where the fortunes and effectiveness of an NSC have waxed and waned depending on the shifting priorities of particular personalities at the helm of government. In Spain, for example, the centre-right government of Jose Maria Aznar (1996–2004) was very preoccupied with national security issues, and was moving towards the establishment of an NSC, considering that it was ill-equipped to face the range of threats with which it was confronted. The Zapatero government that followed, however, was purportedly much less interested in issues of national security and the proposal fell off the political agenda.[14]

In France, which is arguably of more direct significance to the UK government given the 2010 defence treaties between the two countries, a major White

---

[9] P. Cornish and A.M. Dorman, 'Dr Fox and the Philosopher's Stone: The Alchemy of National Defence in the Age of Austerity', *International Affairs*, 87/2 (2011), 339.

[10] T.C. Bruneau, F.C. Matei, and S. Sakoda, 'National Security Councils: Their Potential Functions in Democratic Civil-Military Relations', *Defense and Security Analysis*, 25/3 (2009), 257–8.

[11] Ibid, 255.

[12] Ibid, 257.

[13] Ibid, 266–7.

[14] Ibid, 260–1.

Paper on national security in 2008 saw a number of new bodies being created, including a National Intelligence Council, a National Intelligence Adviser, and a Defence and National Security Council (Conseil de défense et de sécurité nationale (CDSN)). This latter agency, placed under the President's office, broadly equates to an NSC.[15] The aim of the new organization is allegedly very much focused on the coordination function objectives, and particularly the creation of a more unified and collegiate 'intelligence community' in France.[16] However, given the sometimes ambiguous delineation of key responsibilities between the Prime Minister and President in France's system, the new institutions have arguably placed more power in the hands of the President in issues connected with national security, and contributed to a gradual 'presidentialization' of the national security system under Nicolas Sarkozy.[17] As for the new CDSN, Liberti and Blain conclude that it is 'far from becoming the centralised advisory and supervisory body that are the National Security Councils of the US and the UK'. Admittedly, it is early days for these new institutions and time will tell how effective they can become.

Probably the longest serving NSC is that of the United States, which was formed in 1947 under the National Security Act, alongside the Department of Defense and the CIA, and which moved into the President's office in 1949. The general consensus is that the NSC has performed relatively effectively for most of its existence, and certainly throughout the Cold War,[18] with its primary role being the coordination of all-source intelligence assessments for the President in the shape of National Security Study Memorandums (NSSMs), which became Presidential Review Memorandums (PRMs) under Jimmy Carter.[19] By the time of the George W. Bush presidency from 2001, however, problems in its function started to become apparent. A Congressional Research Service report in 2008 noted allegations that the NSC process was 'insufficiently rigorous', failing to ensure 'disciplined, adversarial debate' and running the risk that 'important logical gaps may go undetected or unquestioned'.[20] The historian Hew Strachan noted that the clashes between the powerful and stovepiped Departments of Defense and State, and between the Chiefs of Staff and Centcom within the military during the run-up to the Iraq War of 2003, were not adequately

---

[15] F. Liberti and C. Blain, 'France's National Security Strategy (WP)', Elcano Royal Institute, Security and Defence Working Paper No 3, Madrid, 2011, p 11.

[16] J. Lichfield, 'Sarkozy puts woman in charge of "spy school"', *The Independent*, 11 January 2010, available at <http://www.independent.co.uk/news/world/europe/sarkozy-puts-woman-in-charge-of-spy-school-1863911.html> (accessed 26 August 2011).

[17] Ibid, 15.

[18] Bruneau et al, n 10, at 264.

[19] S. Marrin and P.H.J. Davies, 'National Assessment by the National Security Council Staff 1968–80: An American Experiment in a British Style of Analysis?, *Intelligence and National Security*, 24/5 (2009), 646.

[20] C. Dale, N.M Serafino, and P. Towell, *Organizing the US Government for National Security: Overview of the Interagency Reform Debates* (Washington DC: Congressional Research Service, 16 December 2008), 8.

reconciled by the NSC process, meaning that 'strategy fell between the cracks'.[21] Part of the problem has been perceived by many to be that the system is now too old for the modern range of threats faced by the United State. The Secretary of Defense, Robert Gates, has been one of the leading advocates for a new National Security Act to replace that of 1947, which would 'update the institutions and the framework that helped us wage and win the Cold War'.[22]

The Tower Commission report, which followed the Iran-Contra affair under Ronald Reagan's presidency in the 1980s, concluded that there was 'no magic formula which can be applied to the NSC structure and process to produce an optimal system', and that the NSC 'must adapt to each individual President's style and management philosophy'.[23] This underlines the degree to which the effectiveness of the process is inextricably linked to the political process, and more specifically to the nature and priorities of the particular political personalities in place at any given time. In the United States, the feeling is that the confluence of George W. Bush with key personalities such as Donald Rumsfeld at the helm of a powerful and stovepiped Department of Defense, were contributory factors to an intelligence and policy failure over Iraq in 2003.

Presidentialization and prime ministerialism

In France, debates over 'presidentialization' of the national security system under Sarkozy reflect occasional concerns in the UK about 'prime ministerialism', and the manner in which politics at the top may have changed since Tony Blair's administration from 1997 onwards. By the time of the decision to join the United States in the invasion of Iraq in 2003, many of Blair's detractors were accusing him of having created a 'presidential' style of management, which came to be known in some quarters as 'sofa government'. A more relaxed and intimate form of government in which much of the formal committee proceedings began to be replaced by more informal and ad hoc discussions between the Prime Minister and his key Cabinet ministers and officials (many of the latter being unelected special advisers), shot through with a heightened emphasis on information and media management, led to serious concerns about the traditional process of government and decision-making having broken down. In this environment, the Prime Minister's Director of Communications, Alistair Campbell, became arguably as important as many of the government's senior officials. The nadir of the period, which perhaps reflected the depth of the changes, was the presentation of a dossier of 'evidence' underpinning the case

---

[21] H. Strachan, 'Making Strategy: Civil–Military Relations after Iraq', *Survival*, 48/3 (2006), 69.

[22] Cited in Dale et al, n 20, at 4–5.

[23] 'The White House Crisis: Excerpts from the Tower Commission's Report Part V: Proposals', *New York Times*, 27 February 1987, available at <http://www.nytimes.com/1987/02/27/world/white-house-crisis-excerpts-tower-commission-s-report-part-v-proposals.html> (accessed 26 August 2011).

for going to war in Iraq, which was exposed as being a hastily and amateurishly constructed document commissioned by Campbell, and which the Foreign Secretary of the time, Jack Straw, claimed not to have seen prior to its publication.[24]

The episode of the 'dodgy dossier', as it came to be known, and the furore over the intelligence failure about Iraq's WMD capability, led many to feel that the cultural change instituted by the Blair administration was seriously flawed when it came to critical national security issues. It was felt that both the Cabinet, and Parliament, had come to have a reduced involvement in decision-making over key issues of national security which might entail the commitment of British troops in major conflagrations overseas. By 2007, the opposition Conservatives had drawn up a 'democracy task force', led by the former Chancellor, Ken Clarke, which called for a return to 'proper Cabinet government'.[25] This plan called for a clearer delineation of responsibilities between the Prime Minister and other ministers in the Cabinet, and a reduction in power of unelected special advisers, such as the Director of Communications.[26] The pejorative use of the term 'presidential' to describe the way in which Blair had allegedly changed government,[27] reflects the debate in the United States about the limits of the 'national security state', and particularly the dangers of national security exceptionalism under a president who is also Commander-in-Chief of the armed forces (as is also the case in France). In times of national emergency, this can lead to highly controversial steps being taken with limited parliamentary or congressional input, such as the decision by George W. Bush greatly to expand wiretapping of terrorist suspects within the United States following the 9/11 attacks.

In the UK, fears over such concentration of power in the chief executive, and particularly in areas of national security, have added to the call for a more committee-based process at the heart of government decision-making. In giving evidence to the Foreign Affairs Committee in December 2010 on the role of the FCO in the UK government, Lord Hennessy, a Professor of Contemporary History at Queen Mary, University of London, expressed a feeling that the establishment of the NSC was an 'emblem of the restoration of a much more alive form of collective Cabinet Government', which 'mitigates against excessive prime ministerialism'.[28] He further noted that 'we are a collective Executive or we are nothing'. Historically, this was the way in which the UK system had

---

[24] 'Straw says dossier was "embarrassing"', BBC News, 24 June 2003, available at <http://news.bbc.co.uk/1/hi/uk_politics/3015272.stm> (accessed 26 August 2011).

[25] 'Clarke targets "sofa-style" Blair', BBC News, 27 March 2007, available at <http://news.bbc.co.uk/1/hi/uk_politics/6497751.stm> (accessed 26 August 2011).

[26] Ibid.

[27] Ibid.

[28] House of Commons, 'Minutes of Evidence taken before the Foreign Affairs Committee, 'The Role of the FCO in UK Government', 8 December 2010; 'Corrected transcript of oral evidence to be published as HC 665-I', available at <http://www.publications.parliament.uk/pa/cm201011/cmselect/cmfaff/c665-i/c66501.htm> (accessed 26 August 2011).

evolved since the eighteenth century, and had generally functioned as such to date with just two 'aberrations', which Lord Hennessy identified as the Suez Crisis in 1956, and possibly the Iraq War of 2003 (pending the outcome of the Chilcot Inquiry which was still running at the time).[29]

There is a sense, therefore, that the NSC could actually mitigate against an excessive concentration of power in limited hands and force a more collegiate and process-driven approach to national security, which, in turn, should help to mitigate against making the wrong decisions on major issues of national security. To be fair, Tony Blair's replacement as Prime Minister in the Labour government, Gordon Brown, had also allegedly expressed concerns about the erosion of the traditional process of top-level decision-making under his predecessor, and had pressed for Blair to step down to allow the 'restoration of cabinet government' (an allegation ironically revealed in Alistair Campbell's subsequent memoirs).[30] This may explain why Brown had already started to institute changes to the national security decision-making process which resembled the changes subsequently established by the Cameron government, such as the establishment of the NSID and associated cabinet processes.

It is often said in British political circles that recommendations for moving towards any US system can be dangerous, since the latter is considered to be excessively 'politicized'. This is raised particularly in discussions around the process for assessing intelligence reporting, which, in the UK, has traditionally happened via the JIC process. Davies echoes the sentiments of many British analysts of the JIC, in claiming that it has been 'an enviably successful example to the rest of the intelligence world', noting that 'even American observers' admire its 'collegiality and atmosphere of mutual trust and support as desirable, albeit not necessarily easy to emulate'.[31] The reason that the United States may find it difficult to replicate the consensual and, by and large, successful operation of the JIC (notwithstanding its failures in the run-up to Iraq) may be as much to do with the political and institutional systems and culture in the United States as to the actual structure and process of a JIC-style committee. As Marrin and Davies observe, the difference is as much a quantitative as a qualitative one.[32] In the United States, for example, politically appointed officials occupy almost all the key positions in the four uppermost echelons of the public bureaucracy, reaching down into senior management positions within government departments. This leads to a mammoth task for an incoming administration: Barack Obama had to make around 3,500 appointments in the civil service when he assumed power. In the UK, political appointments cover the top two levels of minister and junior minister, with the civil service below

---

[29] Ibid.

[30] N. Watt, 'Alistair Campbell diaries: MI6 warned Blair over dangers of Brown rift', *The Guardian*, 3 July 2011, available at <http://www.guardian.co.uk/politics/2011/jul/04/alastair-campbell-mi6-blair-brown-rift> (accessed 26 August 2011).

[31] Davies, n 4, at 428.

[32] Marrin and Davies, n 19, at 656.

remaining a non-partisan body. Incoming Prime Ministers therefore have to appoint only 30 people on entering Downing Street.[33]

The issue of politicization arose briefly when it was announced, during President Obama's visit to Britain in May 2011, that a joint UK–US National Security Strategy Board (NSSB) would be established. This would provide unprecedented foreign access to the deliberations of the President's NSC, in a joint group that would discuss not only emergency crises as and when they arose, but also strategic national security issues of significance to both sides of the Atlantic.[34] This would, in future, discuss such issues as policy on Afghanistan, and Libya. Aside from the encouraging underlining of the continued importance of the 'special relationship' between the UK and United States, which exists over and above such fora as NATO, the new NSSB carries with it potential complications. One of these is that the US President's National Security Adviser, currently Tom Donilon, is a political appointee, while the UK's representative, Sir Peter Ricketts, is a civil servant (as is Ricketts' forthcoming replacement, Sir Kim Darroch). The UK will want to make sure that it does not become drawn into any accusation of politicization in national security policy by association with the United States through the NSSB. Much will depend on how the NSSB will operate, and how far it will drive policy rather than provide a political rubber-stamping of already agreed positions on both sides of the Atlantic. By late autumn 2011, the NSSB was still a 'work in progress'.[35]

NSC process and machinery

Early signs are that the weekly rhythm of the NSC in London is providing a welcome focus and structure on national security issues. The group meets every Tuesday after the Cabinet meeting, and is always chaired by the Prime Minister if he is present in Westminster. This slots in with the weekly meeting of the JIC the following afternoon. In his evidence to the Foreign Affairs Committee in December 2010, Lord Hennessy noted with satisfaction the manner in which the NSC was 'genuinely collegial—proper agendas, proper minutes, proper discussions'.[36] He also expressed a belief that the JIC, which is situated just along the corridor from the NSC in the Cabinet Office, had experienced 'a bit of a revival', in that its forward-planning was now 'very much determined by the National Security Council'.[37] Previously, the JIC's programme had been determined by the Joint Intelligence Organisation (JIO) which sits under the Chief of the JIC, broadly comprising the Cabinet Office Assessments Staff in

---

[33] Ibid.

[34] N. Watt, 'Barack Obama agrees to form join national security body with UK', *The Guardian*, 23 May 2011, available at <http://www.guardian.co.uk/world/2011/may/23/barack-obama-security-board-with-uk> (accessed 26 August 2011).

[35] Interview with National Security Secretariat official, September 2011.

[36] House of Commons, n 28, answer to Q8.

[37] Ibid, answer to Q8.

consultation with the JIC members, constituted by the the heads of the intelligence agencies, plus the Chief of Defence Intelligence and the heads of various policy departments. If, as Davies suggests, the role and influence of the JIO has been steadily declining since 2009,[38] then the arrival of the NSC may well have provided a much-needed focus for priorities. Alternatively, it could act as a cause for conflict and competition if not managed correctly.

The NSC itself is split into three commands: Threats, Hazards, Resilience and Contingencies (headed by the Home Secretary); Emerging Powers (headed by the Foreign Secretary); and Nuclear (headed by the Prime Minister). Lead ministers on the NSC will take responsibility for specific issues as they arise, such as the Secretary of State for Energy and Climate Change. Strategic issues involving overseas dimensions will be 'integrated strategies' led by the FCO.[39] Greater coordination of all security-related issues through High Commissioners and Ambassadors in overseas countries is planned, and early experience suggests that it is becoming routine for such diplomats personally to brief the NSC on current issues when they are in London.[40] Issues concerning stability overseas will be led jointly by FCO and DfID, with the MOD when there is a military dimension. Economic interests will be coordinated by FCO, the Department for Business, Innovation and Skills (BIS), and UK Trade and Investment (UKTI). There will be a FCO–UKTI Joint Commercial Task Force to deal with such issues, reflecting another organizational change, albeit one mostly of coordination rather than necessarily establishing a new body. Again, this picture is one of complexity to match that of the threat picture facing the policy-makers.

In terms of working smarter rather than just rearranging the chairs, the NSS talks of 'leaner, better coordinated structures and processes' under the NSC.[41] The body will 'meet and take decisions every week', informed by up-to-date intelligence assessments.[42] In line with the Coalition government's renewed interest in monitoring outcomes of government processes rather than simply generating meaningless metrics (an accusation it frequently levelled at the former Labour administration), the NSC's performance in delivering against its outcomes will be monitored by a cross-departmental Implementation Board, chaired by the Cabinet Office. An annual progress report will be produced for the Joint Parliamentary Committee on the National Security Strategy, and a new—and very important—commitment has been made to update the NSS and SDSR every five years.[43] This last point is interesting in that it places the process of defence and security planning on a rigid timetable for the first time, which is not necessarily connected with electoral, and thus political, cycles. For an

---

[38] Davies, n 4, at 428.
[39] SDSR, n 8, at 66.
[40] Interview with National Security Secretariat official, September 2011.
[41] SDSR, n 8, at 66.
[42] Ibid.
[43] Ibid, 35.

incumbent government it means that difficult decisions and projections cannot necessarily be put off to some time in the future when another government might be picking up the pieces, and thus hopefully has the effect of making such reviews more objective. It also links the review with the spending review cycle, which, argues Chalmers, is critical as it means that the review is conducted simultaneously with fresh spending deliberations, rather than potentially coming some time afterwards when difficult decisions can be ducked on the basis of spending already having been set.[44] A strategy that is shaped only by already-agreed spending cuts and budget allocations is not really a strategy in the truest sense of the word.

For many, therefore, the new Whitehall rhythm around national security may be making a start at fixing the problems that had slowly arisen over the marginalization of the Cabinet and Parliament from key national security policy decisions. For officials in Whitehall, the weekly meeting of the NSC may well be quite onerous, at least in the early days when support structures have not yet been properly established, since the group will be generating a 'torrent of tasks' for civil servants to follow up.[45] The government will need to beware of creating a resource-consuming bureaucracy around the process, particularly when it is supposedly committed to making savings and streamlining the public sector.

Departmental organization outside the Cabinet Office

Outside the Cabinet Office and the immediate NSC structure, a few areas of government are worth examining in terms of institutional adjustments to tackle the new threat picture. In the area of energy security and environmental threat, the new Department of Energy and Climate Change (DECC) was established by the Gordon Brown government in 2008, combining elements of what had been in the Department for Environment, Food and Rural Affairs (DEFRA), and in the Department for Business, Enterprise and Regulatory Reform (BERR). The creation of the new department established a new Cabinet seat on climate change, as distinct from general environmental issues, for the first time, reflecting similar changes in other industrialized countries. (Most European neighbours, such as France, have had ministerial representation on 'environment' or 'ecology' for many years, reflecting the relative strength of Green politics in continental Europe. Australia, meanwhile, created a department very similar to the UK's DECC at the end of 2007.)

---

[44] M. Chalmers, 'The Lean Years: Defence Consequences of the Fiscal Crisis' in M. Codner and M. Clarke (eds), *A Question of Security: The British Defence Review in an Age of Austerity* (London: I.B. Tauris, 2011), 60.

[45] Korski, n 6.

For environmentalists and their supporters, this move represented an unprecedented elevation of the issue of climate change to national policy-making level,[46] at a time when some, such as the Republican Party in the United States, are split about the whole issue. It also places climate change issues, through the representation on the NSC of the DECC Minister, firmly on the national security agenda and shows that this issue has been resolutely securitized in UK strategic thinking.

In other areas of 'new threat', governmental organization is relatively fluid at the moment, while the strategy takes shape. A particularly complex area of policy currently concerns the cyber domain. An overview of government bodies responsible for cyber security published in 2010 identified seven separate official agencies at work, engaged on a variety of policy coordination; strategic analysis; response and analysis; and advice and guidance.[47] Some of these agencies, such as the Centre for the Protection of National Infrastructure (CPNI), are relatively well established and have evolved into cyber security from physical security. But many agencies on the list are new, and I would suggest it is quite likely that the overall picture will undergo a number of further changes before the optimum disposition of agencies and bodies is established. Similar difficulties will be experienced in many other countries as the new and rapidly evolving arena of cyber threats unfolds and takes hold.

In the area of resilience and infrastructure protection, the CPNI has traditionally held primary responsibility. CPNI is an interdepartmental agency, containing staff from a mixture of government (including intelligence agencies), industry, and academia, the primary function of which is to provide infrastructure protection advice (concerning both physical and cyber security) to public and private organizations which form the critical national infrastructure (CNI). On the cyber front, CPNI works closely with the Communications-Electronic Security Group (CESG), based at GCHQ, which is the official government owner of advice and standards on cyber security and protection.

Central coordination of cyber security policy and strategy is coordinated by the Office of Cyber Security and Information Assurance (OCSIA) within the National Security Secretariat at the Cabinet Office, which comes under the Minister for the Cabinet Office, Francis Maude, and feeds directly into the NSC. On the creation of the OCSIA, which also happened under the Brown government in 2009, a separate 'Minister for Cyber Security' was appointed, in the shape of Admiral Lord West. With the change of government in 2010, this specific portfolio passed to Dame Pauline Neville-Jones, although she resigned as Home Office Minister for Security and Counter-terrorism in May 2011 and her responsibilities will remain spread across other existing ministers.

---

[46] 'Greens welcome new climate dept', BBC News, 3 October 2008, available at <http://news.bbc.co.uk/1/hi/7650669.stm> (accessed 26 August 2011).

[47] E. Downing, 'Cyber Security—a new national programme', House of Commons Library, Standard Note SN/SC/5832, 23 June 2011, Appendix 1, p 22.

In the dimension of offensive cyber capability and cyber intelligence, one of the agencies under the OCSIA's remit is the Cyber Security Operations Centre (CSOC), also based at GCHQ in Cheltenham. While much of the work of the CSOC is secret, the initial Minister for Cyber Security mentioned that 'it would be silly to say that we don't have any offensive capability from Cheltenham, and I don't think I should say any more than that.'[48] It is clear that cyber intelligence and cyber security are very much both poacher and gamekeeper activities. Most advanced nations have established cyber capabilities within their defence departments, recognizing that modern warfare now inextricably includes cyber components, both in offence and defence. The leviathan in this area is the Pentagon-based Cyber Command (CYBERCOM) in the United States, which commenced operations in 2010. CYBERCOM specifies that it conducts both the 'defense of specific Department of Defense information networks' and 'full-spectrum military cyberspace operations'.[49] In the UK, the direct corollary is the Defence Cyber Operations Group. The Minister for the Armed Forces, Nick Harvey, outlined the logic of these institutional adjustments, noting that 'action in cyberspace will form part of the future battlefield, but it will be integrated rather than separate, complementary rather than alternative.'[50]

Outside the military and intelligence spheres, other parts of the cyber programme include work by the BIS in raising awareness and expertise in cyber-security issues, such as how to set up resilient business networks and combat cyber fraud, and cross-government public information campaigns such as 'Get Safe Online'.

On the cyber crime front, the picture has again been a complex and changing one over the years, and one beset with some difficulties. Early work on cyber crime was conducted by the National High-Tech Crime Unit (NHTCU), which was an Association of Chief Police Officers (ACPO) agency, and which became subsumed into the Serious Organised Crime Agency (SOCA) in 2006. This appears to have left something of an operational hiatus, however, such that ACPO established a replacement unit called the Police Central e-Crime Unit (PCeU) in 2008. In 2010, the then Metropolitan Police Commissioner, Sir Paul Stephenson, issued a warning to the government about a mismatch between the numbers and skills of officers fighting cyber crime, and those of the criminal fraternity.[51] He noted that, of the 385 police officers in England and Wales dedicated to online work, fewer than 60 were involved in investigating financial crimes such as bank fraud. (The rest were tackling people-trafficking and

---

[48] G. Corera, 'Cyber-security strategy launched', BBC News, 25 June 2009, available at <http://news.bbc.co.uk/1/hi/uk_politics/8118348.stm> (accessed 20 May 2010).

[49] US Cyber Command website at <http://www.stratcom.mil/factsheets/cyber_command/> (accessed 26 August 2011).

[50] 'Armed Forces Minister—responding to Cyber War', MOD, 1 June 2011, available at <http://www.mod.uk/DefenceInternet/DefenceNews/DefencePolicyAndBusiness/ArmedForcesMinisterRespondingToCyberWar.htm> (accessed 26 August 2011).

[51] Cited in Downing, n 47, at 10.

child pornography.[52]) A related warning was issued by the Director of GCHQ, Iain Lobban, to the Intelligence and Security Committee (ISC) in July 2011, that GCHQ was struggling to compete with commercial enterprises to recruit and retain the top-level cyber specialists he needed, as civil service pay could not compete.[53]

The Home Secretary has announced that a cross-cutting Cyber Crime Unit will be established when the National Crime Agency formally replaces SOCA in 2013.[54] While this sounds grand, the serious issues of recruitment, retention, and skills identified above will need to be addressed if the substance is to match the rhetoric. (We saw earlier how such a mismatch may be happening in places with the LRFs, for example.) These issues could yet prove to be very serious ones for the government, and will again be replicated in many other bureaucracies around the world.

In other areas of government activity in the national security sphere, departments and responsibilities are relatively settled, although cross-cutting coordination may place particular new challenges on the overall structure of government. In counter-terrorism, about which I will say more in Chapter 10, a longer experience of the threat as a central national security issue has meant that processes and responsibilities have become relatively set, and the Coalition government does not yet seem to be of a mind to change them substantially. Defence is undergoing some major changes in resourcing, if not in organization, and these are the subject of the next chapter. Intelligence agencies appear to be relatively untouched: indeed, they will receive some of the £650 million of new funding going into cyber-defence activities, although there may be a review of the oversight process currently represented by the ISC. Issues of crisis response, at least in terms of coordination, continued to be covered by the Civil Contingencies Secretariat (CCS), initially established in 2001 and situated in the Cabinet Office. Finally, the Building Stability Overseas Strategy (BSOS), which links the activities of FCO, MOD, and DfID across three pillars of activity (early warning; rapid crisis prevention and response; and investing in upstream prevention) will entail a number of potentially complex projects and arrangements. Measuring the effectiveness of policy in these areas will also be difficult, given the frequently long timescales over which results may manifest themselves. As with all aspects of post-Cold War 'new threats' and the new strategies being proposed to tackle them, we may be very much in the initial stages of thinking how best to respond effectively to such challenges with the current bureaucratic arrangements at our disposal.

---

[52] Ibid.

[53] M. D'Arcy, 'GCHQ can't match Google pay for internet whizzes', PublicService.co.uk, 13 July 2011, available at <http://www.publicservice.co.uk/news_story.asp?id=16889> (accessed 20 August 2011).

[54] SOCA, *Annual Report and Accounts 2010/11* (London: TSO, 2011), 3.

Key points

- The political drivers for the new NSC include a desire for the FCO to be brought back to the centre of foreign policy and national security decision-making, after a period of estrangement. There is also a desire to establish a proper process of strategizing which it not unduly influenced directly by budgetary considerations, but is an objective process.
- A number of countries have an NSC in place, including the United States which established its NSC in 1949. The purpose and function of an NSC can vary a great deal, encompassing any or all of coordination, information, and policy enforcement and oversight functions.
- In France, the NSC body has been criticized as being part of a creeping 'presidentialization' process, while in the UK the new NSC was designed to mitigate a comparable 'prime ministerialism'.
- There are some fears of excessive politicization of the national security decision-making process, particularly when comparisons are made with the United States, which has a much greater degree of political appointments at the heart of government.
- The NSC meets weekly and is usually chaired by the Prime Minister. Early signs are that it is delivering a greater degree of rigour and rhythm to the national security decision-making process. It is also providing some renewed direction for the JIC, with which it interacts closely within the Cabinet Office.
- Outside the Cabinet Office, there is little major reorganization, although the new environment department and minister in the shape of the DECC is a major change. Coordination of cyber activities represents a number of different bodies across government and indeed outside government, and the shape of this area of policy may change further.

8

Boots on the Ground: Restructuring Military Capability

Introduction: the case for restructuring

One of the most politically painful elements of any national security review is the question of defence restructuring, and the launch of the National Security Strategy (NSS) and Strategic Defence and Security Review (SDSR) in 2010 proved to be no different in this respect to earlier reviews. In other respects, there *was* a significant difference in the debate this time, in that all parties around the table had come to accept the enormity of the fiscal crisis facing the British state since the global financial meltdown of 2008. Most agreed that many of the inevitably painful cuts in public expenditure would have to come in the area of defence, as they would in just about every area of public spending. This realization was given further impetus by the apparent evidence of a 'black hole' in defence spending to the tune of some £36 billion, which, as noted in Chapter 2, represents approximately 97 per cent of the entire annual defence budget. To a certain extent this became a political stick with which the incoming government could beat their predecessors, and which they could use to justify the swingeing cuts in expenditure that would inevitably follow. In other ways, the outgoing administration did not necessarily deny that such a problem had accumulated over the years. The outgoing Chief of Defence Staff, Sir Jock Stirrup, for example, noted that there had been 'some pretty unfortunate cases in procurement' during the Labour administration, which had led to such issues as continuing major projects unnecessarily since it would be more expensive to cancel them.[1]

Most agreed, therefore, that the question was not whether to cut and restructure defence, but how. The fiscal pressures, however, are not the only reason that an ongoing and fundamental structuring of the defence capability in Britain is unfolding through the beginning of the twenty-first century (as is indeed the case across the industrialized world). There are two other important reasons, which are very much grappled with in the NSS and SDSR of 2010. The first of these is a reappraisal of Britain's position in the world, in terms of how active a player the British state wishes to be on the international stage. The second concerns the changing character of conflict and warfare, which is increasingly posing difficult questions of a defence posture that still reflects the exigencies of the Cold War in many respects.

Britain's place in the world

As with any waning imperial power, Britain has been grappling with an identity crisis for many decades, and particularly since the end of the Second World War which marked the transition of Britain fully out of its imperial superpower status. During the Cold War, the existential threat of the confrontation with the Soviet Union bound Britain closely to NATO and shaped the defence posture with relatively little debate. To a certain extent, this pushed the question of where Britain wanted to be in the world out to the future, since there was a largely unarguable defence posture to adopt (notwithstanding debates about nuclear disarmament). With the end of the Cold War and the more fluid world system that has since unfolded, this question is very prominently back on the British political table.

No sooner had the Cold War ended than a new and immediate security question flared up within Europe, namely what to do about the implosion of the Balkan states. In Britain, the crisis in the former Yugoslavia coincided with the Labour administration of Tony Blair, under which Britain became committed to military intervention, beneath a NATO umbrella, in both Bosnia and Kosovo. Speaking during NATO's aerial bombardment of Serbia during the Kosovo crisis in 1999, Blair outlined, in what became known as his Chicago speech, what he took to be the principles of military intervention in the modern world.[2] Significantly, he articulated how the notion of 'national interest' had changed

---

[1] Cited in 'Labour vetoed defence cuts plan, says ex-defence chief', BBC News, 31 October 2010, available at <http://www.bbc.co.uk/news/uk-politics-11661151> (accessed 16 September 2011).

[2] 'The Blair Doctrine', PBS News, 22 April, 1999, available at <http://www.pbs.org/newshour/bb/international/jan-june99/blair_doctrine4-23.html> (accessed 16 September 2011).

into a 'subtle blend of mutual self-interest and moral purpose in defending the values we cherish'.[3] Here was a sort of Truman Doctrine that went beyond immediate national self-interest, and partly into the territory of protecting and enhancing 'values' internationally; such as freedom, democracy, and resistance to oppression. For a medium-sized power such as Britain, this is a very important element of foreign and defence policy which other countries, notably some close neighbours in Europe, would not necessarily follow in the sense of translating such noble ideological goals into physical military commitments.

By the time of the NSS and SDSR under the new incoming Coalition government in 2010, experience of a number of post-Cold War military interventions by British troops, including Sierra Leone, Iraq, and Afghanistan (about which I will say more in the next chapter) has deepened the debate about where Britain could and should go in its foreign and defence policies. The NSS contains a detailed section on Britain's position within the multipolar post-Cold War world. Entitled 'Britain's distinctive position', this section starts by explaining that 'Britain will continue to play an active and engaged role in shaping global change'.[4] It presents an equation which, it is argued, makes Britain different from some other countries of comparable size. Despite representing just 1 per cent of world population, for example, Britain is the sixth largest economy in the world. The importance of London as a global financial and business hub, sitting between the trading markets of North America and Asia, provides a further key element of Britain's position in the global economic pecking order. Added to this are the significance of the English language to global economic and cultural life; a large diaspora of population around the world; and a key place at the top table of the most significant international bodies, such as the UN Security Council (of which Britain is one of the five permanent members), the G8, NATO, and the EU, to name but a few.[5]

The question has been posed on occasion, as it was by the chairman of the Public Administration Select Committee (PASC) in a 2010 debate, as to whether Britain ought to consider itself 'a former great power tucked up inside a huge regional organisation'.[6] There are many medium-sized European countries, which, while broadly sharing Britain's ideological and political outlook on the world system, spend considerably less on defence and are much less interested in becoming involved in overseas interventions. During the PASC debate, the historian Lord Hennessy repeated the rather disparaging comment originally

---

[3] Ibid.

[4] HM Government, 'A Strong Britain in an Age of Uncertainty: The National Security Strategy' (London: TSO, October 2010), 21.

[5] Ibid.

[6] House of Commons, Public Administration Select Committee, 'Who does UK National Security?', First Report of Session 2010–11 (HC435, 18 October, 2010), p 5.

made by the Conservative MP for Banbury, Tony Baldry,[7] that Britain would not want to end up being considered a 'Belgium with a nuke'.[8]

The 2010 NSS echoes some of the language of Blair's Chicago doctrine. In its foreword, by the Prime Minister and Deputy Prime Minister, it notes that:

> Our national interest requires us to stand up for the values our country believes in—the rule of law, democracy, free speech, tolerance and human rights. These are attributes for which Britain is admired in the world and we must continue to advance them, because Britain will be safer if our values are upheld and respected in the world.[9]

Indeed, senior National Security Secretariat officials are not averse to speaking of the 'moral' dimension in the work of the National Security Council (NSC).[10] This means that Britain is committed for the foreseeable future to an interventionist role in certain circumstances, unlike many of its European neighbours, and therefore needs to consider the right disposition of military capability with which it can carry out such responsibilities.

The changing character of conflict

The third key dimension that shapes national security strategizing at this time is the question of how conflict and intervention have changed, and continue to change through the beginning of the twenty-first century. In a comprehensive study of the future character of conflict by the Ministry of Defence (MOD) Development Concepts and Doctrine Centre (DCDC), conducted in early 2010 and which fed into the thinking of the newly established NSC, it was noted that conflict is transforming in ways which are 'transcending our conventional understanding of what equates to irregular and regular military activity'.[11] The 'conflict paradigm' is shifting, and Western powers need to adapt their military postures accordingly if they are not to lose advantage significantly on the battlefield.[12]

The scenario described will be familiar to many of those who are conversant with contemporary counter-insurgency and peacekeeping operations, such as those in the Balkans or in Iraq and Afghanistan. The general picture is one of increasing complexity, whereby adversaries become spread across a spectrum from state, to state-sponsored, and non-state groupings. Conventional (military)

---

[7] 'Backbench Business: Strategic Defence and Security Review', 16 September 2010, available at <http://www.tonybaldry.co.uk/2010/09/16/backbench-business-strategic-defence-and-security-review/> (accessed 17 September 2011).

[8] Ibid.

[9] NSS, n 4, at 4.

[10] Interview, September 2011.

[11] MOD, DCDC, 'The Future Character of Conflict', DSDA Operations Centre, 2 March 2010, p 1.

[12] Ibid.

and unconventional threats (involving such issues as environmental and demographic stress) will start to blur together, as will the range of threats, including proliferated weapons of mass destruction (WMD), cyber, and 'other novel and irregular threats'.[13]

As Mackinlay describes in the context of military interventions in conflict overseas, 'forces on the ground find themselves in an environment that continues to grow increasingly complicated'.[14] Not only is the territory increasingly 'crowded by independent actors', from militaries to NGOs and private security companies, but the adversaries have become more organized and lethal,[15] at the same time as becoming harder to identify and to differentiate from the general population. Mackinlay was writing before the war in Iraq in 2003, but many of his observations will have been seen as prescient in that military theatre.

The complex environment described also poses questions for military strategy and equipment. We noted in Chapter 1 that the war to eject Iraq from Kuwait in 1991, which happened simultaneously with the end of the Cold War, led to much discussion about how a Revolution in Military Affairs (RMA) might be changing the face of modern warfare, and very much for the better in terms of the casualty rates, at least for the aggressor. The policy questions here are twofold. First, such experiences run the risk of what McInnes describes as a 'fatal attraction' for Western powers in the use of air power and the strategic benefits that it can offer.[16] During the air campaign against Serbia in 1999, NATO forces flew sorties for 78 days without a single injury.[17] While the complex counter-insurgency environments of Iraq and Afghanistan may have cast some doubt over this strategy, NATO again resorted to surgical airstrikes in the campaign against Gaddafi's regime in Libya in 2011, albeit partly due to restrictions imposed by the relevant UN Security Council resolution.

In the Afghanistan campaign, the benefits of airstrikes have evolved into the domain of unmanned aerial vehicles (UAVs), which have been pivotal in NATO's action against high-value targets (HVTs) of Al Qaeda and the Taliban in the difficult and thinly populated mountainous terrain of the Afghanistan/Pakistan border region. Here, there is another difficult debate, in that the perception of the supposed benefits of such strikes in terms of reduced casualty figures is not shared by both sides in the conflict. US intelligence and security sources will argue that such strikes from UAVs are much 'cleaner' than would be military action against such targets on the ground, as they offer greater speed and precision of strike which minimizes civilian casualties. Public opinion in Pakistan

---

[13] Ibid, p 6.

[14] J. Mackinlay, 'Intervening in Conflict: The Policy Issues', *Conflict, Security and Development*, 7/1 (2001), 175.

[15] Ibid.

[16] C. McInnes, 'Fatal Attraction? Air Power and the West', *Contemporary Security Policy*, 22/3 (2001), 30.

[17] N. Wheeler, 'Introduction: The Political and Moral Limits of Western Military Intervention to Protect Civilians in Danger', *Contemporary Security Policy*, 22/3 (2001), 8.

and elsewhere hotly disputes this argument, however, and suggests that such strikes often kill many more civilians than is claimed.[18] If, as the DCDC's analysis of future conflict suggests, the 'battle of the narratives will be key',[19] then these issues are of the highest importance for national security strategizing.

Inter-service issues

In an address to the International Institute of Strategic Studies (IISS) in January 2010, the then Chief of General Staff and former Commander of ISAF operations in Afghanistan, General Sir David Richards, noted that:

> Hi-tech weapons platforms are not a good way to help stabilise tottering states—nor might their cost leave us any money to help in any other way— any more than they impress opponents equipped with weapons costing a fraction. We must get this balance right.[20]

He was speaking in the context of the counter-insurgency in Afghanistan, in which British and other troops had become bogged-down in a conflict with a Taliban foe armed with little more than Kalashnikov automatic rifles. Using asymmetric techniques, the Taliban have been able to frustrate an enemy equipped with the latest high-tech defence technology, even if the casualty rates between the two sides have been sharply divergent. General Richards made some very specific points about military posture and equipment in his argument, assuming that future conflicts would increasingly look like that in Afghanistan. He was not, as might be supposed, suggesting that all 'heavy-metal' equipment such as aircraft and warships should be ditched in favour of counter-insurgency troops. He was, however, suggesting a significant shift towards smaller and more flexible equipment, such as high-speed littoral naval craft, UAVs, transport aircraft and helicopters, noting that 'one can buy a lot of UAVs or Tucano aircraft for the cost of a few JSF [Joint Strike Fighter aircraft] and heavy tanks'.[21]

The financial logic of this argument, not to mention the need to change military posture in the face of the changing character of conflict, is not disputed. The General's army provenance, however, has fed into some inevitable and heated inter-service debates about the appropriate strategic direction to take in such issues, especially in the light of downward fiscal pressures. A disproportionate amount of the most expensive and technologically sophisticated elements in the military capability tend to be concentrated in the Royal Air Force

---

[18] S. Shane, 'CIA is Disputed on Civilian Toll in Drone Strikes', *The New York Times*, 11 August, 2011, available at <http://www.nytimes.com/2011/08/12/world/asia/12drones.html?pagewanted=all> (accessed 16 September 2011).

[19] DCDC, n 11, at 6.

[20] General Sir David Richards, 'Future Conflict and its Prevention: People and the Information Age', address at IISS, London, 18 January 2010.

[21] Ibid.

and the Royal Navy, be they fighter jets, aircraft carriers, or submarines. The trend in such equipment, furthermore, has been for it to become ever more sophisticated and expensive over time, necessitating rising costs in associated processes such as servicing and training. Much of this equipment is emblematic of the Cold War, when the logic of very large and mobile power-projection capabilities such as aircraft carriers full of fighter jets, and nuclear submarines, made perfect military sense. In a world of counter-insurgency campaigns on land in complex environments, however, if those are to set the tone of all fore-seeable future engagements, such equipment could be argued to be evidence of old thinking that has not embraced the new challenges.

The First Sea Lord, Sir Mark Stanhope, rebutted General Sir David Richards's comments in January 2010 by suggesting that 'we have to look beyond Afghanistan', and to be prepared for 'surprises and strategic shocks' such as the Falklands War of 1982.[22] The BBC's defence correspondent, Caroline Wyatt, interpreted this debate as the two service chiefs setting out their stalls in advance of the SDSR, the preparation of which was underway at the time and which was clearly going to call for substantial cost savings in defence.[23] Invoking the Falklands is perhaps a somewhat predictable strategy, not only because it was a major strategic shock for the UK, but also because naval capability was abso-lutely central to the operation.

Similarly, as the youngest addition to the British armed forces, the Royal Air Force (RAF) has faced some tough questions about its continued role and pur-pose in the post-Cold War future, not least as both the army and navy have air fleet capabilities, and because technology is increasingly moving towards unmanned and computer-controlled aircraft. Eric Grove notes an occasional 'counter-productive defensiveness' in the RAF which 'verges on paranoia'.[24] Given the increasing inter-mingling of capabilities between the three services, talk occasionally arises of scrapping one or more of the services and creating a unitary 'purple' capability, as the Canadians attempted in the 1960s. The experi-ment, which Grove characterizes as a 'dreadful saga of strange green uniforms and unhappy personnel' was later reversed.[25] In the event, the RAF has taken some of the more noticeable hits in the 2010 defence review, including the scrapping of the Harrier jets (another one of the totemic capabilities of the Falklands War), the Sentinel R1 surveillance aircraft, and the cancellation of the Nimrod MRA4 maritime patrol aircraft before the first plane had taken to the air.

---

[22] 'Admiral Sir Mark Stanhope defends Royal Navy's role', BBC News, 19 January 2010, available at <http://news.bbc.co.uk/1/hi/uk/8466961.stm> (accessed 16 September 2011).

[23] C. Wyatt, 'UK military chiefs fight for the future of their services', BBC News, 19 January 2010, available at <http://news.bbc.co.uk/1/hi/uk/8466970.stm> (accessed 16 September 2011).

[24] E. Grove, 'The Case for the RAF' in M. Codner and M. Clarke (eds), *A Question of Security: The British Defence Review in an Age of Austerity'* (London: I.B. Tauris, 2011), 217.

[25] Ibid, 218.

With all of that said, clearly there is some merit in not putting too many strategic eggs in one basket, and in considering that not all future security threats will look as they do today. There is also the 'threshold' argument, as Paul Cornish writes, whereby cuts to capability should not go beyond the point at which 'national "know-how" in design, manufacture, development and deployment might be lost forever'.[26] It is, after all, impossible to put together an aircraft carrier quickly if you suddenly decide you need one. National security and defence should not be 'locked into an economy defined by recession' and 'lacking the practical and intellectual capacity to expand'.[27]

Proposed restructuring

Whatever the government's consideration of such arguments, the 2010 defence review process will deliver armed force personnel numbers of 95,000 for the army (a reduction of nearly 7 per cent, but with infantry remaining at current levels), 30,000 for the navy, and a similar number—35,000—for the RAF. In the case of the latter two services, the proposed cuts in personnel are twice the amount as a proportion of their total strength than for the army.[28] The overall defence budget will be cut by 7.5 per cent in real terms over four years, reducing the percentage of GDP spent on defence from 2.7 per cent to a likely 2.2 per cent by 2014.[29] The emphasis in military posture has therefore indeed shifted slightly towards the army and away from the other services, at least in terms of proposed personnel numbers. As a result, Britain will have 'one of the most land-centric force structures of any modern volunteer military', at 65 per cent of personnel, as compared to around 55 per cent in the United States and France, and 53 per cent in Canada.[30] This suggests that the 'boots on the ground' argument has held sway, and that forthcoming threats are more likely to involve counter-insurgency and low-intensity conflicts (LICs) in complex land-based conflict zones than other scenarios such as 'another Falklands'.

The SDSR describes the changes within and between the armed forces, and the rationale for those changes, in some critical detail. It notes that the navy has been 'locked into a cycle of ever smaller numbers of ever more expensive ships'.[31] The RAF has not been able to support overseas deployments adequately

---

[26] P. Cornish, 'Strategy in Austerity: The Security and Defence of the United Kingdom', Chatham House (October 2010), p 21.

[27] Ibid.

[28] R. Norton-Taylor, 'Strategic defence review means end of Iraq-scale military interventions', *The Guardian*, 19 October 2010, available at <http://www.guardian.co.uk/politics/2010/oct/19/strategic-defence-review-military-cuts> (accessed 16 September 2011).

[29] M. Chalmers, 'Unbalancing the Force? Prospects for UK Defence after the SDSR', RUSI, Future Defence Review, Working Paper no 9, November 2010, p 1.

[30] Ibid

[31] HM Government, 'Securing Britain in an Age of Uncertainty: The Strategic Defence and Security Review' (London: TSO, October 2010), 4.

because of an 'ageing and unreliable strategic airlift fleet'.[32] The army has 'scores of tanks in Germany', but has to face the menace of improvised explosive devices (IEDs) in Iraq and Afghanistan in largely unarmoured vehicles designed for patrolling the streets of Northern Ireland.[33] The conclusion to be drawn, notes the SDSR, is that there has been a 'failure to face up to the new security realities of the post Cold War world'.[34]

In response, as described briefly in Chapter 6, detailed planning has started on a capability called 'Future Force 2020'. The stated intention is that the army will 'continue to have a vital operational role', and that the UK will continue to be 'one of very few countries able to deploy a self-sustaining, properly equipped brigade-sized force anywhere around the world and sustain it indefinitely.'[35] This challenges the assertion, expressed in *The Guardian* following the publication of the SDSR, that 'major operations will be [a] thing of the past',[36] although it is accepted that the nature of operations envisaged under the new force will be lighter in personnel numbers than those deployed to Iraq and Afghanistan at the height of hostilities there. It also underlines the politico-ideological stance discussed earlier, whereby it is accepted that the UK will remain an interventionist force for the foreseeable future, albeit in a slightly different and probably leaner way.

In terms of equipment detail, helicopters are seen as an essential element of a more 'boots on the ground' environment, in the shape of Chinook heavy-lift troop and equipment-carrying aircraft (of which 12 more are to be ordered), and the Puma, Merlin, and Wildcat aircraft, with the operational life of the former being extended.[37] The issue of helicopters has again been one of the emblematic elements of the political debate about military capability and restructuring. The issue found itself at the centre of a political storm in 2009 under Gordon Brown's premiership. Allegations arose at the time that the government had failed to make available sufficient numbers of helicopters for British forces serving in Afghanistan, at a time when British casualties were running at a particular high. The head of the army, General Sir Richard Dannatt, purportedly had to make a visit to his own troops in Helmand Province in a American Black Hawk helicopter as a British one was not available.[38] David Cameron had claimed the issue was a 'scandal', and had used it as part of the narrative that the British forces were not properly equipped for the tasks they were tackling.[39]

---

[32] Ibid.

[33] Ibid.

[34] Ibid.

[35] Ibid, 4.

[36] Norton-Taylor, n 28.

[37] SDSR, n 31, at 4.

[38] N. Allen and R. Prince, 'Gordon Brown faces grilling over Afghanistan helicopters', *The Telegraph*, 16 July 2009, available at <http://www.telegraph.co.uk/news/uknews/defence/5841003/Gordon-Brown-faces-grilling-over-Afghanistan-helicopters.html> (accessed 16 September 2011).

[39] Ibid.

On the Royal Navy, the SDSR decided to press ahead with the construction of two aircraft carriers at a cost of £5 billion, since to cancel them would incur unacceptable extra expense. With the retirement of the vertical take-off Harrier jets, however, there will not be planes to fly from them on their completion in 2020. As an interim measure, one of the carriers will be fitted with a catapult mechanism for launching Joint Strike Fighter (JSF) jets (which has the added benefit of allowing compatibility with the US and French fleets), and the other is likely to be mothballed.[40] Procurement is continuing of a fleet of Type-45 destroyers and Astute nuclear-powered submarines, with the decision point ('Main Gate') on whether to press ahead with construction of the proposed Vanguard replacement submarine due in 2016. If funding is available, a new fleet of more agile, flexible, and—crucially—less expensive frigates is also planned, of the type described by General Sir David Richards above. This will aim to break the navy's vicious cycle of continually moving up the cost and sophistication scale.

On the air front, the fleet will comprise modernized Typhoon (Eurofighter) jets, and the US-made JSF. Further investment will be made into UAVs, and the heavy-lift capability will be spearheaded by the introduction of the Airbus A400M, constructed at Seville in Spain. Perhaps in an effort to calm fears about unification of the armed services, the Prime Minister and his deputy mention in the preamble to the SDSR that, on the 70th anniversary of the Battle of Britain, the RAF 'has a vital continuing role'.[41]

The central tenets of the Future Force 2020 plan are four 'R's and a 'D', namely:

- Readiness (in which a small number of forces will be held in a state of high readiness close to immediate deployability);
- Reconstitution (a state of 'extended readiness' close to, but not synonymous with the mothballing of certain capabilities such as amphibious vehicles and equipment);
- Reinforcement (in which the Reserve Forces are central);
- Regeneration (primarily involving certain skills and expertise which may be needed in the future, and working with partners who may have capabilities that we do not currently);
- Dependency (meaning 'we rarely deploy alone', but usually do so under the NATO umbrella).[42]

The aim is to develop a more flexible and agile force more suited to 'boots on the ground' military interventions in complex conflict environments, and to move away from a force designed for fighting a Soviet invasion in Central Europe. By its very nature, such a range of capabilities, as General Richards

---

[40] Norton-Taylor, n 28.
[41] SDSR, n 31, at 6.
[42] Ibid.

described, potentially includes considerable cost-savings in terms of the types of equipment and capabilities, since army personnel are cheaper than state-of-the-art fighter jets and ships. At the same time, the government is dancing around the 'threshold' line described by Cornish above,[43] whereby the reconstitution and regeneration elements of the strategy may prove to be more complicated and less achievable than envisaged within acceptable timescales. The logic of such a strategy is sound, but further work will be needed on exactly how effective these processes can be made to be in serving the UK's essential national security interests, both in terms of its own interests and in supporting those of partners.

Most of the capability issues above describe existing areas of activity, but the cyber realm is one in which it is recognized that new military capabilities will need to be developed and resourced. It was noted in Lord Levene's report into the structure and management of the MOD, published in summer 2011, that the Defence Cyber Operations Group (DCOG) ought to be a cross-cutting body, and ought to sit within a new Joint Forces Command.[44] In September 2011, it was announced that a senior officer in the RAF, Sir Stuart Peach, would head-up the new Joint Forces Command, which would be in charge of military intelligence, cyber operations, and strategic planning. In this role, Sir Stuart would sit at the same level as the heads of the three Services.[45] While the precise nature and shape of this command is not yet clear, it does reflect that certain issues such as cyber, as discussed in Chapter 7, do not readily fall into existing organizational silos and will need to be part and parcel of activities across government. In this, the military is no different.

The nuclear question

One issue we have not yet explored is that of the UK's nuclear capability. At one level, this could be reasonably assumed to be the archetypal relic from the Cold War period of national security strategy, which must surely be a prime candidate for cutting, not least as it is one of the heaviest of the 'heavy-metal' capabilities in terms of cost. Under the logic of General Sir David Richards, the Taliban are probably not terribly deterred by the fact that we possess nuclear weapons, nor is this submarine-based capability particularly useful or appropriate for resolving such a situation as Afghanistan. The Liberal-Democrat component of the Coalition government in Britain has always signalled its clear

---

[43] Cornish, n 26.

[44] MOD, 'Defence Reform: an independent report into the structure and management of the Ministry of Defence' (London: TSO, June 2011), 77.

[45] R. Norton-Taylor and N. Hopkins, 'Sir Stuart Peach appointed head of UK's new Joint Forces Command', *The Guardian*, 15 September 2011, available at <http://www.guardian.co.uk/news/defence-and-security-blog/2011/sep/15/stuart-peach-defence-appointment?INTCMP=SRCH> (accessed 16 September 2011).

opposition to the nuclear deterrent and its intention to place this very much within the purview of defence reform and rationalization. This was one of the trickiest issues in striking an agreement between the Conservatives and Liberal Democrats in forming a governing coalition.

The two major political parties in the UK, however, are firmly of the belief that the nuclear deterrent still makes sense in the post-Cold War world and that it should be retained. The logic for this argument, as outlined in the NSS and the SDSR, is that the nuclear capability is the 'ultimate deterrent'.[46] In an age of uncertainty, such a deterrent is arguably more, not less, appropriate since one never knows what types of threat are over the horizon. The equation is a complex one, and includes two further considerations. First, a nuclear capability is probably a classic 'threshold' issue, in the sense that once a state relinquishes such a capability built up over several years, it would be difficult if not impossible to re-establish it—certainly not within any rapid timescales and not without considerable political risk. Secondly, the issue is related to the question discussed at the beginning of this chapter, of the place in the world that Britain considers itself to occupy. By holding a nuclear capability, Britain is at the political and military 'top table', representing one of just five states identified as Nuclear Weapons States (NWS) under the provisions of the Nuclear Non-Proliferation Treaty (NPT). (Four other states are believed to possess nuclear weapons, but are not signatories of the NPT, namely India, Pakistan, North Korea, and Israel.) The five NWS are synonymous with the five permanent members of the UN Security Council. In this way, possession of a nuclear capability while remaining within the NPT is central to the UK's political and military standing. To abolish its capability would entail a very symbolic change in the UK's status in this regard, and could be very damaging to the UK's status internationally. It may be that such a change could be detrimental to the leadership role and Truman Doctrine aspirations that the UK wishes to pursue.

For the time being, therefore, a compromise has been struck in that it has been agreed to retain the nuclear deterrent, while reducing the number of operational launch tubes on the submarines from 12 to eight, and the number of operational warheads from 48 to 40, thus achieving a saving of £3.2 billion over ten years.[47] This also allows the UK to say that it is 'vigorously' pursuing 'global nuclear disarmament'.[48] There has also been agreement with France, through a set of defence treaties signed in November 2010, to cooperate on future nuclear capability development (more on this in Chapter 11). The political battle in the UK on the nuclear issue, meanwhile, has been put off to another day. The Liberal Democrats are still of the view that the capability should be on the

---

[46] The SDSR (n 31, at 5) describes it as the 'ultimate insurance policy'.
[47] Ibid, 5.
[48] Ibid.

agenda for future defence reviews, and have continued to work on policy options for alternative deterrent strategies.[49]

Key points

- Most have accepted that defence has to be cut and restructured given the financial crisis, but there is disagreement over how to do so.
- Part of the question concerns the role that Britain wishes to play in the international community. The NSS points out that Britain has a 'distinctive position in the world', which belies the mere 1 per cent of world population it represents. For many, this means Britain should aim to be a more active player on the world stage than many of its European neighbours.
- The changing nature of conflict, which has manifested itself particularly in the Iraq and Afghanistan campaigns, has, arguably, bolstered the case for further defence restructuring towards more expeditionary and agile 'boots on the ground' and supporting infrastructure.
- This has led to considerable inter-service rivalries within the UK military, not least as the cuts in personnel will fall more heavily on the RAF and Navy, making the UK's military the most army-oriented of any in the industrialized world.
- At the centre of the plans is a proposal to build a Future Force 2020. The principles of this are enshrined within the five concepts of readiness, reconstitution, reinforcement, regeneration, and dependency (on partners).
- Whether the UK should continue to have a nuclear deterrent is still a political issue, not least as the two partners in the Coalition government fundamentally disagree on this point. For the time being, the plan is to reduce, but not to eliminate the capability altogether. There is also a treaty in place with France to cooperate on future nuclear capability development.

---

[49] See eg the 2010 launch of a review paper on 'Policy options for the future of the UK's nuclear weapons', available at <http://www.libdems.org.uk/news_detail.aspx?title=Menzies_Campbell_launches_review_of_UK_nuclear_weapons&pPK=691e8ca2-8766-450b-a3ce-400f214cc641> (accessed 16 September 2011).

9

Fighting Asymmetric Conflicts

The challenge of Afghanistan

At the time of writing, the decade-long war in Afghanistan is reaching a critical
stage for the International Security Assistance Force (ISAF). President Obama set
July 2011 as the first period in which US forces would start to hand over to their
Afghan counterparts in significant numbers, with 2014 being the target date for
a comprehensive handover and return of the country to full Afghan government control. 2011 was also set as the year that Canadian, Dutch, and Spanish
forces would withdraw. The British Prime Minister, David Cameron, had said
that an initial withdrawal of British troops in the same year was 'possible',
depending on situations on the ground.[1] Germany's Parliament also voted to
start withdrawing its troops by the beginning of 2012.[2] The plan that underpins
the withdrawals is dependent on the appropriate establishment of Afghan
National Army (ANA) and National Police (ANP) forces across the country.
This is part of the Security Sector Reform programme (SSR) in Afghanistan,
which also includes reform of the Afghan intelligence agency (the National
Directorate of Security (NDS)). The programme is a large and substantial element of Afghanistan's rebirth, representing $30 billion in aid up to 2010.[3] Afghan
President Hamid Karzai has underlined its importance, noting that 'Security
Sector Reform, in short, is the basic pre-requisite to recreating the nation that
today's parents hope to leave for future generations.'[4]

---

[1] 'Afghanistan withdrawal possible from 2011, says Cameron', BBC News, available at <http://
www.bbc.co.uk/news/uk-politics-10708063> (accessed 29 January 2011).

[2] J. Dempsey, 'Germany plans start of troop withdrawal', *New York Times*, 28 January 2011,
available at <http://www.nytimes.com/2011/01/29/world/europe/29germany.html> (accessed
29 January 2011).

[3] J. Richards, 'Intelligence burden: Afghanistan grapples with security reforms', *Jane's
Intelligence Review* (February 2011), 30.

[4] M. Sedra, 'Security First: Afghanistan's security sector reform process', *The Ploughshares
Monitor*, 24/4 (2003), 2.

Afghanistan's SSR process was formally agreed upon in Geneva in April 2002. As with many similar processes in post-conflict states, the programme is structured around five 'pillars', namely: military reform (led by the United States); police reform (led by Germany); the disarmament, demobilization, and reintegration (DDR) of former militants and combatants (led by Japan); judicial reform (led by Italy); and reform of the counter-narcotics programme (led by the UK). Despite positive statements occasionally made by both the Afghan government and its ISAF guests on the progress of the SSR agenda, however, Sedra has noted that conditions in Afghanistan fall somewhat short of those normally required for a successful SSR process, and notably the requirement for a 'minimal degree of security and institutional capacity' on which to build the process.[5] For Afghanistan, a long history of bitter conflict overlaid on a weak state has meant that security is heralded as the first and most important aspect needed to move the country forward. In this way, the SSR agenda has been seen as a potential 'panacea' by many.[6]

Selling the strategy—the battle of the narratives

As noted in the previous chapter, the Ministry of Defence (MOD) Development Concepts and Doctrine Centre (DCDC) study of the future character of conflict noted that the 'battle of the narratives' is critical in an operation such as Afghanistan.[7] This refers not only to winning the support of the local population in the conflict zone itself, but also to winning the backing of the electorate at home. In Afghanistan, the Taliban insurgents are using asymmetric hit-and-run tactics to try to derail ISAF's process of handing over security to the Afghan government and to create a general impression of lacking security, thus suggesting that the security handover is not going very well. A 19-hour siege by armed militants of the US Embassy, NATO HQ, and National Directorate of Security (NDS) offices in Kabul during September 2011, which ended in the deaths of 14 militants and Afghan soldiers, was described by the US Ambassador, Ryan Crocker, as 'not a very big deal'.[8] The NATO Secretary General, Anders Fogh Rasmussen, was perceptive about the Taliban's motives, noting that 'we are witnessing the Taliban trying to test transition but they can't stop it. Transition is on track and it will continue.'[9] Here we can clearly see a battle of narratives underway.

---

[5] M. Sedra, 'Security Sector Reform in Afghanistan: The Slide Towards Expediency', *International Peacekeeping*, 13/1 (2006), 95.

[6] Sedra, n 5.

[7] MOD, DCDC, 'The Future Character of Conflict', DSDA Operations Centre, 2 March 2010, p 6.

[8] '14 killed as Kabul siege ends', *The Hindu*, 15 September 2011, available at <http://www.thehindu.com/todays-paper/tp-international/article2454396.ece> (accessed 17 September 2011).

[9] J. Kelly, 'Militants attack government and NATO buildings in Kabul', *The Guardian*, 14 September 2011, available at <http://www.guardian.co.uk/world/2011/sep/13/kabul-explosions-afghan-capital-blasts> (accessed 17 September 2011).

For those in the West confronted with a situation such as Afghanistan, the first problem is what McInnes describes as the 'body bag problem'.[10] For the US public at least, this reflects a bitter memory of the Vietnam conflict, which fed into the removal of US Marines from Beirut after the Hizbollah bombing in 1983, and the aborting of the UN mission to Somalia after the death of 18 US servicemen in 1993.[11] We can also see that Spain's decision to remove its troops from the coalition fighting in Iraq following the Madrid terrorist bombings of March 2004 was an example of where a low threshold of tolerance to casualties (in this case civilian casualties) can have a major effect on national security policy formation. Wheeler further examines this issue, and claims that 'Western publics are not prepared to accept the loss of members of the armed forces unless it is believed that vital national interests are at stake'.[12]

Under this formulation, the key is adequately and appropriately to define 'vital national interests' and to bring public support along with the notion that intervention overseas is necessary to establish national security at home. Such a notion has been seen in the developing process of securitization since the end of the Cold War, in which transnational threats within a globalizing world are seen to be creating new linkages between conditions of instability and conflict abroad, and domestic security. The 9/11 terrorist attacks in the United States represented a new high-water mark in this thinking, and spawned a greater degree of interest in how 'ungoverned spaces' such as Afghanistan could act as places in which radical ideologies and groups could develop their international plans. We saw in Chapter 4 how Tony Blair described the effect of the 9/11 attacks as being one that changed the 'calculus of risk' for Western states.[13] Crucially, what this meant for Western leaders was that the definition of 'vital national interests' had changed in such a way that military intervention by Western states became a viable and sensible option again, after the traumas of the Balkans and Somalia in the 1990s (to which could be added the failure to intervene in Rwanda). This led very quickly to the campaign in Afghanistan, which started just 26 days after the 9/11 attacks, and, less than two years later, to the invasion of Iraq and removal of the Saddam Hussein regime. Of course, the equation can also work in reverse: the former Director-General of the Security Service (MI5) in the UK, Baroness Eliza Manningham-Buller, has often said that the wrong foreign policy options can actually worsen national security at home. She refers specifically to the campaign in Iraq, which, in her view,

---

[10] C. McInnes, 'Fatal Attraction? Air Power and the West', *Contemporary Security Policy*, 22/3 (2001), 34.

[11] Ibid.

[12] N. Wheeler, 'Introduction: The Political and Moral Limits of Western Military Intervention to Protect Civilians in Danger', *Contemporary Security Policy*, 22/3 (2001), 8.

[13] T.A. Peter, 'Blair Iraq War Enquiry: Calculus of Risk on WMD Changed after 9/11, *The Christian Science Monitor* (29 January 2010), available at <http://www.csmonitor.com/World/terrorism-security/2010/0129/Blair-Iraq-war-inquiry-Calculus-of-risk-on-WMD-changed-after-9-11> (accessed 2 July 2011).

'increased the terrorist threat' and 'spurred some young British Muslims to turn to terror'.[14]

Whatever the merits of this point of view, there is general acceptance in the National Security Strategy (NSS) that Britain will remain an interventionist country in certain circumstances, which will 'use all the instruments of national power to prevent conflicts and avert threats beyond our shores'.[15] This will occasionally entail a need to 'tackle potential risks at source'.[16] The process of so doing is described in the NSS as 'shaping a stable world',[17] and one of the key strategies in this area is the joint Foreign and Commonwealth Office (FCO)/ MOD/Department for International Development (DfID) programme called the Building Stability Overseas Strategy (BSOS). The BSOS reiterates the dual principles of intervening overseas to establish stability, namely that it is 'both morally right and in Britain's national interest'.[18] In the case of the latter, the strategy explains that:

> In our interconnected world, the effect of violence in one region can spread to other more stable areas through refugee movements, terrorist activity, and organised crime groups, all of which can have an impact on our own security. . . . In the long term, our prosperity and security is [sic] intertwined with peaceful development and security across the globe.[19]

'Poorly governed spaces' around the world can be launch pads for terrorist movements (as in the cases of Somalia, Yemen, and Afghanistan), and for organized crime groups such as international drugs traffickers or people smugglers. Conflict, once started, can disrupt trade and flows of vital commodities on a wide regional scale and generally depress economies. It can also lead to very costly and complicated military and humanitarian interventions to resolve. All these factors can be security issues for the UK at various stages, to say nothing of the basic moral and humanitarian issues of allowing possibly millions of people to live in conditions of severe underdevelopment and insecurity. In these ways, it is no longer good enough to tackle security threats once they reach our shores, but to think about 'upstream' work to prevent and resolve conflict and strengthen governance in those places where it is weak.

---

[14] Baroness Eliza Manningham-Buller, 'Securing Freedom: Lecture One—Terror', BBC Reith Lectures 2011, BBC Radio 4, 6 September 2011.

[15] HM Government, 'A Strong Britain in an Age of Uncertainty: The National Security Strategy' (London: TSO, October 2010), 9.

[16] Ibid, 22.

[17] Ibid, 11.

[18] HM Government, 'Building Stability Overseas Strategy' (London: DfID/FCO/MOD, July 2011), 4.

[19] Ibid, 8.

Peacekeeping, peace-enforcement, and counter-insurgency

These are the calculations against which Western governments must balance the risk of death and injury to troops and other personnel when deployed overseas in such places as Afghanistan. The resultant policy is a complex one that combines military activity with development projects and use of 'soft power' tools, such as cultural links and diplomatic activity. All these factors mean that the landscape in which such activities must take place can be, as discussed in the previous chapter, a complex and crowded place involving an increasing number of actors.

At one end of the process is a recognition that security is the bedrock on which strong governance and viable state structures are built: an essentially Weberian notion of the state. In terms of when and how British and other personnel may become committed to operations abroad, the spectrum of scenarios is a wide and complex one, ranging from situations in which conflict has ended and the post-conflict 'stabilization' process must be embedded, to those where the conflict is still very much underway and the immediate task is more akin to warfighting. Afghanistan, as we will discuss, represents a complicated mix of these scenarios, and is arguably still located towards the latter end of the spectrum. The Taliban's strategy is to keep things at this end of the spectrum, so that the international forces and their Afghan government ally cannot develop a convincing narrative that the country is moving along the developmental scale.

As Mackinlay describes, it is generally accepted that there are three types of intervention along this developmental scale, which he describes as three 'force options', comprising intervention; containment; and 'traditional peacekeeping'.[20] By the mid-1990s, the UN had mandated the deployment of approximately 100,000 troops in operations generally described as 'complex humanitarian emergencies', and thus outwardly occupying the peacekeeping end of the spectrum.[21] Broadly speaking, peacekeeping and containment operations, typified by the NATO operations in the Balkans during the 1990s, meant keeping a lid on the situation locally in such a way that it did not unfold into a wider regional or global security problem. With the advent of the 9/11 attacks, however, Mackinlay argues that national security thinking, especially and not surprisingly in the United States, lurched towards the more comprehensive intervention end of the spectrum, whereby a realization that the West could no longer hide behind the 'safety curtain' in the face of the threat from ungoverned or rogue states, led to operations which removed whole regimes and set about rebuilding the state in a shape that would be more beneficial to the

---

[20] J. Mackinlay, 'Intervening in Conflict: The Policy Issues', *Conflict, Security and Development*, 7/1 (2007), 169.
[21] Ibid, 170.

West's security.[22] Thus were born the extraordinarily complex and traumatic episodes in Afghanistan and Iraq.

From a UN peacekeeping point of view, as Jones describes, the shift has been one in which peacekeeping operations are increasingly operating in 'non-consensual environments', where a group of actors generally known in the business as 'spoilers' (organized criminals, extremists, terrorists, and other interest-groups opposed to the activities of foreign interveners) are becoming more prevalent, organized, and lethal.[23] The actions described at the beginning of this chapter by the Taliban in Kabul during September 2011 are a classic example of 'spoiler' activity.

These are the types of factors which have definitely characterized the operations in Iraq and Afghanistan, and which must be taken to be the types of situations in which British troops and other personnel must expect to deploy in the foreseeable future. That said, it is important to heed one of the conclusions of the UK's joint-departmental Stabilisation Unit, that every situation of intervention and stabilization is different and assumptions about the environment must never be made.[24]

The Stabilisation Unit also recognizes that counter-insurgency (or COIN) will, by the end of the 2000s, often be 'at the heart of stabilization'. COIN is not a new concept, not least for countries with an imperial past such as Britain, which have had to fight anti-colonial uprisings and insurgencies at various stages in their history. The traditional view is that Britain has gathered a great deal of experience in such issues over the years, through such experiences as the 'Malayan emergency' in the late 1940s and 1950s. Nagl, for example, argues that Britain learned a great deal from this experience and adapted its methods to great effect, in a way that the United States did not throughout the Vietnam experience.[25]

Donald notes how, in Kosovo, the British earned respect and set themselves apart from their US counterparts by employing tactics developed in such places as Northern Ireland. These included patrolling outside their operating bases in smaller groups, with soft caps rather than hard hats, in a non-confrontational way which brought them into closer contact with the locals and developed local trust.[26] In Afghanistan, of course, the British had been present some years before in a colonial capacity, albeit not with particularly happy memories! Such confidence in experience and ability in counter-insurgency situations, however, has taken some severe hits in the maelstroms of Iraq and Afghanistan in the

---

[22] Ibid, 173.

[23] B. Jones, 'Peacekeeping in Crisis?', *RUSI Journal*, 154/5 (2009), 79.

[24] HM Government, 'The UK Approach to Stabilisation: Stabilisation Unit Guidance Notes' (London: FCO/DfID/MOD, November 2008), 18.

[25] J.A. Nagl, 'Learning to Eat Soup with a Knife: British and American Army Counterinsurgency Learning during the Malayan Emergency and Vietnam War', *World Affairs*, 161/4 (1999), 193.

[26] D. Donald, 'The Doctrine Gap: The Enduring Problem of Contemporary Peace Support Operations Thinking', *Contemporary Security Policy*, 22/3 (2001), 138 n 105.

early twenty-first century. As Ucko describes, the British experience of its occupation of Basra in the Iraq War 'has left many asking what happened to Britain's prowess in such missions'.[27] Initially, the operation went well, in that the uniquely British 'soft and unobtrusive approach'[28] seemed to reap dividends in the local community and administration. Ultimately, however, the 'gradual takeover of Basra by sectarian militias, criminal networks and other predatory actors'—the spoilers of modern counter-insurgency and peacekeeping environments—led to a collapse in security.[29] By the end of operations in 2007 when the British garrison withdrew, the British force was bunkered in its base outside the city, dodging daily mortar attacks from Shia militia groups such as *Jaish al-Mahdi*. A senior British officer, Colonel Tim Collins, concluded that the reputation of the British army had been 'badly damaged' as a result.[30]

Similarly, the latest Afghanistan experience for the British military has proved to be an extremely difficult episode. It has not helped that the British have been deployed in the southern Helmand Province, one of the most restive and difficult areas of the country, where the battles with the Taliban have been among the fiercest. King's analysis of British operations in Helmand notes that the continual problem has been 'attempting to turn recurrent tactical successes into strategic gains'.[31] Part of the problem may be a tactical one of concentrating forces in dispersed Forward Operating Bases (FOBs), with areas between policed periodically through patrols. The initial British deployment was probably too small (at 3,500 troops in 2006) to cover the area effectively in any other way. Despite an increase of the troop strength to 19,000 by early 2010, however, the tactic of concentrating troops within dispersed FOBs seems to have continued.[32]

Some observers have drawn a historical parallel with British campaigns in Afghanistan in the nineteenth century, equating today's FOBs with the 'forts' of the colonial forces in British India's frontier.[33] Then, as now, with a relatively small force covering a huge area, and a hostile attitude among the local population to the presence of foreign forces, jurisdiction often extended just a few yards beyond the immediate boundaries of the garrison. In Helmand, the particular ferocity and persistence of the Taliban campaign has meant that the British forces have been constantly chasing shadows and failing to ensure continued security in the areas that they take.

---

[27] D.H. Ucko, 'Lessons from Basra: The Future of British Counter-Insurgency', *Survival*, 52/4 (2010), 131.

[28] Ibid, 133.

[29] Ibid, 134.

[30] H. Strange, 'Basra pull-out leaves UK military "damaged", says Colonel Tim Collins', *The Times*, 17 December 2007.

[31] A. King, 'Understanding the Helmand Campaign: British Military Operations in Afghanistan', *International Affairs*, 86/2 (2010), 311.

[32] Ibid, 315.

[33] Sir Sherard Cowper-Coles, former British ambassador to Afghanistan, Speech at the Pluscarden Programme, St Antony's College, Oxford University, 27 January 2011.

Ucko draws two very important conclusions from the British experience in Basra. First, the myth of an innate British capability in counter-insurgency has been severely questioned, if not laid to rest. Secondly, there was an 'absence of a well-conceived and resourced strategy', and a 'low understanding of and priority for state-building'.[34] The issue of resources is probably the most critical, since in both Iraq and Afghanistan one of the key criticisms of the British contingents is that they have had simply too few troops and supporting infrastructure to be able to cover the ground adequately. As a result, they have very often ended up isolated within their bases, unable to achieve anything more than defensive actions. The implications of this in the context of the defence cuts proposed by the Strategic Defence and Security Review (SDSR) are clear: either the military has to find a way of 'working smarter', or operations of the scale and complexity of Iraq and Afghanistan cannot be attempted by Britain again for the foreseeable future, or certainly not outside a large and robust international coalition.

In the United States, an understanding of counter-insurgency has developed enormously since the invasion of Iraq in 2003, and particularly since the tactical shift in the operation achieved by General Petraeus in 2008. Petraeus's Counterinsurgency Field Manual, which stresses the importance of a highly developed sociopolitical understanding of the environment in which the intervening force is operating, has become recommended reading for all militaries subsequently involved in overseas interventions. Supporters of his doctrine, such as the Australian former army officer and Special Adviser for Counterinsurgency to the US Secretary of State, David Kilcullen, have also been extensively read and followed in the post-9/11 period.[35] A word of caution must again be raised, however. As discussed, there is a severe danger in developing formalized doctrine which can be applied 'off-the-shelf' to any situation, when the reality is that every conflict environment is likely to have important differences from any other. One of the key elements of Petraeus's doctrine in Iraq, for example, which helped to turn the campaign around for the United States, was the policy of arming local militias to take on the Al Qaeda insurgents themselves. The Anbar Awakening, or Sons of Iraq as the local militants became known,[36] proved to be enormously successful both in deflecting attention from the occupying US forces and driving a wedge between the insurgents and the local population. As the UK's Stabilisation Unit noted, however, 'Iraq and Afghanistan are fundamentally different contexts'. To arm local militias in

---

[34] Ucko, n 27, at 132.

[35] See eg Kilcullen's *The Accidental Guerrilla* (London: Hurst, 2009).

[36] G. Bruno, 'The Role of the "Sons of Iraq" in Improving Security', Council on Foreign Relations, 28 April 2008, available at <http://www.washingtonpost.com/wp-dyn/content/article/2008/04/28/AR2008042801120.html> (accessed 16 September 2011).

Afghanistan might be 'highly counterproductive' in that the arms are much more likely to be turned ultimately on the providers.[37]

Future force requirements

As Kraska observes, one of the outcomes of the increasing complexity of peace-keeping and counter-insurgency operations is that the distinction between police and military functions and activities in the field become blurred. Traditionally, the modern nation-state has sought a demarcation between the two functions, and seen a crossover between them as evidence of 'repressive-ness and lack of democracy'.[38] However, many tasks in a COIN situation see a distinct overlap between these two functions. Typically, troops deployed in Iraq and Afghanistan, as well as periodically undertaking combat operations, will spend much of their time on such activities as routine patrolling; house-to-house searches looking for contraband and suspects; and arresting law-breakers.[39]

Such roles are sometimes described as 'gendarmerie' functions, after the French security force created in the eighteenth century, which has always been under the dual governance of the Ministries of Interior and Defence. These forces combine civil policing functions (eg powers of investigation and arrest) with military functions (eg the use of firearms and other military equipment), and will often be deployed in such activities as riot control. While unfamiliar to security structures in the UK, United States, and many other countries, many continental European countries have a long tradition of gendarmerie functions, for instance Italy, Spain, Portugal, and Austria (some of which evolved during periods of military rule). Various countries outside Europe also have paramilitary forces, for example the Army Rangers in Pakistan, which is an army detachment but can be deployed by the Interior Ministry to quell civil disturbances. As Lutterbeck describes, the post-Cold War security landscape has seen gendarmeries which combine policing and military capabilities come back into fashion in the two areas of peacekeeping and border patrols in particular.[40]

The peacekeeping mission in Bosnia saw the creation of Multinational Specialised Units (MSUs) to take over public-order and law-enforcement tasks from the SFOR (Stabilisation Force in Bosnia-Herzegovina) troops. These units were composed exclusively of gendarmeries, headed by the Italian caribinieri.[41]

---

[37] HM Government, Stabilisation Unit, 'Responding to Stabilisation Challenges in Hostile and Insecure Environments: Lessons Identified by the UK's Stabilisation Unit' (London: FCO/DfID/MOD, November 2010), 6.

[38] P.B. Kraska, 'Militarization and Policing—Its Relevance to 21st Century Police', *Policing*, 1/4 (2007), 501.

[39] Ibid, 510.

[40] D. Lutterbeck, 'Between Police and Military: The New Security Agenda and the Rise of Gendarmeries', *Cooperation and Conflict*, 39/1 (2004), 51.

[41] Ibid, 61.

Similar units were subsequently deployed in Kosovo and East Timor. Within the EU, the four member states of France, Italy, Spain, and Portugal, have linked together their gendarmerie capabilities in an initiative (called FIEP), which has links to similar forces outside Europe, and aims to become a type of rapid reaction police force deployable in a number of environments.

The NSS and SDSR do not use the word 'gendarmerie', although this has occasionally entered the debate about what type of armed forces Britain should have in the future, and particularly the skillsets that an 'expeditionary force' should possess.[42] For all the difficulties of Iraq and Afghanistan, a much more positive example is sometimes mentioned in this respect, namely the British military intervention in Sierra Leone in 2000, known as Operation Palliser. In May of that year, 1,300 troops of the Joint Rapid Reaction Force (JRRF) were deployed to Sierra Leone for approximately six weeks, during the civil war in which the Revolutionary United Front (RUF) were besieging the capital, Freetown. At the end of the deployment, 200 British troops remained to assist the UN peacekeeping force in the country, known as UNAMSIL. Later in the year there was a further brief deployment of 650 troops including the Amphibious Ready Group to bolster the UN force, which was coming under renewed pressure from the RUF. The Secretary-General of the UN at the time, Kofi Annan, was able to take comfort that the ignominy of failed intervention in Rwanda six years earlier would not be repeated, and the 'spoiler' efforts of the RUF, who were hoping to emulate the disasters for the UN in Mogadishu and Kigali, ultimately proved a failure.[43] Interestingly, the operation was led by Brigadier David Richards, who later became Chief of Defence Staff and Commander of ISAF in Afghanistan.

As Williams points out, the operation had much to commend it, including the fact that it represented a willingness to live up to the rhetoric of the 'ethical foreign policy' that the relatively newly installed Labour government had espoused.[44] It was also a situation in which there were few strategic interests for Britain beyond the humanitarian factors, other than the protection and evacuation of some British nationals. Subsequent history has looked kindly upon the operation, as it proved to be something of a turning point, and Sierra Leone is now proceeding on a road of post-conflict recovery after years of appalling violence and disruption. Writing shortly after the completion of the operation in 2000, Connaughton observed that Palliser was 'rich in both lessons and promise'.[45] The subsequent operations in Iraq and Afghanistan, which are admittedly considerably larger and more complex situations than that of Sierra

---

[42] See eg D. Rodin, 'Defence review is an opportunity, not a threat, to our military', *The Guardian*, 13 October 2010, available at <http://www.guardian.co.uk/commentisfree/2010/oct/13/defence-review-is-opportunity-not-threat> (accessed 16 September 2011).

[43] R.M. Connaughton, 'Organizing British Joint Rapid Reaction Forces', *Joint Forces Quarterly* (Autumn 2000), 91, 93.

[44] P. Williams, 'Fighting for Freetown: British Military Intervention in Sierra Leone', *Contemporary Security Policy*, 22/3 (2001), 163.

[45] Connaughton, n 43, at 94.

Leone in 2000, will have swept aside much of the pride and confidence that accompanied the successful completion of Operation Palliser. As the government and the military work hard on restructuring forces in 2011 to become much more flexible and 'expeditionary', however, many will be dusting off the Palliser reports and considering how its lessons can be built upon.

Key points

- The conflict in Afghanistan is at a critical stage. Many have seen SSR, in which the UK is playing a part within an international coalition, as being central to Afghanistan's future.
- The campaign in Afghanistan has turned into something of a 'battle of the narratives', in which the ISAF forces and the insurgents compete with one another to present a picture of what is happening in Afghanistan, and how successfully the security handover to Afghan government forces is proceeding.
- Success in Afghanistan, in Western eyes, is to establish a strong Weberian state on which the foundations of future security can be built. This means that peacekeeping and conflict resolution operations become a sensible long-term strategy in which to invest in a national security context.
- Recent experiences of counter-insurgency have been mixed, and the UK may have suffered some tarnishing of its military reputation through the difficulties experienced in Iraq and Afghanistan.
- Future force requirements include a notion of 'gendarmerie' capability, which brings defence capabilities closer to policing functions. This is a very different defence posture from that required during the Cold War.

10

Domestic Policies: Counter-Radicalization and Counter-Terrorism

Old and new threats

We have seen how the threat from international terrorism has been identified as being in the top tier of threat to the UK within the National Security Strategy (NSS), as has a 'significant increase in the levels of terrorism relating to Northern Ireland'.[1] In many ways, we tend to think of terrorism, certainly in the Western world, as the archetypal transnational threat that is inextricably linked to processes of globalization accelerating at the end of the twentieth century. Such a view has been reinforced by the tenth anniversary commemorations of the 9/11 attacks in the United States. The original attacks in 2001, as we have noted, are seen by many to have caused a fundamental strategic shift in national security strategizing in the post-Cold War world. Reference in the UK context to terrorism relating to Northern Ireland, however, reminds us that the phenomenon has a much longer history than Al Qaeda, and that it can manifest itself in a number of ways.

The official terrorist 'threat level' is set in the UK by a joint analytic team based within the Security Service's (MI5) London headquarters, called JTAC (Joint Terrorism Analysis Centre). The threat level was only made public in 2006, after London suffered a coordinated terrorist attack on its Underground system and on a bus in July of the previous year, which killed 56 people including the four suicide attackers and injured hundreds more. Since this time,

---

[1] HM Government, 'A Strong Britain in an Age of Uncertainty: The National Security Strategy' (London: TSO, October 2010), 27.

the threat level has fluctuated between its highest level (Severe) and the next level down (Substantial) which mean respectively that a serious terrorist incident in the UK is either 'a strong possibility' or 'highly likely'.[2] In summer 2011, the level in mainland UK was reduced from Severe to Substantial due to a variety of factors, including an analytical judgement that a 'Mumbai-style' terrorist attack in a crowded place was less likely than had been previously assessed, and that the Al Qaeda organization seemed to be suffering a substantial reduction in capability following actions based on intelligence obtained after the raid on Osama Bin Laden's compound in Pakistan in May 2011. The level in Northern Ireland has remained at Severe, following an upsurge in dissident Irish Republican violence.

The threat from terrorism affects the UK directly in a number of ways. First, the Northern Ireland threat is specifically about the UK, and, while it was assumed to have been dissolved with the 1998 Good Friday agreement and power-sharing arrangement that followed, it has proved to be stubbornly persistent. The Al Qaeda phenomenon, which arose in the late 1990s, is a very different phenomenon, and affects a great number of countries. Where this comes home to roost for the UK, the NSS notes, is in the process of radicalized recruits to the cause travelling abroad with ease and relative anonymity, then bringing terrorist techniques they have subsequently learned to deploy on operations within the UK.[3] Similarly, British interests abroad have come under attack by terrorist groups. This is one result of a more interventionist and 'upstream' foreign policy as described earlier, namely that not every group will approve of UK actions abroad and may undertake terrorist actions in response. For counter-terrorism policy, therefore, as I will describe, the equation is a complex one combining actions overseas with activities domestically within the UK.

The evolving nature of the terrorist threat

Activities that could be described as terrorism are probably as old as time, although this partly depends on how 'terrorism' is defined: an intellectual pursuit that has consumed a great deal of academic and institutional activity over the years. At one level, this is a moot question but, at another, it is critically important for policy in the sense that terrorist activities need to be defined in close legal terms if people are to be prosecuted for them. As Saul describes, governments have grappled with whether to pursue military or criminal justice responses to terrorist acts, especially since the 9/11 attacks,[4] and this has led to

---

[2] JTAC website, at <https://www.mi5.gov.uk/output/threat-levels.html> (accessed 17 September 2011).

[3] NSS, n 1, at 14.

[4] B. Saul, 'International Terrorism as a European Crime: The Policy Rationale for Criminalization', *European Journal of Crime, Criminal Law and Criminal Justice*, 11/4 (2003), 323.

a number of complicated issues, such as confusion over the status of detainees in Guantanamo Bay. In the UK, from 1977 onwards and into the Thatcher government that followed, a gradual process of 'criminalization' towards the terrorist problem was instituted, which shifted action from a 'military-security' model to one involving police primacy.[5] This was not without its reaction: the 1981 hunger strike by terrorist prisoners within the high-security Maze Prison in Northern Ireland, in which ten inmates ultimately died, was triggered by protests over the change of status of the prisoners to the category of standard criminals. We have seen that the debate has continued after the 9/11 attacks, and the launch of the controversial 'War on Terror' by the United States, which many see as shifting the balance dangerously back again towards a military-security model. As Baroness Eliza Manningham-Buller noted in the September 2011 Reith Lecture series, on the question of the 9/11 attacks on the United States by Al Qaeda:

> I call it a crime, not an act of war. Terrorism is a violent tool used for political reasons to bring pressure on governments by creating fear in the populace . . . For me what happened was a crime and needs to be thought of as such. What made it different from earlier attacks was its scale and audacity, not its nature.[6]

We saw in Chapter 3 how the terrorist threat affecting the UK has evolved, as it has in many other countries, into a multifaceted threat involving a number of different groups with different motivations and ideologies. The longest running threat to the British state has been that associated with Irish Republicanism, which is now entering its third century of continuous activity. Despite the hopes unleashed across British and Irish communities with the signing of the Good Friday Agreement in 1998, and the undoubted radical reduction in violence under the banner of the 'Troubles' in the province of Northern Ireland (which claimed an estimated 3,500 lives between 1969 and 1998),[7] dissident Irish Republican terrorism has resurged somewhat since 2009 and has caused the terror threat level in Northern Ireland to be raised again to its highest level.

Meanwhile, the 'new terrorism' threat epitomized by Al Qaeda and its affiliates,[8] which has emerged since the 1990s, has come to take a central place in the UK's counter-terrorism prioritization since the 9/11 attacks in the United States in 2001, and accelerating after the 2005 attacks in London. As we saw in Chapter 3, the number and range of attacks under this banner are almost too

---

[5] C. Campbell and I. Connolly, 'A Model for the 'War against Terrorism?' Military Intervention in Northern Ireland and the 1970s Falls Curfew', *Journal of Law and Society*, 30/2 (2003), 368–69.

[6] Baroness Eliza Manningham-Buller, 'Securing Freedom: Lecture One—Terror', BBC Reith Lectures 2011, BBC Radio 4, 6 September 2011.

[7] HM Government, Home Office, 'Prevent Strategy' (London: TSO, June 2011), 14.

[8] Walter Laqueur, *No End to War: Terrorism in the Twenty-First Century* (New York: Continuum, 2004), 143.

numerous to mention, but 79 people with a specifically 'Islamist'-related affili-
ation found themselves in custody in early 2011 on terrorism charges. Despite
the fact that the terror threat level was reduced in summer 2011, the Home
Secretary stressed that 'there is still a real and serious threat to the UK and I
would ask the public to remain ever vigilant'.[9]

The terrorist attacks in Oslo in July 2011, apparently by a man who transpired
to be a Far Right extremist, emphasized a point made with great care in the
review of the UK's counter-terrorism 'Prevent' policy in 2011, to which I will
return below, that terrorism can come from a variety of extremist ideologies and
should not necessarily be seen as emerging from one particular religio-political
strand. This is the case even if, as the refreshed Prevent Strategy document
points out, the threat from Al Qaeda and its ideology remains very much the
most serious and highest priority for the UK at the present time.[10] Part of the
issue here is again a political one that has arisen from the early experience of
the Prevent Strategy, which was launched by the previous Labour administration
and about which I will say more below.

Counter-terrorism strategy in the UK

As Campbell and Connolly describe, the British experience of counter-terrorism
in the Northern Ireland period after 1969 went through a number of phases,
starting with an initial military-led phase, which, in their view, did not in
retrospect provide a suitable model for how best to deal with such terrorist
threats in a liberal democracy.[11] As described earlier, experience later shifted
towards a more civilian police and intelligence-led model, although this was
also not without its problems. Throughout that period, a number of techniques
and approaches were used to strengthen security and intelligence against the
threat, many of which caused a great deal of controversy and echoes of which
were heard again some years later as the Al Qaeda threat emerged and counter-
terrorism policy developed in response.

The key issues included questions of interrogation, internment, surveillance,
and legal process for suspects. In the first of these, the initial military phase
included the highly controversial deployment of the 'five techniques' for
enhanced interrogation (standing in stress positions, hooding, exposure to continuous noise, and deprivation of food and sleep). The Prime Minister, Ted Heath,
announced that such techniques had been banned from further use in 1972, following attempts by the government of the Republic of Ireland to bring a case
against Britain for contravention of the articles of the European Convention on

---

[9] 'UK terror threat level reduced to "substantial"', BBC News, 11 July 2011, available at
<http://www.bbc.co.uk/news/uk-14111281> (accessed 17 September 2011).

[10] HM Government, n 7, at 5.

[11] Campbell and Connolly, n 5, at 341–2.

Human Rights (ECHR).[12] Other difficult issues revolved around a brief period of internment without trial launched in 1971, allegations of collusion between Loyalist paramilitaries and the local police, the Royal Ulster Constabulary (RUC, now renamed as the Police Service of Northern Ireland (PSNI)), and the introduction of jury-less trials in special cases, dubbed 'Diplock courts', after Lord Diplock who had advocated such a measure in an inquiry presented to Parliament in 1972. All these measures were eventually phased out, and many are of the view that they were ultimately counter-productive in radicalizing the Republican community further against the British state. It is interesting to note, however, as Bamford observes, that the intelligence war against the IRA gradually achieved considerable success over the years through ever-greater penetration of the movement's plans and activities.[13] This suggests that, while 'one successful attack can have devastating consequences', good intelligence 'greatly reduces that possibility'.[14]

With the advent some years later of the Al Qaeda-related threat, there was recognition that the threat had evolved into something somewhat different from that faced in Northern Ireland, although many of the same debates about policy rights and wrongs were rehearsed. Debates over the extension of pre-trial detention periods (which, at 28 days in the UK, are now the longest in Europe) and Control Orders which impose curfews on certain terrorist suspects on the basis of intelligence alone, reprise many of the difficult discussions held in the 1970s about balancing strong anti-terror security with civil liberties and human rights. Control Orders were renamed Terrorism Prevention and Investigation Measures (TPIMs) under the Coalition government, although they have changed little in essence. The Coalition government has committed itself to a full review of counter-terrorism legislation in autumn 2011.

The July 2005 suicide attacks in London by a group of four young British Muslim men using improvised home-made explosives raised the new realization that 'home-grown' terrorists were a threat on the British mainland, as much as individuals travelling into the country from outside, as had been the case with the 9/11 attacks in the United States. The policy response was the Counter-Terrorism Strategy, or CONTEST, which was first launched in 2006. The strategy, as discussed briefly in Chapter 6, takes a four-pronged approach,[15] called the 'four P's'. The strands in question are Pursue (which is about finding, disrupting, and interdicting terrorist individuals and groups through intelligence, security, and military action); Prevent (countering the process by which individuals become drawn into terrorism, through counter-radicalization);

---

[12] S. Newbery, B. Brecher, P. Sands, and B. Stewart, 'Interrogation, Intelligence and the issue of Human Rights', *Intelligence and National Security*, 24/5 (2009), 634.

[13] B.W.C. Bamford, 'The Role and Effectiveness of Intelligence in Northern Ireland', *Intelligence and National Security*, 20/4 (2005), 603.

[14] Ibid.

[15] The prongs were originally called 'pillars', but this was later changed to 'strands' to avoid any unhelpful religious allusions.

Protect (making the UK's national infrastructure as resilient as possible to terror-ist attack); and Prepare (ensuring emergency response capabilities are in place and are exercised frequently, so that the impact from a terrorist attack can be mitigated as quickly and efficiently as possible).

The overall headline of CONTEST is a stated intent to 'reduce the risk to the UK and our interests overseas from terrorism, so that people can go about their lives freely and with confidence.'[16] This, in many ways classically British under-statement, contains within it some very important principles when compared with similar strategies in other countries. Unlike the policy statements around such issues as intervention overseas, as described earlier in the book, the counter-terrorism strategy is not about promoting particular ideologies or principles or 'exceptionalist' policy responses, but is almost the opposite of that, namely about promoting normality and continuity. The former Intelligence and Security Coordinator, Sir David Omand, explains the intent of this statement by describ-ing the logic in terms of how best to thwart the desired impact sought by the terrorists. The aim of the terrorists is

> to alter the equation sufficiently in their favour by creating conditions of abnormality so that the government is regarded . . . as impotent in controlling risk. . . . Such an expression of the *power of normality* would directly deny the terrorists part of what they most seek. [Emphasis added.][17]

In these terms, one of the points about living in a liberal democracy (and one of the things that ideological extremists wish to constrain or destroy) is that people are free to pursue their lives in the way they see fit, within the bounds of the rule of law. To greatly constrain freedoms through dramatic counter-terror-ist reactions runs the risk of giving the terrorists exactly what they want. A steadfast normality has the potential to deny this objective, and is similar to the logic of 'criminalization' discussed earlier. One of the reasons that this pro-cess caused the furore in the Maze Prison in 1981 and led to the hunger strikes was that prisoners were being denied the special privileges that went along with being essentially political prisoners, such as the right to wear one's own clothes. By being reduced to the level of a 'normal criminal', the allure of ideological rhetoric was deflated.

Aside from this difference in approach, CONTEST also recognizes that a notion of risk and resilience in the face of 'new threats' in the post-Cold War and globalizing world, such as terrorism, mean that a strategy response cannot focus on one front alone. The government says in the latest CONTEST docu-ment that 'we do not believe it is possible to resolve the threats we face simply by arresting and prosecuting more people.'[18] In this way, the current situation *is* different from that during the Northern Ireland 'Troubles' in two

---

[16] HM Government, Home Office, 'CONTEST: The United Kingdom's Strategy for Countering Terrorism' (London: TSO, July 2011), 6.

[17] D. Omand, *Securing the State* (London: Hurst, 2010), 89, 91.

[18] HM Government, n 16, at 11.

important ways. First, there is recognition that the situation cannot be won by the state solely with strong security and intelligence. The change in the Northern Ireland situation was brought about ultimately through negotiation and political dialogue, but, for the IRA, it must surely have been the case, as Bamford observes, that this started to look like a more attractive option when it was clear that the security and intelligence war against the British state was being lost.[19] In the case of the current Al Qaeda-related threat, the situation is structurally different in that it mitigates against the same types of intelligence successes by the state. This is so first because there does not appear to be the same sort of unitary and hierarchical organizational structure in Al Qaeda as there was in the IRA, which could be penetrated with the right sources and informants. Al Qaeda is perhaps as much an idea as an actual organization, although it should be stressed that there is academic disagreement about this point. Marc Sageman, for example, supports this idea of an ideological movement through his 'Leaderless Jihad' concept.[20] Bruce Hoffman, on the other hand, disputes the 'myth of grass-roots terrorism', suggesting that Sageman's thesis is a 'fundamental misreading of the Al Qaeda threat'.[21] Events at the time of writing point in both directions. On the one hand, newspaper reports suggest that the intelligence dividend from the raid on Bin Laden's redoubt in Pakistan is decimating the Al Qaeda organization and causing the US Under Secretary of Defense for Intelligence, Michael Vickers, to talk of the possibility of the 'strategic defeat of Al Qaeda'.[22] If this is true, it suggests that the organization is important.

On the other hand, as I type these words, news is coming in of the arrest of seven individuals in Birmingham as part of a counter-terrorist investigation relating to Islamist extremism.[23] While the outcome of this operation is not yet known, it underlines the fact that multiple investigations into suspect terror groups are ongoing, and are doing so a long way away (in all respects) from Bin Laden's former office in Pakistan. This is the second way in which the security and intelligence fight against Al Qaeda-related terrorism will always struggle to attain the outcomes achieved against the IRA, namely that the scale and geographical spread of the threat is much greater. The IRA was essentially a geographically contained British issue, and had little if any connections to other parts of the world, aside from attempts by the IRA to gain arms and munitions from dealers overseas, and the issue of funding of the movement by Irish diaspora communities, notably in the United States. Al Qaeda and its supporters, on the other hand, are a truly international phenomenon with manifold

---

[19] Bamford, n 13, at 585.

[20] M. Sageman, *Leaderless Jihad: Terror Networks in the Twenty-First Century* (Philadelphia, PA: University of Pennsylvania Press, 2008).

[21] B. Hoffman, 'Review Essay: The Myth of Grass-Roots Terrorism—Why Osama bin Laden Still Matters', *Foreign Affairs*, 87/3 (2008), 134.

[22] C. Lamb, 'Al Qaeda to be smashed apart "within two years"', *Sunday Times*, 18 September 2011, p 27.

[23] 'Seven held in Birmingham anti-terror operation', BBC News, 19 September 2011, available at <http://www.bbc.co.uk/news/uk-14969893> (accessed 19 September 2011).

international connections. In the UK alone, the Director-General of the Security Service (MI5) claimed in 2007 that his service was investigating around 2,000 individuals who 'posed a direct threat to national security and public safety'. This was an increase on the figure mentioned by his predecessor, Eliza Manningham-Buller, a year previously of 1,600 individuals, and reflected a 'steady flow of new recruits to the extremist cause'.[24] If such a scale of targets is accurate, then the size of the task for the state intelligence agencies is very considerable.

Prevent

The second key way in which the current counter-terrorism challenge is different from that presented by the Northern Ireland period is related to this organizational factor, and specifically to the question of the role of ideology. The IRA's underpinning objectives were crucially different from Al Qaeda's. The IRA was fighting for a specific nationalist political goal, with finite boundaries to it. The updated Prevent Strategy of 2011 placed increased emphasis on 'terrorist ideology', noting that:

> We judge that radicalisation is driven by an ideology which sanctions the use of violence; by propagandists for that ideology here and overseas; and by personal vulnerabilities and specific local factors which, for a range of reasons, make that ideology seem both attractive and compelling.[25]

The robust emphasis on the ideological factor was the result of an extensive review of the work in this area following the experience of the years since 2006, when Prevent was first launched as part of the CONTEST Strategy. The Prevent strand of CONTEST, which was articulated as 'Preventing Violent Extremism' (PVE) was led jointly by the Department for Communities and Local Government (DCLG), the Foreign and Commonwealth Office (FCO), and the Home Office. For DCLG, the objective was to focus on 'community cohesion' in breaking down supposed barriers and degrees of alienation between communities. Through a process of prioritization based broadly on the size of the Muslim community in each area, local government was tasked with coordinating a multi-agency process around a local 'Prevent Strategy'. Under this local strategy, depending on the amount of funds allocated to any particular area, money was made available for projects in the local community which were assessed to meet the broad objectives of community cohesion. These objectives usually overlapped locally with those of a Local Authority Agreement (LAA)

---

[24] MI5, 'Intelligence, Counter-Terrorism and Trust: Address to the Society of Editors by the Director General of the Security Service, Jonathan Evans', Society of Editors, 'A Matter of Trust' Conference, Manchester, 5 November 2007, available at <https://www.mi5.gov.uk/output/intelligence-counter-terrorism-and-trust.html> (accessed 17 September 2011).

[25] HM Government, n 7, at 5.

'national indicator' (NI35) entitled 'Building Communities Resilient to Violent Extremism', again allocated to each area depending on the size and nature of its local socio-ethnic picture, and specifically the Muslim component.

For the police in relevant local authorities, Prevent-related action would tend to be fronted by the deployment of resources interfacing with the local community, either in the shape of existing Community and Diversity Officers (CADOs), or, in some areas, in the shape of new and dedicated police staff posts called Prevent Engagement Officers (PEOs). There were also other important processes in some areas, notably the 'Channel Project': a multi-agency forum for raising potential cases of vulnerability to radicalization among the local community and deciding on the best local authority or other agency 'intervention', where appropriate. (This could involve any number of a wide range of actors, from the police to health, education, or criminal justice authorities, to name a few.) The FCO work was mostly concerned with communications activities overseas concerned with Britain's foreign policy and, in some cases, working with foreign partners on counter-radicalization initiatives.

In 2007, an initial tranche of £6 million was allocated to 70 local authorities with a Muslim population of 5 per cent or more (the funding was called the 'Pathfinder' fund), and this was increased in 2008 to a three-year, £45 million fund for qualifying areas[26] within an overall Prevent budget of £140 million.

Right from the start of the programme, a range of problems emerged. Application of the requirements were variable regionally, but in some areas the process engendered considerable friction between the local Muslim community and the local authority. In Reading, a 'PVE Crisis Group' was formed which protested formally about the manner in which the NI35 local authority indicator 'in effect singles out the Muslim community as a problematic community'.[27] Arun Kundnani conducted a detailed report for the Institute of Race Relations which outlined many of the issues.[28] He noted that PVE was structured in such a way that it singled out the Muslim community as being the key community of concern as a whole. He also identified fears in the community that the programme was a front for gathering intelligence on the community; that funding that would previously have been basic community project funding was now linked to 'signing up to' Prevent objectives; and that there was a misguided and slightly sinister attempt underway by government to promote a particular strand of Islam as being 'moderate' and 'mainstream', while certain strands of the faith (primarily non-Sufistic strands) were demonized as being 'extremist'. Ironically, these distinctions were overlooked or not understood where certain

---

[26] P. Thomas, 'Failed and Friendless: The UK's 'Preventing Violent Extremism' Programme', *British Journal of Politics and International Relations*, 12 (2010), 443.

[27] Reading Muslim PVE Crisis Group, 'Letter to Reading Council: Position of the Muslim community in relation to PVE in Reading', 27 October 2008, available at <http://pvecrisisgroup.com/letter-to-reading-local-authority/> (accessed 17 September 2011).

[28] A. Kundnani, *Spooked: How not to prevent violent extremism* (London: Institute of Race Relations, 2009).

groups outwardly signed up to Prevent objectives in order to obtain funding, meaning that, in some cases, exactly the wrong type of groups may have been receiving funding when more moderate elements of the community felt stigmatized and alienated.[29]

At the end of 2009, the House of Commons Communities and Local Government Committee reviewed progress on the programme. Its findings set the stage for the refreshed Prevent Strategy, issued by the Coalition government in 2011, and in particular identified the key difficulty with the programme, namely that counter-terrorism work did not sit comfortably alongside community cohesion work. The report noted that Prevent was 'unlikely ever to be accepted in its existing form by those it is most important to engage'.[30] In addition to problems noted in the Muslim community about being thrust 'into an uncomfortable limelight', the report also identified other 'unintended consequences'.[31] Principle among these was a divisiveness engendered with other minority communities, who felt resentment about special funding going specifically to the Muslim community at what they perceived to be their expense, and discomfort about interfaith dialogue issues having to be framed within the context of extremism and terrorism.[32] Finally, there was a widespread feeling that, in prioritizing Al Qaeda-related extremism, the Prevent programme did not take adequate notice of other types of extremism which could emerge in other communities, such as that relating to the Far Right, or to Northern Irish sectarianism.

On the question of Prevent being seen as a thinly veiled front for spying on the Muslim community, the accusations have been that, by coupling community cohesion projects and activities with a counter-terrorism agenda, the thrust of such work in the community inevitably felt as though it was a way for the authorities to gather data on the community for intelligence purposes. The police were placed in a particularly difficult position in this respect, since they were tasked simultaneously with liaising with the community through such activities as the work of the PEOs, sitting on Channel Project committees and chairing community liaison meetings and committees of various descriptions, and with gathering intelligence on potential counter-terrorism cases and liaising with the Security Service (MI5) in so doing. As many in the British Muslim community will say, as taxpayers, Muslims are no less keen than any other citizen for MI5 and the other intelligence agencies to fulfil their role in catching terrorists and keeping us safe. But they expect this to be an unseen business, and not for it to be undertaken semi-covertly through community cohesion

---

[29] Ibid, 6–7.
[30] House of Commons, Communities and Local Government Committee, 'Preventing Violent Extremism: Sixth Report of Session 2009–2010' (HC65, 16 March 2010), p 3.
[31] Ibid, p 18.
[32] Ibid.

and liaison activities.[33] In some ways these remain a classic dilemma of intelligence-gathering on a subject such as terrorism within a modern liberal democracy, where the distinction between domestic and overseas individuals and activities are distinctly blurred. There is a need to gather intelligence from 'within the community', including situations where members of the community themselves take responsibility for flagging up potentially significant information to the police or to the intelligence agencies. At the same time, no one wants to see a Stalinist situation emerging where neighbour informs on neighbour for the wrong purposes, or where the police start to look like a repressive secret police.

Following a relatively extensive review with a range of stakeholders, the Coalition government eventually issued its 'refreshed' Prevent Strategy in June 2011. The principle points to note about this are, first, that it retained the core principles of Prevent within the CONTEST framework, in the sense that it recognized the continuing need to identify and disrupt processes of violent radicalization where they could be identified, and that this should be central to the overall counter-terrorism strategy.[34] Beyond that, it made the expected change of decoupling counter-terrorism work more clearly from community cohesion work, focusing Prevent itself on the process of people 'becoming terrorists', and leaving the issue of 'wider extremism' to DCLG and local government. This clarifies the position for the police somewhat, and allows them to concentrate on what had previously been seen as their 'core business'.

On the question of stigmatizing Muslim communities, the new strategy does two interesting things. First, it talks more generically about 'violent extremism', and notes that this can emerge from any number of communities and terrorist threat areas, in a way that the strategy had largely failed to do previously. At the same time, it does not shrink from using the term 'Islamist' and 'Islamism' in relation to a political ideology: these terms are mentioned 18 times in the main body of the text of the new strategy, when they had been scrupulously avoided in previous policy documents in this area on the ground that some observers feel they unhelpfully link terrorism with a wider religion. The 2007 DCLG document, 'Preventing Violent Extremism—Winning Hearts and Minds', for example, does not use either of these terms once. The change of rhetoric is partly evidence of the 'muscular liberalism' that Prime Minister Cameron advocated at the Munich Security Conference in February 2011. In this speech, Cameron spoke of the problems of what he described as 'state multiculturalism', which had led to a 'hands-off' situation in which communities could grow apart and become alienated from one another.[35] The political territory here is

---

[33] Interview with various local Muslim community representatives, southern England, May/June 2010.

[34] HM Government, n 7, at 6.

[35] 'PM's speech at Munich Security Conference', Number10.gov, 5 February 2011, available at <http://www.number10.gov.uk/news/pms-speech-at-munich-security-conference/> (accessed 16 September 2011).

dangerous, and some accused the Prime Minister of pandering to xenophobic groups, such as the relatively newly formed pressure group, the English Defence League (EDL).[36] It did not help that, in a curious twist of fate, the EDL happened to have been holding a large rally in Luton on the same day as David Cameron's Munich speech.

Prevent, therefore, continues as a key plank in the UK's counter-terrorism strategy, but with a slightly altered focus. Many of the original elements, and notably the Channel programme for spotting and developing cases of violent radicalization are being retained and built upon, although there are potential question marks over its continued resourcing under new arrangements and general public sector cutbacks. It is fair to say that, in the grand sweep of national security strategizing, CONTEST and Prevent are still relatively new concepts and it is not surprising that they will take some years to refine and embed, especially given their complexity and community sensitivity. One of the key problems with the strategy and particularly with the Prevent strand is the difficulty over monitoring the effectiveness of any actions taken. It is virtually impossible to measure whether a particular intervention or strand of funding ever successfully stops someone from going down a path of violent radicalization, or if they would otherwise have become a terrorist. Despite robust statements to the effect that 'evaluation and performance monitoring have been weak and they must be improved',[37] it is likely that this will remain a particularly difficult thing to achieve in practice.

In the meantime, the UK's ongoing experience of Prevent within the counter-terrorism strategy has highlighted the extraordinarily difficult questions posed by a transnational threat such as terrorism, where the security targets are not only overseas but also deeply embedded within the domestic community. Providing strong security across these dimensions in ways that do not compromise core values in a liberal democracy will continue to be a very difficult balancing act.

Key points

- The UK's current terrorist threat comprises both the old threat of violence from dissident Irish Republican groups, and the newer threat from Al Qaeda-related groups and individuals. JTAC recently reduced the mainland UK's threat level to 'Substantial', but this still represents a heightened risk of a terrorist attack.

---

[36] T. Helm, M. Taylor, and R. Davis, 'David Cameron sparks fury from critics who say attack on multiculturalism has boosted English Defence League', *The Guardian*, 5 February 2011, available at <http://www.guardian.co.uk/politics/2011/feb/05/david-cameron-speech-criticised-edl> (accessed 16 September 2011).

[37] HM Government, n 7, at 9.

- There has been disagreement over how to define terrorism and how to treat it within the state. The UK has occasionally experimented with the 'criminalization' of terrorism, and the Director-General of MI5 at the time of the 2005 London terrorist attacks is strongly of the opinion that this is the right course to take, even with an attack as grandiose as 11 September 2001 in the United States.

- The UK's counter-terrorism strategy is enshrined within CONTEST, launched in 2006. This comprises four strands of activity (the 'four P's'), namely Pursue, Prevent, Protect, and Prepare.

- The Prevent strand, initially launched as Preventing Violent Extremism (PVE), became one of the most important—and most controversial—strands of activity in CONTEST.

- A major review and refresh of Prevent was published under the Coalition government in 2011, which aimed to address the problems that had built up of the confusion between community cohesion work at the local level, and police-led counter-terrorism work. One of the problems that had emerged from this confusion was a feeling in the Muslim community at large that they were being stigmatized.

- At the same time, the Prime Minister has expressed a desire for 'muscular liberalism', which does not shrink from the idea that radical and sometimes religiously-derived ideology is a problem in the counter-terrorism struggle. This is likely to remain an extraordinarily difficult area of national security policy and strategy.

11

Partnerships: EU, UN, NATO, and the 'Special Relationship'

Chance encounters and shifting alliances

On 6 February 2009, the French defence ministry reported that one of its nuclear submarines, *Le Triomphant*, had collided with a 'submerged object' in the mid-Atlantic. It transpired shortly afterwards that the object in question was in fact *HMS Vanguard*, one of Britain's nuclear submarines. Both vessels limped back to their respective bases, carrying minor injuries and assertions from both defence ministries that there had been 'no danger of a nuclear incident'.[1]

This chance and clumsy encounter in the middle of the world's second largest ocean presaged a more developed and concrete defence relationship between Britain and France, unveiled in late 2010, which goes much further forward than any previous agreement between the two European neighbours. This development has proved to be one of the most substantial and controversial elements of the latest defence review in Britain, and marks a significant new strategic direction in national security thinking. In particular, it underlines the central importance of partnerships in twenty-first century national security strategizing, and, perhaps, a subtle rebalancing of the priority relationships for both France and the UK.

The National Security Strategy (NSS) explains the rationale in terms of the need to place the UK's national interests within an 'international context'.[2] This means thinking about national security strategy in relation to 'key alliances', headed by that with the United States, and closely followed by NATO and the

---

[1] 'Nuclear subs collide in Atlantic', BBC News, 16 February 2009, available at <http://news.bbc.co.uk/1/hi/7892294.stm> (accessed 16 September 2011).

[2] HM Government, 'A Strong Britain in an Age of Uncertainty: The National Security Strategy' (London: TSO, October 2010), 10.

'vital partnership in the European Union'.[3] Beyond this triumvirate, however, the strategy notes that the 'relative weight of economic activity around the world is shifting' from Europe and the industrialized world towards Asia, Latin America, and the Gulf.[4] This means that the UK has 'strategic and economic imperatives to build closer ties with the new economic powers'.[5] The G20 is becoming a more significant economic forum than the G8, but over and above active membership in international fora, the UK must also 'strengthen our network of bilateral ties with new partners as well as traditional allies, recognising that many emerging powers put a premium on direct relationships.'[6]

In this way, the UK is setting forth a strategy on partnerships which aims to be flexible and ready for future developments, using the barometer of 'national interests' to evolve and reappraise existing partnerships while being open to developing new relationships with emerging powers. This is another way in which Britain, under this strategic line, sees itself as an outward-looking world power within the emerging multilateral environment, not only in terms of projecting values and influence in an interventionist manner, but also in terms of developing new diplomatic and economic relationships. Some of those new relationships may have their complications politically, as is the case with China and Russia for example, or indeed with certain relationships forged for counter-terrorism purposes, but what the strategy is stressing is that Britain does not want to cut itself off from the world or to be dogmatic about such relationships.

The 'special relationship'

There is some continuity in the strategy—the United States, NATO, and the EU are very much at the top of the list—while at the same time there are hints that such relationships should not necessarily be considered as set in stone. Nowhere is this more the case than in the relationship with the United States, which has often been described in history as the 'special relationship', but which has undergone a complex reappraisal with recent changes of government on both sides of the Atlantic. As the NSS notes, 'our relationship with the US is and will remain central but we must expect it to evolve'.[7] This process of evolution is an oblique reference to the way in which the incoming Conservative-led government has tackled the delicate issue of the UK's apparent change in relationship with the United States, particularly since the rise to power of President Obama.

---

[3] Ibid.
[4] Ibid, 15.
[5] Ibid.
[6] Ibid.
[7] Ibid.

Here, two subtle shifts have been perceived to have happened. First, Obama made it clear in his early months in power that Europe was less of a priority in his foreign policy than other parts of the world. Bettiza posed the question of whether the relationship in the 'age of Obama' was 'drifting or rifting'.[8] Issues such as Iran, the Middle East, and the relationship with China took centre stage in the President's early diplomatic priority list (as did a host of domestic problems, such as the faltering economy). In the UK, which historically feels very sensitive about its 'special relationship' with the United States, the first meeting between Obama and the Prime Minister at the time, Gordon Brown, was a brief discussion in the kitchen of the UN building in New York: a situation which elements of the UK press interpreted as showing that the UK–US relationship was at its 'lowest ebb for nearly 20 years'.[9]

At the same time, there is a strand in British politics which feels that Britain has, on occasion, been too passive in its relationship with the United States. Tony Blair's decision to take Britain into the Iraq War alongside the United States was lambasted by many in the media and the public, some elements of the former of which regularly portrayed Blair as 'Bush's poodle'. The opposition Conservatives at the time, not surprisingly, shared this view and have made it an element of their strategizing on international partnerships. The incoming Conservative Foreign Secretary, William Hague, has recast the relationship as 'solid, not slavish', and pointed out that the UK has and will continue to criticize some elements of US foreign policy where it feels it appropriate to do so.[10] Part of the rationale for this political line is the warning from the coalition partner in government, the Liberal Democrats, of the 'dangers of a subservient relationship with the US'.[11] This is a delicate political balancing act within the Coalition government, but it will also strike chords with many in the electorate. At the same time, it makes logical sense, as Lindley-French observes, that 'there can be no romantic or nostalgic attachment to past structure and relationships in the pursuit of influence'.[12] National interests will be a moveable feast to a certain extent, much as the world itself is shifting and evolving in multipolar directions.

---

[8] G. Bettiza, 'Drifting or Rifting? America and Europe in the Age of Obama', *LSE Ideas, Ideas Today* (23 April 2010), 13.

[9] A. Porter, 'Barack Obama rebuffs Gordon Brown as "special relationship" sinks to new low', *The Telegraph*, 23 September 2009, available at <http://www.telegraph.co.uk/news/politics/gordon-brown/6224813/Barack-Obama-rebuffs-Gordon-Brown-as-special-relationship-sinks-to-new-low.html> (accessed 16 November 2010).

[10] C. McGreal, 'William Hague says Britain will pursue "solid not slavish" relationship with the US', *The Guardian*, 14 May 2010, available at <http://www.guardian.co.uk/politics/2010/may/14/hague-uk-us-clinton-afghanistan> (accessed 15 September 2011).

[11] Ibid.

[12] J. Lindley-French, 'Britain and France: A Dialogue of Decline?', Chatham House, International Security Programme Paper ISP PP 2010/02, September 2010, p 2.

Existing alliances

With all that said, it should be stressed that the position of the United States in the UK's table of strategic interests is likely to remain firmly at number one for the foreseeable future. The extraordinarily close security relationship between the two countries, particularly since the Second World War and epitomized by such agreements as the UKUSA agreement on intelligence sharing, signed in 1946,[13] is a firm bedrock to the UK's national security architecture in intelligence, security, and defence spheres. There is no prospect of this being seriously unravelled in the immediate future. In its section on 'Alliances and Partnerships', the Strategic Defence and Security Review (SDSR) identifies five 'priorities for international engagement', in which the 'pre-eminent defence and security relationship with the US' is number one.[14] The other priorities are identified as 'new models of practical bilateral' relationships with various allies and partners; an 'effective and reformed UN'; continued involvement with NATO as the 'bedrock of our defence'; and an 'outward-facing European Union that promotes security and prosperity'.[15]

A number of interesting points are raised by this list in terms of what it tells us about the UK's proposed international strategy on national security. Aside from the continued importance of the United States despite the rocks in the road of the relationship, there is specific reference to 'bilateral' relationships, which means that the UK sees potentially more merit in these than in multinational organizations. One of the most important of these bilateral relationships is emerging in the direction of France, as I will discuss below. Aside from such relationships, the EU itself, as an organizational entity, is seen as something which can work in such areas as conflict resolution, peacekeeping, and post-conflict reconstruction, but not necessarily in the area of warfighting. This reflects the UK's general distrust of the European Security and Defence Policy (ESDP), which aims to develop a European defence capability largely independent of the United States, and on which European neighbours such as France and (to a lesser extent) Germany have been very keen in the past.

In the place of such an independent European defence capability, the UK clearly places high and continued trust in NATO, the formation of which was introduced at the beginning of this book. In many ways, as Krahmann identifies, NATO has somewhat confounded the predictions of security analysts, who foresaw that a Cold War and essentially 'Realist' defence organization that was structured around the notion of state-on-state conflict, would naturally wither

---

[13] Details of the agreement were recently released by the National Archives: see R. Norton-Taylor, 'Not so secret: deal at the heart of UK-USA intelligence', *The Guardian*, 25 June 2010, available at <http://www.guardian.co.uk/world/2010/jun/25/intelligence-deal-uk-us-released> (accessed 16 May 2011).

[14] HM Government, 'Securing Britain in an Age of Uncertainty: The Strategic Defence and Security Review' (London: TSO, October 2010), 59.

[15] Ibid.

away in the re-ordered post-Cold War environment of transnational threats, the proliferation of non-state actors, and the blurring of civil and military boundaries.[16] Instead, NATO has continued to be involved in a number of major military operations, from the Balkans to Afghanistan and Libya, not to mention specific roles in numerous other situations, such as in Iraq, and in counter-piracy patrols off the Horn of Africa. These operations, starting with NATO's position at the centre of the International Security Assistance Force (ISAF) force in Afghanistan, have taken the organization into military activities outside Europe for the first time, and thus started to redefine its parameters.

Despite these activities, there has clearly been a growing need to redefine NATO's role following the end of the Cold War, how it can re-orient its activities, and whether it is still the right forum in which to undertake collective Euro-Atlantic defence. There have also been complex questions about how far it can or should expand its borders.

The 9/11 attacks in the United States caused Article 5 of the NATO Treaty to be invoked, whereby an attack on one member is seen as an attack on the whole alliance and should prompt a subsequently appropriate collective response. This provided the philosophical mandate for offensive operations in Afghanistan against Al Qaeda and its Taliban hosts, but it has raised a question mark about other means by which the alliance is best suited to respond to a threat such as international terrorism. One of the activities which symbolizes the conceptual difficulties is the maritime operation in the Mediterranean region, called Operation Active Endeavour (OAE). This operation involves collective naval patrols in the Mediterranean designed to detect and deter maritime terrorism activities. NATO itself describes OAE as 'a vivid example of the added value that NATO can bring to the complex, global fight against terrorism',[17] and there is no doubt some deterrent value in the operation's activities in boarding vessels and establishing multilateral information-exchange networks. But difficult questions have to be asked about how effective such a deterrence has been, and whether the considerable cost of maintaining a fleet of highly capable military vessels designed for naval warfare and sailing them around the Mediterranean is a cost-effective approach to the threat in hand.

Of course, such questions are virtually impossible to answer, and no criticism is implied of an organization which found itself thrown into a new threat dynamic in which much of the old rule book needed to be thrown away. Some action is probably better than none. But NATO itself has recognized the need to reappraise its position. The new 'Strategic Concept' emerged from the NATO Lisbon Summit in November 2010, around the same time as the UK's new NSS. Described as NATO's 'roadmap for the next ten years', the declaration re-affirmed the alliance's commitment to work together for collective

---

[16] E. Krahmann, 'Conceptualizing Security Governance', *Cooperation and Conflict*, 38/5 (2003), 7.
[17] NATO, Allied Command Operations, 'Operation Active Endeavour', available at <http://www.aco.nato.int/page1367412.aspx> (accessed 16 September 2011).

Euro-Atlantic defence 'in a changing world, against new threats, with new capabilities and new partners'.[18] The Strategic Concept reaffirms the three core NATO objectives of collective defence, crisis management, and cooperative security. While recognizing the continued need for 'conventional' military capabilities and threat assessments (within which the nuclear deterrent is retained), it also recognizes the emergence of new security threats, including the proliferation of weapons of mass destruction (WMDs), terrorism, threats such as organized crime and extremism arising from unstable states, cyber threats, and security problems arising from environmental issues.[19] In this way, the Strategic Concept mirrors contemporary national security assessments across the industrialized world, not least the UK's NSS, in firmly securitizing the range of post-Cold War 'new threat' issues. It also takes these new threats very seriously. In the cyber domain, for example, the United States has urged the alliance to consider cyber attacks on NATO member states as akin to military attacks, necessitating the collective response, up to and including military action.[20] Jamie Shea, the NATO Deputy Assistant Secretary General, sees it as a 'powerful political signal', that NATO should consider cyber attacks as 'just as unacceptable as an attack by tanks or aircraft'.[21]

Significantly, the Strategic Concept also stresses the importance of interfacing with other multinational organizations, and particularly the EU and UN, while simultaneously having an 'open door' policy to new members which share the liberal democratic values of the NATO countries and meet its requirements.[22] One of the trickiest issues here is the question of Russia, and the former Soviet Union's sphere of influence in Central and Eastern Europe. While the Strategic Concept stresses that 'NATO poses no threat to Russia', and that cooperation between the two will create a 'common space of peace, stability and security',[23] there is no doubt that a great deal of mutual suspicion still exists between the two foes. Shevtsova explores the fluctuating official opinions of Russia towards NATO expansion into the former Soviet territory, and the manner in which an apparent initial ambivalence has gradually become more hostile.[24] Many analysts of the Russia–Georgia war of 2008, such as Ronald Asmus, saw the seeds of

---

[18] NATO, 'Strategic Concept for the Defence and Security of the Members of the North Atlantic Treaty Organisation, Adopted by Heads of State and Government in Lisbon: Active Engagement, Modern Defence', available at <http://www.nato.int/lisbon2010/strategic-concept-2010-eng.pdf> (accessed 16 September 2011).

[19] Ibid.

[20] NATO, 'NATO Chronicles: Fighting the Invisible Enemy'. NATO Channel TV, 20 September 2011.

[21] Ibid.

[22] NATO Strategic Concept, n 18.

[23] Ibid.

[24] L.F. Shevtsova, *Lonely Power* (Washington DC: Carnegie Endowment for International Peace, 2010), 141.

the conflict as being partly to be found in Georgia's interest in accession to NATO.[25]

A NATO–Russia dialogue continues, however, aiming to build on areas of shared interest such as counter-terrorism. From the UK's point of view, continued dialogue and engagement with Russia is seen as important to national security strategy, particularly in such areas as trade and competition, and energy security, recognizing that Russia is now the world's largest exporter of oil and gas, and that Europe as a whole is the largest importer of Russian gas.[26] On his visit to Russia in September 2011, Prime Minister Cameron talked of a desire for 'a new approach based on cooperation' between the two countries.[27] He made this statement while recognizing that relations had been tense for some years, and that his visit to Moscow was the first by a British Prime Minister since 2005, the year before the Russian dissident, Alexandr Litvinenko, was murdered in London by radioactive poisoning. The incident had led to the expulsion of the Russian intelligence agency, the FSB, from London, along with a number of diplomats. Thus, the UK recognizes that its international role is one of pragmatism, where certain alliances and partnerships need to be pursued despite serious differences in certain values and political strategies. This applies as much to China as it does to Russia. It means UK national security strategy in this particular area is very much in line with NATO's new principle of broadening and deepening its international connections and relationships beyond the traditional Cold War Euro-Atlantic heartland.

NATO will also be conducting a detailed review of its operation in Libya, which appeared to have been instrumental in facilitating a victory for the rebel uprising against Colonel Gaddafi's regime. Not surprisingly or unreasonably, NATO and many of its supporters have seen Operation Unified Protector in Libya not only as a great success, but as an encouraging model for the alliance's strategy in the twenty-first century. NATO Secretary General, Anders Fogh Rasmussen, claimed that the lessons learned from the Libya operation were almost all positive, emphasizing how the crisis had demonstrated the alliance's flexibility, openness (in working in tandem with partners in the Middle East) and strength.[28] He stressed how the operation had been largely led in the field by the Europeans and Canada, countering to some extent the accusations made by outgoing US Secretary of Defense, Robert Gates, earlier in 2011, in which he

---

[25] R. Asmus, *A Little War that Shook the World: Georgia, Russia and the Future of the West* (New York: Palgrave Macmillan, 2010), 5–6.

[26] S. Paltesev, 'Russia's Natural Gas Export Potential up to 2050', MIT Center for Energy and Environmental Policy Research, CEEPR WP 2011–12, July 2011, p 2.

[27] 'PM's speech in Moscow', Number10.gov, 12 September 2011, available at <http://www.number10.gov.uk/news/pms-speech-in-moscow/> (accessed 13 September 2011).

[28] 'Monthly press briefing by NATO Secretary General Anders Fogh Rasmussen', NATO, 5 September 2011, available at <http://www.nato.int/cps/en/natolive/opinions_77640.htm> (accessed 16 September 2011).

predicted a 'dim if not dismal future' for the alliance and accused the European allies of complacency over international security.[29]

However, amidst the jubilation and congratulation in Europe, few are blind to the difficulties that were highlighted by the Libyan operation. RUSI Director General, Michael Clarke, describes the victory in Libya as a 'curious' one, and that the operation created 'an image of NATO's limitations rather than its power'.[30] Despite the European and Canadian lead, most of the air sorties were reliant on US Suppression of Electronic Air Defence (SEAD) capabilities backing up the fighter jets, and US reconnaissance was extensive throughout the operation.[31] The resource strain on Britain and France was considerable, and it is doubtful whether both could have sustained the same level of intensity of operations for a much longer. Within the alliance, some countries prohibited their aircraft from flying attack missions (Spain and Turkey), and Germany not only did not take part, but criticized the whole venture throughout.[32] So, the final verdict is a mixture of satisfaction and relief at what appears to have been an ultimately successful operation, tempered with a great deal of reflection about whether, how, and to what extent the NATO alliance can undertake similar types of military operations in the future.

There is also a particular question for the UN, which, as a 2004 update to the Brahimi Report acknowledged, saw the number of personnel it deployed in peacekeeping missions overseas drop by about 50 per cent since the mid-1990s to the immediate post-9/11 period.[33] The reasons for this are partly ascribed to a changed threat perception post-9/11 which sees international operations as more complex and lethal, but also that unilateral and NATO-led interventions of a more military nature have been consuming resources which might otherwise be used on UN-led peacekeeping operations. While operations in Iraq have largely ceased and those in Afghanistan will also be scaled back, defence cuts across the industrialized world may pose a similar constraint on UN-led operations.

With respect to the Libya operation, NATO sees itself (as does the EU) as an 'implementer' of UN resolutions.[34] This has not always been the case, of course. In 1999, for example, vetoes in the UN Security Council by China and Russia

---

[29] I. Traynor, 'US defence chief blasts Europe over NATO', *The Guardian*, 10 June 2011, available at <http://www.guardian.co.uk/world/2011/jun/10/nato-dismal-future-pentagon-chief> (accessed 16 September 2011).

[30] M. Clarke, 'Curious victory for NATO in Libya', RUSI, Analysis, Commentary, 2011, available at <http://www.rusi.org/analysis/commentary/ref:C4E53CF030EB3B/> (accessed 16 September 2011).

[31] Ibid.

[32] Ibid.

[33] T. Thardy, 'The Brahimi Report: Four years on. Proceedings of a workshop held at the Geneva Centre for Security Policy', Geneva, Centre for Security Policy (GCSP), p 4.

[34] 'NATO Secretary-General statement on NAC decision to extend Libya mission', NATO, 21 September 2011, available at <http://www.nato.int/cps/en/natolive/news_78355.htm> (accessed 22 September 2011).

over authorization for military force to back-up UN condemnations of Serbia for crimes of humanity against the Kosovar people, led to NATO deciding to intervene militarily anyway, albeit on 'expressly humanitarian' grounds.[35] Such a situation arising in the future cannot be ruled out. However, Jones sees grounds for optimism for the role of the UN, particularly in peacekeeping operations, noting that 'it is the only organisation through which the forces of the permanent five nations (P5), and all the major powers, including the rising and regional powers, can jointly participate in providing stability.'[36] The renewed commitments by the Obama administration to supporting peacekeeping, and China's growing commitment to operations, both augur well for the UN as a vehicle on this front.[37]

The UK, meanwhile, has expressed strategic goals in making the UN more 'effective and reformed'. In particular, there is recognition of—and support for—the notion that the Security Council ought better to represent the changing power balances in the increasingly multilateral world, which means supporting candidacies for seats on the Council by such countries as India and Brazil. This goal of enlargement is shared by France, partly, suggests Patrick, to forestall notions of combining the two European members of the Security Council into a single EU seat.[38] There is a strategic objective here which fits with Britain's (and France's) continued desire to remain at the 'top table' of international diplomacy and decision-making, as discussed in Chapter 8.

Europe, and France

On the EU front, the politics are complex for Britain. Generally, the UK has been keen to broaden the EU, in terms of expanding its membership, rather than deepening it, in terms of embedding the EU's centralized power structures and institutions. In this way, the UK is a supporter of Turkey's accession to the EU, for example.[39] Such sentiments are also reflected in Britain's stance on defence capability. The SDSR stresses that the UK will 'work to persuade other member states to direct effort and resources towards improved national military and civilian capabilities, rather than institution building and bureaucracy.'[40] From a national security perspective, the UK sees the EU's strengths as being in such areas as peacekeeping, humanitarian, and post-conflict reconstruction activities.

---

[35] N. Wheeler, 'Introduction: The Political and Moral Limits of Western Military Intervention to Protect Civilians in Danger', *Contemporary Security Policy*, 22/3 (2001), 3–4.

[36] B. Jones, 'Peacekeeping in Crisis?', *RUSI Journal*, 154/5 (2009), 82–3.

[37] Ibid, 83.

[38] S.M. Patrick, 'Security Council reform in sight?', Council on Foreign Relations, 7 July 2011, available at <http://blogs.cfr.org/patrick/2011/07/07/security-council-reform-in-sight/> (accessed 16 September 2011).

[39] SDSR, n 14, at 62.

[40] Ibid, 63.

Additional areas of focus on which the UK would like the EU to concentrate include border security, terrorist finance-tracking, and counter-drugs work.[41]

In this way, the UK sees the EU's competencies as being situated more towards the policing end of the civil–military spectrum, while the military lead should sit with NATO. Such humanitarian and policing 'Petersberg tasks',[42] as they are known, sit well alongside the 'soft power' capabilities of the EU, represented by diplomatic effort and the occasional application of large amounts of money in aid and grants. As Toje recalled, the former EU Council of Ministers Director General, Robert Cooper, had once characterized the desired policy of the EU to be 'speak softly and carry a big carrot'.[43] In this way, the EU would play to its strengths and not trespass on NATO's turf.

The European nation with whom this British approach to the EU's foreign policy objectives has most been at odds, is France. Under De Gaulle, France formally left NATO's Integrated Military Command structure in 1966, following the aftermath of the Suez crisis in which France took a different strategic route from the UK in deciding to develop a defence capability independent from the United States. With the EU Council of Cologne in 1999, the ESDP was launched, and this fitted with France's aspirations for an independent European capability. The Helsinki Council six months later, with strong French backing, called for the formation of a European Rapid Reaction Force (ERRF), which could undertake quick reaction military interventions and post-conflict reconstruction operations. However, ten years later, Lindley-French argues that the ESDP (which became the Common Security and Defence Policy (CSDP) at the Lisbon Council in 2009) and the Helsinki Declaration have palpably failed to make any significant progress on the original aspirations.[44] In 2009, President Sarkozy reversed the trend and agreed to take France back into NATO's integrated command structure, and 2011 found Britain and France operating side-by-side in an offensive NATO military operation in Libya.

One of the most important and much-analysed aspects of the UK's security and defence review at the end of 2010 was the announcement of a major bilateral Franco-British defence agreement, which, Gomis argues, is much more ambitious than, and distinctive from, any previous agreement, such as the St Malo accord of 1998.[45] At the core of the agreement, announced on 2 November 2010, is an unprecedented level of naval integration, whereby each nation agreed to contribute to a common force one aircraft carrier on which to station

---

[41] Ibid.

[42] Derived from the 1992 Western European Union (WEU) Petersberg Declaration, which forged an agreement between the WEU and the EU on the provision of military forces for humanitarian missions.

[43] A. Toje, 'The Consensus-Expectations Gap: Explaining Europe's Ineffective Foreign Policy', *Security Dialogue*, 39/1 (2008), 138.

[44] J. Lindley-French, 'Britain and France: A Dialogue of Decline?', Chatham House, International Security Programme Paper ISP PP 2010/02, September 2010, p 20.

[45] B. Gomis, 'Franco-British Defence and Security Treaties: Entente while it lasts?', Chatham House, Programme Paper ISP PP 2001/01, March 2011, p 5.

each other's planes (although Britain would not have any immediately compatible planes on the completion of its new aircraft carrier in 2020), and sharing in their naval protection. There was also an agreement to create a Combined Joint Expeditionary Force (CJEF), combining two brigades of 5,000 personnel from each country, which could be deployed in a rapid-reaction manner either under NATO or bilaterally.[46] Additionally, agreement was struck on defence industry and research and development collaboration; traditionally areas of great national sensitivity. In a second treaty, both nations agreed to work together on developing and testing their respective nuclear capabilities, which, argues Gomis, represents a 'historic leap forward in Franco-British relations'.[47]

The politics around these historic agreements are not uncomplicated on either side of the Channel. In both countries, the battle of the narratives could be seen as one of national prestige versus pragmatism. In the UK, the political right within David Cameron's Conservative Party are distrustful of France's longer term intentions, seeing them as another method of achieving the cherished goal of ESDP through a different route.[48] David Cameron was at pains to point out that the agreement would not 'lead to [some] sort of European armies',[49] but detractors on the political right are likely to continue to watch developments with some unease, worried about a situation in which 'British troops could take orders from a Frenchman'.[50] The pragmatists in both countries, meanwhile, share De Durand's view that this is an agreement forged through economic necessity, and, as such, makes perfect sense. 'If nothing is done', he argues, 'British and French military capabilities will rapidly diminish beyond repair, both in terms of overall volume and critical capabilities.'[51]

Counter-terrorism

Beyond the purely military sphere, the 9/11 attacks and subsequent sharply increased focus on counter-terrorism, have led most countries in the industrialized world greatly to expand the number and depth of relationships they have with foreign security and intelligence agencies. The difficulties and political risks of intelligence and security relationships with certain countries have always existed to a certain extent, but there is no doubt that the advent of the 'War on Terror' has changed the dynamics and brought many of these

---

[46] Ibid.

[47] Ibid, p 6.

[48] Ibid, pp 7–8.

[49] J. Kirkup, 'British combat troops to come under French command', *The Telegraph*, 2 November 2010, available at <http://www.telegraph.co.uk/news/uknews/defence/8103057/British-combat-troops-to-come-under-French-command.html> (accessed 16 September 2011).

[50] Ibid.

[51] E. De Durand, 'Entente or Oblivion: Franco-British Defence Co-operation' in M. Codner and M. Clarke (eds), *A Question of Security: The British Defence Review in an Age of Austerity* (London: I.B. Tauris, 2011), 92.

difficulties into sharper focus. As Lefebvre observed, the immediate impact of 9/11 meant that NATO allies found themselves conducting intelligence-exchange conversations with such unlikely bedfellows as the Russians, Chinese, Pakistanis, and Libyans,[52] most of whom could accurately have been described as adversaries just a short time before. More importantly, many of these countries posed serious questions of the degree to which they respected the human rights of detainees.

As Reveron noted:

> the current counterterrorism strategy requires cooperation of all interested states, no matter how distasteful they may be. . . . The challenge is to extract useful information from these foreign intelligence services without becoming tainted by their tactics.[53]

The issue is the much-discussed paradox of 'dirty hands' in politics.[54] Such issues become more difficult in a situation of conflict, counter-terrorism. or counter-insurgency, where considerations such as the rights and wrongs of using torture to extract confessions from potential terrorists begin to raise their heads.

The NSS attempts to grapple with the question of the application of values and standards when dealing with overseas partners in counter-terrorism relationships. Under the heading 'National Security and British Values', the strategy states that:

> Protecting our security requires us to work with countries who do not share our values and standards of criminal justice. In working with them to protect our country from terrorist attacks and other threats we do not compromise on our values. . . . As the Foreign Secretary has said, 'we cannot achieve long-term security and prosperity unless we uphold our values.'[55]

This statement at once recognizes the need to work with states that 'do not share our values and standards of criminal justice', while also stating that there can be no compromise on core values. The somewhat unsatisfactory instrument that has been used to tackle this problem politically has been that of 'Diplomatic Assurances', under which a partner country will pledge to uphold human rights in dealing with shared detainees. In the case of Afghanistan, for example, this process has been represented in part by an 'exchange of letters' undertaken in 2007 between a coalition of NATO members comprising the United States, Canada, the UK, the Netherlands, Norway, and Denmark, and the Afghan government on the question of detainee transfers.[56] The letters provide for officials

---

[52] S. Lefebvre, 'The Difficulties and Dilemmas of International Intelligence Cooperation', *International Journal of Intelligence and Counterintelligence*, 16/4 (2003), 528.

[53] S. Reveron, 'Old Allies, New Friends: Intelligence-Sharing in the War on Terror', *Orbis* (Summer 2006), 458.

[54] M. Walzer, 'Political Action: The Problem of Dirty Hands', *Philosophy and Public Affairs*, 2/2 (1973), 161.

[55] NSS, n 1, at 23.

[56] 'US Monitoring of Detainee Transfers in Afghanistan: International Standards and Lessons from the UK and Canada', Human Rights Institute, Columbia Law School, December 2010, p 6.

to have access to Afghan detention facilities, to interview transferees in private if required, and for the same privileges to be accorded to the International Committee of the Red Cross, UN human rights bodies, and the Afghanistan Independent Human Rights Commission (AIHRC). Such an agreement has taken on an extra impetus in the light of a number of reports alleging very serious human rights abuses in the detention facilities of the Afghan national intelligence agency, the National Directorate of Security (NDS), including torture and extra-judicial killings.[57] The Afghan government pledged that the NDS would issue instructions to all regional offices informing them of these agreed procedures.[58] It was a breakdown in this agreement in early 2009 which led to the UK military to join the Canadians in placing a temporary freeze on all transfers of detainees to the NDS.

Similar diplomatic assurances have been obtained with a number of other partner countries with whom the West is working on counter-terrorism intelligence cooperation. Human rights organizations have been scathing about the utility of such diplomatic instruments. In its 2005 report 'Diplomatic assurances no safeguard against torture', Human Rights Watch claimed that states striking such diplomatic agreements with partner countries with a history of systematic torture of detainees 'are either engaging in wishful thinking or using the assurances as a figleaf to cover their complicity in torture and their role in the erosion of the international norm against torture.'[59] The report went on to pronounce that the practice of diplomatic assurances 'should stop'.[60] Amnesty International echoed this sentiment in noting that 'the best way to prevent torture is to refuse to send people to places where they risk being harmed'.[61] In the case of the 2011 NATO operation against Libya, some of the gloss came off for the UK, with allegations made by a senior Libyan rebel leader, Abdul Hakim Belhaj, that he was tortured by the Libyan authorities, with the knowledge of Britain's MI6 intelligence agency, after he was detained and rendered out of Thailand in 2004 due to his purported connections with the Islamist group LIFG (Libyan Islamic Fighters Group).[62]

Such embarrassing allegations will feed into an official enquiry in the UK, to be conducted by Sir Peter Gibson, called the Detainee Inquiry. The problems

---

[57] See eg A. Prasow, 'Afghan Torture is no Secret', Human Rights Watch, 4 May 2010, available at <http://www.hrw.org/en/news/2010/05/04/afghan-torture-no-secret> (accessed 13 June 2011).

[58] Human Rights Institute, n 56, at 7.

[59] 'Still at Risk: Diplomatic Assurances no Safeguard against Torture', *Human Rights Watch*, 17/4(D) (2005), 3.

[60] Ibid.

[61] 'Europe must halt unreliable "diplomatic assurances" that risk torture', Amnesty International, 12 April 2010, available at <http://www.amnesty.org/en/news-and-updates/report/europe-must-halt-unreliable-diplomatic-assurances-risk-torture-2010-04-12> (accessed 13 June 2011).

[62] M. Chulov, 'MI6 knew I was tortured, says Libyan rebel leader', *The Guardian*, 5 September 2011, available at <http://www.guardian.co.uk/world/2011/sep/05/abdul-hakim-belhaj-libya-mi6-torture> (accessed 16 September 2011).

underline the difficulty of articulating a strategy that stresses a 'firm commitment to human rights, justice and the rule of law',[63] while dealing with the daily realities of striking pragmatic and effective relationships with foreign partners, whether they be large and strategic relationships with the likes of Russia or China, or tactical relationships with the likes of the Afghan national intelligence agency. In both cases there will be constant pitfalls, which will allow detractors both at home and abroad to pick holes in the strategy, and for there to be substantial damage to Britain's perceived standing in the world.

Key points

- Britain's defence treaties with France signed in November 2010 may represent a new approach to bilateral defence strategy.
- The 'special relationship' with the United States has hit some bumps in the road, and many in the UK government have expressed a desire for the relationship to become close but not 'slavish'. The United States will, however, remain very much the pre-eminent defence partnership for the UK for the foreseeable future.
- The UK sees NATO as the most important defence coalition, linked to the UN's decisions. The new 2010 NATO Strategic Concept promises to re-orient the alliance towards the new threat picture. The EU is also seen as important, but much more in the area of peacekeeping and conflict resolution, and in the use of 'soft power' to tackle foreign policy issues. The UK maintains a position of 'broader not deeper' in the EU.
- Bilateral relationships with countries such as Russia and China are seen as important, if politically tricky. The UK is also keen to widen the UN Security Council to newer powers, notably India and Brazil. The new defence relationship with France goes further than any previous agreement and will be an interesting test politically and operationally for both countries.
- International counter-terrorism work has caused the UK to work closely with a wider range of partners in the security and intelligence field, some of which are posing grave questions in the area of adherence to human rights. The forthcoming Gibson Inquiry will examine allegations of complicity in torture of terrorist detainees by foreign partner agencies.

---

[63] NSS, n 1, at 10.

12

Conclusions

At the end of September 2011, the British Prime Minister, David Cameron, made his inaugural speech to the UN General Assembly in New York. Buoyed by the apparent victory of the rebel uprising in Libya, in which NATO had played an important role, Cameron took the UN to task. The Arab Spring showed that 'the UN needs a new way of working', he claimed. 'Because the Arab Spring is a massive opportunity to spread peace, prosperity, democracy and vitally security, but only if we really seize it.'[1] He noted that, in the case of Libya, the international community had shown a 'will to act', which had prevented Benghazi from becoming another case in the 'painful roll call of massacres the world failed to prevent', such as Srebrenica in Bosnia, and Rwanda.[2] He also took the opportunity to lambast President Ahmadinejad of Iran, who had preceded him in speaking at the meeting, accusing the Iranian President of presiding over a system where they 'violently prevent demonstrations and detain and torture those who argue for a better future'.[3]

This was a robustly made statement about the imperative of interventionism in the modern world, backed by the international community and working through the UN. The need was identified as spreading freedom and democracy where there was tyranny, although Cameron noted that 'we should not be trying to impose Western values or a single template. . . . Democracy is a process, not an event.'[4] Inevitably, the British press has interpreted Cameron's speech as akin to Tony Blair's Chicago speech of 1999, delivered during the height of the military campaign over Kosovo, which was interpreted at the time as delivering a new 'Blair doctrine' of humanitarian interventionism backed by

---

[1] 'Prime Minister's first speech to the UN General Assembly', Number10.gov, 22 September 2011, available at <http://www.number10.gov.uk/news/pm-speech-to-unga/> (accessed 23 September 2011).

[2] Ibid.

[3] Ibid.

[4] Ibid.

force, under a NATO lead.[5] Cameron's aides have tried to distance him from such a notion, stressing that 'this is not a doctrine', but many are drawing parallels with the late 1990s and a time when Britain asserted itself within a NATO umbrella as a robustly interventionist force in the world.[6]

The questions for the UK in 2011 were slightly different, however, since the Libya intervention came on the back of one of the most substantial and controversial defence and security reviews for many years. The two key questions were: first, what sort of country Britain wished to be within the international community and, secondly, whether it had the resources and the will to be able effectively to take an interventionist line given the extent of the cuts and restructuring being undertaken in the defence budget, and the general economic climate.

A paper for the Henry Jackson Society, by Bernard Jenkin MP and George Grant, called 'The Tipping Point',[7] stresses that this is a strategic moment for the UK of the utmost seriousness. It suggests that the UK is currently at a fork in the road, where it must decide whether it wishes to remain a 'global power with a global role', or 'just another European country with only a regional one'.[8] The danger arising from the National Security Strategy (NSS) and Strategic Defence and Security Review (SDSR) process in 2010, it suggests, is that the British government wishes to be the former, while the reductions in its military capability consign it in reality to the latter. This is a much repeated argument in Britain today, and the most frequent criticism levelled at the NSS and SDSR outcome, especially from some senior members of the military who are smarting at the degree of defence cuts. We saw in Chapter 8 how the head of the navy had invoked at the beginning of 2010 what might be called the 'Falklands factor' in the debate, noting that the war with Argentina in 1982 was the classic 'strategic shock' that necessitated a strong military response using heavy naval and air force capabilities, in addition to ground troops. 'The Tipping Point' expands on this example, suggesting that the Falklands exemplifies many of the issues on the critical side of the debate. Not only was there evidence that Argentina decided to invade Las Malvinas, as they called the islands, following a strategic assessment that Britain was losing interest in defending them as a territory (the 1981 defence review had led to a decision to withdraw *HMS Endurance* from the area), but the decision by the Thatcher government to launch an ultimately successful military operation to regain the captured islands had reverberations well beyond the South Atlantic region.[9] Many around the world came to see that the UK was not necessarily the post-imperial spent force that it

---

[5] See eg M. Savage, 'Words not enough against tyrants, Cameron tells UN', *The Times*, 23 September 2011, p 7.

[6] Ibid.

[7] B. Jenkin and G. Grant, 'The Tipping Point: British National Strategy and the UK's Future World Role', Henry Jackson Society, July 2011.

[8] Ibid, p 1.

[9] Ibid, p 25.

had appeared to be. 'Power', argues the paper, 'is an essential guarantor of prosperity.'[10]

There are flaws, I would contend, in this argument. 'The Tipping Point' also quotes the example of the 9/11 attacks as being one in which a threat—Al Qaeda—made an assessment that the United States was a declining power with a will to fight that had palpably declined over the years, as evidenced by its decision to pull out of Beirut in 1983 and Somalia ten years later having suffered casualties on a miniscule scale when compared to the Vietnam conflict or the Second World War.[11] While it is undoubtedly true, as we saw in Chapter 9, that a 'body bag problem' has increasingly afflicted Western states in the post-Cold War period and possibly had an impact on the willingness of such states to become involved in complex conflict environments, the 9/11 attacks showed that a determined enemy using asymmetric techniques can turn the traditional 'balance of power' equations on their head. With the 9/11 attacks, the most militarily powerful nation the world has ever seen, which spends more on defence than the rest of the world combined, was humbled by a group of individuals armed with little more than box-cutters.[12]

In this way, the standard thinking about projection of power and defence equations possibly become much more complex and much more difficult to establish in the face of transnational, post-Cold War threats such as sub-state international terrorism. The emergence of cyber warfare as a concept could also be a game-changer, whereby the very complexity of our military arsenals and their increasing reliance on networked systems, could become their greatest weakness. Certainly the risk of a traditional state-on-state conflict involving the UK directly, or its interests overseas, has to be pondered and factored into the thinking somewhere, even if the likelihood is low. Similarly, the risk of a nuclear attack cannot be completely ruled out for ever more, not least as the general trend is for such technologies to proliferate to a greater number of countries. This, in turn, means the risks of a non-state actor gaining such technology cannot be ruled out in the long term. Globalization, meanwhile, is not necessarily unfolding in even and monolithic ways across the globe, and does not appear to be inextricably linked to the spread of democracy as we understand it in the West. As Clarke pointed out:

China and Russia maintain that they can play the globalisation game without being liberal, democratic, or even particularly open. They proclaim a model that is attractive to dictatorships in many parts of the world, and which may yet bring the major powers into confrontation.[13]

---

[10] Ibid, p 3.

[11] Ibid, p 25.

[12] M. Parenti, *The Terrorism Trap* (San Francisco, CA: City Light Books, 2002), 4–5.

[13] M. Clarke, 'The United Kingdom's Strategic Moment' in M. Codner and M. Clarke (eds), *A Question of Security: The British Defence Review in an Age of Austerity* (London: I.B. Tauris, 2011), 18.

In Russia, we have seen that far from joining the West European democratic family following the collapse of the Soviet Union, the new state has so far decided to follow its own course, which has included a lurch towards centralization of power around the President and increased authoritarianism. The rise of 'Putinism' may have been a reaction to the corrupt and chaotic days of the immediate post-Soviet period under Yeltsin, but it strikes a chord with many Russians. China, meanwhile, is extending its influence relentlessly around the globe, particularly in the African continent, bringing with it ideas of a state and its commitments to such issues as human rights that are very different from those held to be appropriate in the West.

All these issues call for advanced thinking and analysis of situations in the foreign policy spheres. First, I would argue there is a risk of 'mirror-imaging' in the deterrence logic when applied to some contemporary threat actors, namely that all contemporary adversaries will understand and respond to traditional military power projection in ways that we would as a nation-state. An Argentina might do so, but an insurgent or terrorist group probably will not. The 'aura of power' argument used in 'The Tipping Point'[14] may not apply always in quite the same ways as before to contemporary threat actors, who may be able to make the aura quickly dissipate with an unconventional attack. At the same time, we should not restrict ourselves to one line of thinking or to categorize all threats as being of the transnational, sub-state variety. Despite the Globalization School's thinking that nation-states will wither in importance as global society becomes more transnational, some states, such as Russia, China, or indeed the United States, are still highly significant players in the international field and are likely to remain so for the foreseeable future.

One thing on which critics of the 2010 SDSR process and the government agree is that uncertainty is the essence of the contemporary challenge for national security strategizing. The NSS process has taken a 20-year look into the future, since this is considered to be the furthest horizon within which any trends can be postulated, and even here there is a great deal of uncertainty.[15] In many ways, the Arab Spring, which began to unfold just after the 2010 NSS and SDSR processes had completed, was the epitome of this strategic uncertainty. It seems clear that no government or intelligence agency had predicted the way events would unfold in the Middle East at the beginning of 2011, or the extent of them. No one would have anticipated, when discussions over the NSS process were underway, that Britain would find itself in an offensive military operation against Libya just a few months later. In this way, the National Security Council (NSC) calculates that flexibility is the key, such that responses can be undertaken to a range of unexpected situations. Indeed, the whole strategy itself needs to be 'flexible, to take account of uncertainty and change'.[16]

---

[14] Jenkin and Grant, n 7, at p 31.

[15] Interview with Cabinet Office official, September 2011.

[16] HM Government, 'A Strong Britain in an Age of Uncertainty: The National Security Strategy' (London: TSO, October 2010), 10.

We saw in Chapter 8 Cornish's argument that there is a lower threshold below which the cuts and restructuring towards a more 'expeditionary' and flexible military force can become dangerous in the face of the unexpected re-emergence of more traditional state-based military threats.[17] This is an extra dimension to the loss of prestige and deterrence argument above, namely that in pure operational military terms, Britain could become unable to undertake the types of military response to threats that it would previously have been able to take, and would be irretrievably far from being able to reverse the situation. In many ways, this was the essence of the warning issued by the former US Secretary of Defense, Robert Gates, in July 2011. Not only would European nations such as Britain be unable to undertake any meaningful military operations in the future, he warned, but the United States may no longer be willing to prop up the NATO military alliance when its partners offered so little to match the United State's massive contribution.[18] This warning, argue Jenkin and Grant, affects 'the fundamental assumptions of Europe's security architecture'.[19] Since the Second World War, Western Europe has sat under the security blanket offered by the United States. With dwindling military capabilities and a 'complacency' over security, we may no longer be in a position to rely on this state of affairs in the future. For Britain in particular, there are questions about the 'special relationship' we have with United States over security, and whether we will be able to continue to offer a deal that is worth maintaining for our transatlantic cousins.

We can see an anxiety over which direction Britain should take at this fork in the road in a number of quarters, both within the military and beyond it. At the time of writing, the Minister for Cyber Security under the previous Labour government, Admiral Lord West, has found himself having to apologize over a curious outburst in which he had reacted to a suggestion that Britain was becoming a second-tier military power by exclaiming that 'we are not bloody Denmark or Belgium'.[20] This echoes the 'Belgium with a nuke' quip made originally by the backbench MP, Tony Baldry, and repeated by Lord Hennessy in a Public Administration Select Committee hearing in the House of Commons in 2010 about national security policy.[21] Aside from being somewhat offensive, as the then Defence Minister, Liam Fox, was quick to point out to Lord West, to two of Britain's NATO partners which have served alongside the UK in

---

[17] P. Cornish, 'Strategy in Austerity: The Security and Defence of the United Kingdom', Chatham House (October 2010), p 21.

[18] I. Traynor, 'US defence chief blasts Europe over NATO', *The Guardian*, 10 June 2011, available at <http://www.guardian.co.uk/world/2011/jun/10/nato-dismal-future-pentagon-chief> (accessed 16 September 2011).

[19] Jenkin and Grant, n 7, at p 28.

[20] N. Hopkins, '"Not like bloody Belgium" blunder by admiral causes outrage', *The Guardian*, 22 September 2011, available at <http://www.guardian.co.uk/politics/2011/sep/22/admiral-lord-west-diplomatic-blunder?newsfeed=true> (accessed 23 September 2011).

[21] House of Commons, Public Accounts Select Committee, 'Who does UK National Security?', First Report of Session 2010–11 (HC435, 18 October, 2010), p 5.

Afghanistan and lost a number of troops in the process, these comments reflect a deep anxiety in some quarters in Britain about taking the direction of being 'just another European power'. The route that other European countries have taken is reflected in declining defence expenditures across the continent, such that only four countries outside the United States now spend above the 2 per cent of GDP on defence that the United States considers the minimum effective contribution to NATO: the UK, France, Albania, and Greece. Many now spend considerably less, such as Germany (1.4 per cent), Italy (1.4 per cent), and Spain (1.2 per cent).[22]

In this way, the comprehensive defence cooperation agreement with France announced in November 2010 would seem to make perfect pragmatic sense. Not only are these two nations the largest defence spenders within the European component of NATO, but in 2010 were the third and fourth largest military spenders in the world.[23] Both share very similar national security assessments of the world, and both need to make substantial cuts in, and rationalization of, their military disposition in the face of serious fiscal pressures. If the historical and political enmities between the two nations can be put to one side, the agreement offers the opportunity to make a real difference in capability in the face of the bleak economic climate.

Of course, grand military and defence policy issues are not the only consider-ations on the NSC's agenda. The 2010 NSS marks the culmination of resolutely broadened post-Cold War national security assessments across the industrial-ized world, in that it completely incorporates a wide range of transnational, non-state, and 'human security' factors into the strategizing alongside those of traditional statist military threats. Indeed, three of the four threats identified in the top tier of both likelihood and impact in the 2010 NSS are such issues, namely those arising from international terrorism, cyber attack, and from a major natural accident or hazard. The strategy recognizes that, in securitizing these issues alongside the threat of military action, the response is a complex one which both cuts across multiple areas of government and across actors outside government such as business, while also stating the need to develop a response capability which is flexible and agile, and can be brought to bear in any number of situations. As the Copenhagen School of security analysts iden-tified in their seminal 1998 study, this process shifts the 'referent object' in national security conceptualization out from purely military issues (which are easier to identify) and into a much broader and potentially 'fuzzier' set of issues to define in existential terms.[24]

---

[22] M. Chalmers, 'The Lean Years: Defence Consequences of the Fiscal Crisis' in Codner and Clarke (eds), n 13, at 69.

[23] J. Madslien, 'World military spending soars inspite of recession', BBC News, 2 June 2010, available at <http://www.bbc.co.uk/news/10184610> (accessed 23 September 2011).

[24] B. Buzan, O. Waever, and J. de Wilde, *Security: A New Framework for Analysis*' (Boulder, CO: Lynne Rienner, 1998), 23.

Such a broadened security environment is not necessarily accepted as appropriate by everyone, as we have discussed, and critics argue that it delivers a long shopping list of issues which lack focus and thus constrain the formation of sensible national security policy. Whatever the merits of this point of view, the 2010 NSS (and similar recent strategy documents in France, the United States, and many other countries) now takes a broad and interconnected view of security encompassing a wide range of issues as being the normative approach to national security strategizing in the twenty-first century. As far as the UK is concerned, in some of these areas, for instance terrorism, the experience is deep and expertise is developing all the time, even if newer policies such as the 'Prevent' strand of the counter-terrorism policy have taken the government into complex and fraught areas of inter-community relations and tested our notions of 'what it is to be British'. In this way, the question of how Britain wishes to see itself is not simply a question affecting foreign policy, but is also existential in an avowedly domestic sense. Many European countries are grappling with the same issues in the post-industrial era, and some are seeing a polarization of national politics as a result.[25]

In other areas of security threat, especially the cyber realm, an understanding of the nature of threat and the required disposition of capabilities to tackle it are at a very early stage of evolution. Responses to major natural hazards and accidents similarly involve a broad range of actors, and in this way, the UK government has established coordinating secretariats on both issues within the National Security Secretariat in the Cabinet Office. These, and the NSC into which they feed, do not constitute a national security 'department' in government per se (which better describes the NSC model in the United States, for example) but are rather coordinating processes involving a small number of staff orchestrating policy and activity across government. In this way, much as security delivery on the ground through the process of globalization has increasingly involved a loosely connected 'network' of security actors, including not only government and militaries but also private companies, non-governmental organizations, and the public,[26] then the governance of national security in the contemporary world may also need to look more like a coordinated network rather than a centralized departmental process. Whether this light-touch UK model proves to be the right one to tackle a broadened security strategy, only time will tell.

In addition to the geostrategic questions of changing security threat and 'existential' questions about Britain's place in the world at the beginning of the twenty-first century, we have seen how issues of government machinery and indeed politics were also drivers in the development of the new NSC process

---

[25] See J. Richards, 'Globalization and the Rise of Far Right Militancy in Europe: A UK Perspective' in B.A. Szegál and I. András, *Conflict in a Society in Transition.* (Dunaújváros: Dunaújváros College Press, 2011).

[26] P. Gill, 'Not Just Joining the Dots but Crossing the Borders and Bridging the Voids: Constructing Security Networks after 11 September 2001', *Policing and Society*, 16/1 (2006), 28–9.

in 2010. There is no doubt that many ministerial participants in the newly instituted NSC would consider that one of the main catalysts for the new process has been a need to end the 'sofa government' of the Blair administration.[27] The trauma of the Iraq War and Britain's decision to be part of it, have left some in Whitehall determined to introduce a greater degree of scrutiny, rigour, and dialogue to the process of making major national security decisions. It is early in the experience of the new process at the time of writing, but initial signs are that the NSC, which meets every week and is usually chaired by the Prime Minister himself, not only drives national security discussion and policy-formation in Whitehall in a much more structured and rigorous way than before, but also provides a 'centre of gravity' and a regular battle-rhythm for the process of decision-making on the big issues in government.[28] It is the case that the need for this change had been recognized to a certain extent and had commenced before the incoming Coalition government, in the shape of the launch of the National Security, International Relations and Development Committee (NSID) under Gordon Brown. But experience of the NSID suggests it was somewhat more ad hoc in its regularity of meeting and in the attention it gave to the major national security issues of the time: those involved in the process would probably not equate the regularity and rigour of the current NSC process with that experienced under the NSID.[29]

There are risks in this heightened process of ministerial activity. First, having numerous meetings looks good, but can risk being more style than substance. (From the beginning of military action in Libya in March, to September 2011, for example, there had been at least 70 meetings of the NSC's Libya sub-committee, which equates to several meetings per week.[30]) As any large organization knows, meetings are not necessarily productive if decisions are not taken and outcomes not achieved. It is also the case that a frantic programme of meetings, all of which require briefings before and after, can lock ministers and supporting civil servants into a spiralling workload at a time when public sector cuts are starting to be felt. For the ministers themselves, furthermore, national security issues will not always be the whole of their portfolio, and most will have a much wider waterfront of issues to cover than the crisis in the Middle East. This feeds into a further risk identified by some observers that David Cameron could become 'the latest Prime Minister to be distracted by foreign affairs'.[31] Tony Blair has admitted that his 'Blair doctrine' activity meant that he may have taken his eye off the ball of crucial domestic issues.[32] David Cameron is clearly investing a huge amount of energy into foreign policy issues at present, shuttling between Russia, Libya, and the UN to name but a few, and this is to his credit. But it could

---

[27] Interview with National Security Secretariat official, September 2011.
[28] Ibid.
[29] Ibid.
[30] Ibid.
[31] Savage, n 5.
[32] Ibid.

mean that less time is available for domestic issues in a period when Britain is facing some very severe economic and social issues at home.

There is not yet any particular sign that these risks are being realized. Those involved with the process claim that while it has been 'pretty intense' since the beginning of 2011, the 'discipline' of having ministers meeting weekly on key national security issues, in a properly briefed and supported meeting, has 'driven greater coherence across Whitehall' on the key questions of the day.[33] It has also been observed that the Prime Minister is very keen for the meetings to be about taking decisions, and forming policy, rather than merely chewing over the issues. The atmosphere at the beginning of 2011 was 'brisk and businesslike'.[34] On the question of the interface with intelligence, the distinction has been kept between the Joint Intelligence Committee (JIC) process and its work programme and papers, and the NSC process, for the express purpose not only of keeping a 'Butler distinction' between analysis and policy, but also in order to engender a healthy creative tension and challenge in the process.[35] As Lord Butler wrote in 2004, intelligence assessment 'must avoid being so captured by policy objectives that it reports the world as policy-makers would wish it to be rather than as it is.'[36] There is evidence that the NSC is starting to provide some strategic direction for the JIC in developing the topics on its work programme.[37] This is a good thing, but the risk identified above must continue to be heeded.

A Chatham House report in October 2010 by Paul Cornish about the UK's NSS process questioned whether it was a proper 'strategy' at all, conducted in an appropriately objective way. First, the rapid pace at which the White Paper was produced that led to the NSS (less than six months from the election of the Coalition government) was such that it 'largely precluded a wide-ranging discussion of ideas and options, involving research institutes, independent analysts and others outside government.'[38] (Such a view is disputed by officials within the Cabinet Office itself, who point out that government has a wide and ongoing network of analysts who are producing assessments all the time, and have outreach to academics in so doing.[39]) Secondly, despite the purported lack of academic input, the strategy was developed in a climate of feverish discussion about expected cuts to defence, and specific debates about which elements of the three services should be cut or rationalized. Cornish claims these are 'second order' factors which should flow from the strategy, not drivers in its formation.[40] Indeed, which areas to cut are questions of policy, not strategy. Additionally, the NSS is seen as lacking by some through not properly being a

---

[33] Interview with National Security Secretariat official, September 2011.

[34] Ibid.

[35] Ibid.

[36] The Rt Hon The Lord Butler of Brockwell, 'Review of Intelligence on Weapons of Mass Destruction: Report of a Committee of Privy Councillors' (London: TSO, 14 July 2004), 16.

[37] Interview with National Security Secretariat official, September 2011.

[38] Cornish, n 17, at p vi.

[39] Interview with National Security Secretariat official, September 2011.

[40] Cornish, n 17.

'Grand Strategy', that not only considers national security factors themselves, but places these firmly within a much wider context of where Britain wants to be in the world order, in terms not only of security, but also of trade and industry, culture and society. In many ways, the current moment in history is perhaps a key 'strategic moment' for Britain, as Clarke describes it.[41]

To a certain extent, whether these criticisms of Britain's 2010 NSS are valid and whether they mean the strategy is flawed in relation to the experience of subsequent national security threats, remains to be seen. What is certain is that much has changed in the UK's process of national security strategizing since the beginning of 2011, and that Prime Minister David Cameron seems determined to make the ongoing process a rigorous and structured one. The experience of Libya, which was certainly unexpected at the beginning of the process, provided a fierce initial test of the NSC's workings, and of the UK's ongoing military capacity and capability. Much has been, and will be learned; some of it good, much of it not. One thing for certain is that the 2010 NSS and SDSR in the UK provide a fascinating, and perhaps highly indicative case study of national security strategizing in the twenty-first century world, not only for Britain but also for the wider world.

Key points

- Prime Minister Cameron, in his first address to the UN General Assembly, delivered an interventionist vision for the UK which echoed Blair's Chicago speech of 1999.
- Critics have suggested that the UK is at a strategic 'tipping point', whereby it wishes to be more than 'just another European power', but is unable to be so given the cuts and restructuring of its defence capability. The Libya crisis provided an incomplete test, in that it appeared to be successful while simultaneously exposing serious operational difficulties within NATO.
- There may be flaws in the argument, in that traditional power-projection approaches may not work the same way with transnational post-Cold War threats. Cyber threats are a classic example of where this may be the case.
- The new NSC process appears to have brought about a greater degree of rigour to the process of making decisions on major national security issues, and the Libya crisis was one of many early tests for it. Whether it will continue to be sustainable as a process, and whether it will make the differences that are required, only time will be able to tell.

---

[41] Clarke, n 13.

Index

Administration
departmental organization outside
Cabinet Office 111–14
key points 115
mapping of response activities 88–9
National Security Council
political origins 101–3
process and machinery 109–10
rationale for 103–6
presidentialism in France 106
prime ministerialism in UK 106–9
Afghanistan
asymmetric conflict 129–30
'battle of narratives' 131
changing character of
conflict 119–20
impact of organized crime 60
instability 47–9
inter-service issues 121–3
peace-keeping and
enforcement 133–5
public perceptions 12–13
Armed conflicts
changing character of
conflict 119–20
fighting asymmetric conflicts
Afghanistan 129–30
'battle of narratives' 130–2
future force requirements 137–9
key points 139
peace-keeping role 133–6
Armed forces
'boots on the ground'
Britain's changing place in the
world 117–19
case for restructuring 23, 116–17
changing character of
conflict 119–21
inter-service issues 121–3
key points 128
nuclear question 126–8
proposed restructuring 123–6
role of NATO 11
international military crises 48–50

restructuring military capability
anxiety over way forward for
Britain 171–2
Britain's place in the world 117–19
changing character of
conflict 119–20
inter-service issues 121–3
key points 128
need for cuts 116–17
proposed restructuring 123–5
UK's nuclear capability 126–8
Revolution in Military Affairs
(RMA) 10–11
Asymmetric conflicts
Afghanistan 129–30
'battle of narratives' 130–2
future force requirements 137–9
key points 139
peace-keeping and enforcement 133–6

'Battle of narratives' 130–2
Border security
classification of threat 19
Tier Three risk 78–9

**Chemical, biological, radiological, or
nuclear weapons (CBRN)** *see*
'Unconventional' weapons
Chicago doctrine 119
Civil emergencies
classification of threat 19
flooding 47
nuclear emergencies 76–7
Climate change 46
Copenhagen School 11–12
Counter-insurgency
experience and
understanding 134–6
future force requirements 137–9
Counter Terrorism Strategy (CONTEST)
national security 'tasks' 92–3
Prevent 147, 151
proposed responses 84
risk reduction 145–6

Cyber-threats
classification of threat 19
Defence Cyber Operations Group
(DCOG) 126
departmental organization outside
Cabinet Office 112–14
new approach of NSS to
globalization 27–8
new challenges 173
responses
'adaptable posture' towards
capability 90
administrative strategies 86–7
Tier One 41–4

**Defence Cyber Operations Group
(DCOG)** 126
Disasters *see* **Natural hazards and
disasters**
Disease outbreaks 47

Energy security
classification of threat 19
Tier Three risk 72–6
Environmental security
French ministerial
representation 111–12
Tier One threat 45–6
Europe
see also **NATO**
backdrop to Tier Three risk 67–70
national security 'tasks' 93
political backdrop to NSS 24
post-war security response 7
UK's relationship with EU 161–2

Failed states *see* **Unstable and failed
states**
Foreign relations *see* **Partnerships**
France
creation of new security bodies 104–5
ministerial representation 111–12
national security 'tasks' 96
pragmatic approach from UK 172
presidentialism of security system 106
relationship with UK 162–3
Future Force 2020 125

Globalization
Britain's place in the world 168–70
humanitarian interventions 50
impact on organized crime 62–3

key points 30–1
new approach of NSS 25–30
'Gendarmerie' functions 137–9

Human rights 143–4, 165
'Human security'
challenge to Realist thinking 23
concept to rival national
security 17–18
effect of climate change 23
focus on development 45
interconnectedness with energy
security 72
NSC policy agenda 172
'operations of political choice' 72
response framework 83
Humanitarian interventions 48–50
UK criticisms of UN 167–8

International military crises
'adaptable posture' towards
capability 90
Tier One threat 48–50

Key points
administration 115
conclusions 176
counter-terrorism strategy 151–2
fighting asymmetric conflicts 139
National Security Strategy 2010 17–18
partnerships 166
responses 96–7
restructuring military capability 128
Tier One 50–1
Tier Three risks 80
Tier Two 66

Media
'battle of narratives' 130–2
central importance 13
Middle East
'battle of narratives' 131–2
challenge of uncertainty 170
continuing importance of
NATO 159–61
energy security 74–5
humanitarian interventions 49
nations and states
distinguished 15
peace-keeping and
enforcement 133–4
post-Cold War priority 10

National security
Britain's place in the world 168–70
defined 14–17
modern history 7–14
'tasks' 91–6
National Security Council (NSC)
broadening of strategy 172–3
mapping of response activities 88–9
political origins 101–3
priority setting 86
process and machinery 109–10
rationale for 103–6
National Security Strategy 2010 (NSS)
'adaptable posture' towards
capability 90
administrative strategies 87
breaking new ground 3–5
Britain's place in the
world 118, 168–9
classification of threats 19–20
complexity of problems faces 14
criticisms of process 175–6
humanitarian interventions 49
key points 17–18
new approach to global and
transnational threats 25–30
partnerships
importance 153–4
political backdrop 20–5
priority risks and threats 5–6
proposed responses 83
risk assessment
Tier One 34–5
Tier Two 53
National Security Strategy Board
(NSSB) 109
NATO
backdrop to Tier Three risk 68, 70
continuing importance to UK 156–61
establishment 7
importance of partnerships 164
national security 'tasks' 93
political backdrop to NSS 24
post-war security response 8
preference for surgical bombardment 11
problems faced by Yugoslav
conflict 9–10
relationship with Britain 117–18
Natural hazards and disasters
'adaptable posture' towards
capability 90
Tier One threat 44–8

Non-governmental organizations
(NGOs)
importance 29
presence in armed conflicts 120
North-South divide 48
Nuclear emergencies 76–7

Organized crime
administrative response 86–7
border security 78–9
classification of threat 19
cyber-threats 42–3
key threats 62
Tier Two threat 60–4

Pandemic disease 47
Partnerships
counter-terrorism 163–6
Europe 161–2
France 162–3, 172
importance 153–4
key points 166
NATO 156–61
'special relationship' 154–5
Peace-keeping and enforcement
experience and
understanding 133–6
future force
requirements 137–9
Political perspectives
backdrop to NSS 20–5
breaking new ground with NSS 3–5
Chicago doctrine 119
energy security 76
National Security Council
origins 101–3
process and machinery 109–10
rationale for 104
national security systems
departmental organization outside
Cabinet Office 111–14
presidentialism in France 106
prime ministerialism in
UK 106–9
need for change in government
machinery 173–5
origins of instability 11–12
'special relationship' 109, 155
'speech acts' 12
strategy documents 86
UK's nuclear capability 127
Prevent 147–51

Regional conflicts 70–2
Resilience
  departmental organization outside
    Cabinet Office 112
  disruption of satellite
    communications 64
  NSC command process 110
  Tier One risk assessment 33–5
Responses
  'adaptable posture' towards
    capability 90–1
  administrative organization 86–7
  key points 96–7
  key principles 83–6
  national security 'tasks' 91–6
Revolution in Military Affairs (RMA)
  post-Cold War priority 10–11
  satellite communications 65
Risks
  'adaptable posture' towards
    capability 90–1
  Counter Terrorism Strategy
    (CONTEST) 145–6
  mapping of response activities 88–9
  NSS priorities 3–5
  Tier One 32–3
  Tier Three
    border security 78–9
    energy security 72–6
    European backdrop 67–70
    key points 80
    nuclear emergencies 76–7
    wider regional conflicts 70–2
Rogue states
  origins 11–12
  use of 'unconventional' weapons 55

Satellite communications 64–6
'Special relationship'
  politicization 109
  reappraisal 154–5
'Speech acts' 12–13
Strategic Defence and Security
    Review 2010 (SDSR)
  administrative strategies 87
  assessment of energy security risks 74
  Britain's place in the world 168–70
  changes within and between armed
    forces 123–4
  classification of threats 19–20
  key points 17–18
  national security 'tasks' 92

nuclear emergencies 77
proposed responses 83
Strategies
  administrative organization 86–7
  challenge of uncertainty 170
  counter-terrorism
    evolving nature of threat 143–6
    key points 151–2
    Prevent 147–51
  criticisms of NSS process 175–6
  fighting asymmetric conflicts
    Afghanistan 129–30
    'battle of narratives' 130–2
    future force requirements 137–9
    key points 139
    peace-keeping role 133–6
  partnerships
    counter-terrorism 163–6
    Europe 161–2
    France 162–3, 172
    importance 153–4
    key points 166
    NATO 156–61
    'special relationship' 154–5
  restructuring military capability
    Britain's place in the world 117–19
    changing character of conflict 119–20
    inter-service issues 121–3
    key points 128
    need for cuts 116–17
    proposed restructuring 123–5
    UK's nuclear capability 126–8

'Tasks' 91–6
Terrorism
  classification of threat 19
  continuing importance of NATO 157
  counter-terrorism strategy
    evolving nature of threat 143–6
    importance of partnerships 163–6
    key points 151–2
    Prevent 147–51
  cyber-threats 42
  departmental organization outside
    Cabinet Office 114
  domestic threats
    evolving nature of terrorist
      threat 141–3
    old and new threats 140
  encouragement in 'poorly governed
    spaces' 132
  exploitation of unstable states 47–8

new approach of NSS to global
        threats 27–30
responses
    'adaptable posture' towards
        capability 90
    Counter Terrorism Strategy
        (CONTEST) 84
    national security 'tasks' 92–3
risks 32–3
Tier One threat
    Al Qaeda 37–40
    Northern Ireland 35–7
use of 'unconventional'
        weapons 53–4
Threats
classification 19–20
NSC command process 110
NSS priorities 3–5
terrorism
    evolving nature of terrorist
        threat 141–3
    old and new threats 140
    Prevent 147–51
Tier One
    cyber-threats 41–4
    international military crises 48–50
    key points 50–1
    natural hazards and
        disasters 44–8
    overlap with Tier Two 52–3
    resilience 33–5
    risk 32–3
    terrorism 35–40
Tier Two
    disruption of satellite
        communications 64–6
    key points 66
    organized crime 60–4
    overlap with Tier One 52–3
    'unconventional' weapons 53–6
    unstable and failed states 56–9
Tier Three
    border security 78–9
    energy security 72–6
    European backdrop 67–70
    key points 80
    nuclear emergencies 76–7
    wider regional conflicts 70–2
Tier One
cyber-threats 41–4
international military crises 48–50
key points 50–1

natural hazards and
        disasters 44–8
overlap with Tier Two 52–3
priority risks 6
resilience 33–5
risk assessment 32–3
terrorism 35–40
Tier Two
disruption of satellite
        communications 64–6
key points 66
organized crime 60–4
overlap with Tier One 52–3
priority risks 6
'unconventional' weapons 53–6
unstable and failed states 56–9
Tier Three
border security 78–9
energy security 72–6
European backdrop 67–70
key points 80
nuclear emergencies 76–7
priority risks 6
wider regional conflicts 70–2
Transnational threats
key points 30–1
new approach of NSS 25–30

'Unconventional' weapons
classification 53
Tier Two threat 53–6
United Nations
nations and states
        distinguished 15
peace-keeping and
        enforcement 133–4
UK criticisms 167–8
United States
see also **NATO**
administrative response 86
longest serving NSC 105–6
'special relationship'
    politicization 109
    reappraisal 154–5
understanding of counter-
        insurgency 136
Unstable and failed states
classification of threat 19
humanitarian interventions 48–50
problems created by Yugoslav
        conflict 9–10
Tier Two threat 56–9

Weapons
  classification of threat 19
  cyber-threats 42
  origins of proliferation 11–12
  UK's nuclear capability 126–8

Weapons of mass destruction *see*
  'Unconventional' weapons
'Westphalian state' 16
Wider regional conflicts 70–2